Thank You,
Billy Graham

A Tribute to the Life and
Ministry of Billy Graham

Thank You,
Billy Graham

A Tribute to the Life and Ministry of Billy Graham

Compiled by Billy Graham's Grandchildren
Jerushah Armfield, Aram and Boz Tchividjian
Foreword by Michael Reagan

SHILOH RUN  PRESS

The compilers are represented by Bruce R. Barbour, Literary Management Group, Inc., Nashville, Tennessee.

Print ISBN 978-1-62836-634-1

eBook Editions:
Adobe Digital Edition (.epub) 978-1-63058-015-5
Kindle and MobiPocket Edition (.prc) 978-1-63058-016-2

Front cover image: Gamma-Rapho via Getty Images;
Back cover image: Edward Miller/Stringer/Getty Images

Published by Shiloh Run Press, an imprint of Barbour Publishing, Inc., P.O. Box 719, Uhrichsville, Ohio 44683, www.shilohrunpress.com

Our mission is to publish and distribute inspirational products offering exceptional value and biblical encouragement to the masses.

 Member of the
Evangelical Christian
Publishers Association

Printed in the United States of America.

Contents

Foreword

As the son of Ronald Reagan, I have enjoyed a unique perspective on the ministry of Billy Graham.

People call him "America's pastor," and with good reason. We've had presidents, including my father, who knew that they could pick up the phone—any time of the day or night—and Billy Graham would pray with them. And he wasn't only praying with and for presidents. If Billy Graham had not been interceding regularly for our whole nation, where would the United States be today?

I've had the privilege of knowing Dr. Graham and his family since my father was governor of California. And it was in two of Billy Graham's California crusades that I experienced moments I will never forget.

In 1985, during a ten-day crusade at Anaheim, I watched Billy Graham preach to a full stadium. I had walked away from the church years before, but had recently been drawn back by the influence of my wife and the ministry of Pastor Jack Hayford of The Church on the Way. Billy's message that night was so powerful and compelling, I almost felt badly that I'd accepted Christ just weeks before!

Nearly twenty years later, in 2004, the Billy Graham Evangelistic Association asked me to speak during his Los Angeles crusade. My first thought was that his staff had called the wrong Reagan—but if Billy Graham asks you to give a testimony, it really is like a message from God. With an earnest prayer for the Holy Spirit's help, I told the huge Rose Bowl crowd my own story of God's grace and forgiveness.

"As you listen to Dr. Graham tonight," I said in my wrap-up, "I want you to think of our Lord and Savior Jesus Christ.

He's standing at the doorway of your life with His arms wide open, waiting to give you a hug."

Turning from the podium, I came face-to-face with Billy Graham, who shook my hand and said, "Michael, you should have stayed out there and kept speaking!" I was so grateful to hear those words from a man who has accomplished so much in his long life of service to God.

Now, in this book, we all have the opportunity to say "thank you, Billy Graham." Millions of people have heard him preach the gospel, and many of them have posted messages of gratitude on the web site ThankYouBilly.com. In the pages to follow, you'll read real-life stories of people who are thankful that Dr. Graham helped them find Jesus. . .inspired their Christian walk. . . touched the lives of their loved ones. . .and set such an example of honesty and integrity.

Billy always told us that "God loves you." Thank you, Billy Graham, for faithfully communicating that simple, but incredibly profound, message. Billy, we love you!

MICHAEL REAGAN
Author of *Twice Adopted* and *the New Reagan Revolution:
How Ronald Reagan's Principles Can Restore America's Greatness*

Introduction

For as long as we can remember, people from all walks of life have approached us to say they came to know Jesus Christ through the work and ministry of Billy Graham. Beyond all the White House visits, magazine cover photos, worldwide crusades, books, movies, and television appearances, the true testimony of his life are the masses of ordinary people whose lives have been transformed by God through an ordinary man we've always known simply as "Daddy Bill."

As grandchildren, we have been blessed to spend more time with Daddy Bill than most who have come to know and love Billy Graham during his seventy-plus years of public ministry. After the cameras have been turned off and the crowds have gone home, he is our grandfather. We know him as a man who simply loves people, who is as comfortable conversing with a cab driver or busboy as he is with a president, CEO, or movie star. And we can honestly say it never mattered where he was or what he was doing—Daddy Bill always had time for us. We consider ourselves so very blessed.

Not only has Daddy Bill been a blessing to us, but what a joy to know that he has blessed and inspired countless other people, in their own times and places and ways. Daddy Bill has affected literally millions of individuals around the world since he first entered the ministry so many years ago. With every changed life comes a story worth sharing—stories from those who sat in the stadiums, watched him on television, listened to him on the radio, read his many books, or enjoyed a personal encounter of some sort.

Daddy Bill's own story is best told by the people God touched through his life. Through the website ThankYouBilly.com, hundreds of people have shared stories of hope, forgiveness, joy, redemption, and God's amazing grace. These are stories of how God chose an ordinary North Carolina farm boy for an extraordinary purpose. Whether they address him as Rev. Graham, Dr. Graham, Mr. Graham, Brother Graham, or just plain Billy, these precious individuals all share the joy of knowing Jesus through Daddy Bill's preaching.

These stories cover many years—several decades, actually—of our grandfather's ministry. They come from many states and several countries. They describe people of all ages—from young children to the elderly—who were impacted by the simple but profound gospel message communicated by Daddy Bill. The stories have been lightly edited for readability, but retain the voice of each contributor and the raw power of their faith experiences. Last names have been dropped to protect the privacy of those who contributed, and not everyone who responded on the website provided a name. But every testimony you're about to read came from someone whose life was touched by Daddy Bill.

As we compiled this powerful book, each of us found ourselves encouraged to examine our own faith. Our hope is that as you read these amazing stories of God's love, you will also be encouraged to examine your own faith and understanding of the gospel and the indescribable love of Jesus.

Through the dozens of testimonies that follow, you'll be encouraged by the ringing affirmation that God is the God of all comfort and strength. Most importantly, we pray that this book will remind you of the most beautiful truth that Daddy Bill so often told packed stadiums, "God loves you!"

We are so grateful to God for Daddy Bill, and the amazing love and awesome power of the God who introduced this man to us and to the world.

JERUSHAH ARMFIELD
BOZ TCHIVIDJIAN
ARAM TCHIVIDJIAN

Thank You, Billy Graham. . .
for Inspiring My Christian Walk

ALWAYS THERE

I first heard Billy Graham when he was preaching in a crusade on the radio. I felt God's presence through the message and came under the influence of Billy's preaching from that night on. As a youngster, I wanted to be a preacher like Billy; my sister thought I would be. Well, I never became a Billy Graham, but I did become an ordained minister and am now completing my career as a Veterans Administration chaplain.

My tribute to Billy Graham is that he has been a constant in my life. I have heard him preach numerous times over the radio and have seen many of his crusades on TV. It seems that Billy Graham has always been there for me, whether I was watching him on TV, listening to him on the radio, or reading an article in *Decision* magazine. I never heard Billy Graham speak without being inspired or challenged to a closer walk with God. The Holy Spirit's presence in Billy's sermons has always uplifted me and encouraged me in my daily walk with God. The simple message of the Gospel that he preaches is so clear and convicting.

I once got to meet him personally. While at the Jackson, Mississippi, crusade, he visited Reformed Theological Seminary, where I was attending at the time. Our whole study body was invited to hear him speak to the local clergy in Jackson. George Beverly Shea sang, and Billy preached a message to encourage us pastors and would-be pastors. After the sermon, I had the privilege of shaking his hand. He looked more like Christ to me than any other person I have ever met.

I don't know how it would have been not having Billy Graham's touch on my life through his ministry. I truly think that God gave him to the church as the "Evangelist of the World." There may be other evangelists, but there will never be one of the stature of Billy Graham. Thank you, Billy, for faithfully preaching, teaching, and living out God's Word in your life.

Ron

DEDICATED FOR MINISTRY

My youth director took a busload of teenagers to your crusade at the Los Angeles Coliseum in 1963. I was thirteen and seeking to know God more deeply. I remember we sat in a top section, and it was a long way down, but I was determined to make a public statement of my desire to completely follow Jesus.

I was raised in a Christian home but knew I had to make a personal decision for myself. My mother had desired to sing in your choir, but she was at my father's bedside in the hospital. The week your crusade ended, my father died of a stroke. Though it was a tragedy to lose my earthly father, your crusade reminded me that my heavenly Father would now come alongside me.

I went on to start a Youth for Christ club at my public junior high school, worked at the InterVarsity Christian Fellowship book table at my secular university, taught in an inner-city Christian school, graduated from seminary, became an ordained minister, and served as a hospital chaplain.

In November 2005, I was privileged to serve as a ministerial counselor at your crusade at the Rose Bowl in Pasadena.

Near the end of the week, a thin, fair-haired young man ("Roman") sat down next to me. I learned that he was from Russia and had been in the country for just a year. He had seen the crusade ads in a store and had come on his own. He had never heard of Billy Graham but was curious to attend such a large public, religious gathering. He said he had never accepted the atheistic curriculum taught to him in Russia but believed there was a living God. He had sneaked into the backs of cathedrals to try to experience God. Roman accepted Christ that night at the crusade and was delighted to receive the Bible on CD-ROM. I couldn't help but think that someday he will take his faith back home to Russia.

Debbie

I FOUND PURPOSE

As a restless fourteen-year-old, with no understanding of God and no awareness of Jesus, I saw no purpose to my life. Then my sister invited me to a free film, which turned out to be *Oil Town USA*. I remember little of the story and none of the facts about Jesus, but I do remember that these people clearly had a purpose and it seemed to be connected with Jesus. A few weeks later, I went to the Harringay crusade and discovered that this Jesus was real and important! Now, over fifty years later, twenty-seven as an ordained minister, I thank Billy Graham for showing me the purpose of my life—serving Jesus!

SALVATION IN SOUTH FLORIDA

In the spring of 1985, my mother and I went to your crusade. I went forward, and my mother said she accepted Jesus in her seat. (She was a very private person and had cancer at the time.) When she died in January 1986, it was nice to know I would see her again in heaven. Her last words to me (in German) were, " 'Til we meet again."

After that, my sons accepted Jesus, and last year I believe my dad called on Jesus before he died. *Thank you for leading us to Christ!*

It will be great to have the family together in heaven. I'll introduce you to them when we're all there, to thank you.

God's blessings to you, your family, and all the people who sacrificed so my family and I would be saved through Jesus Christ.

PRAYER

During my time at Moody Bible Institute (1954 to 1957), Billy Graham came to speak to the student body. The class I had before chapel let out early so we could get good seats. I was in the third row, center section of Torrey-Gray Auditorium. I had been to his crusades before in Upstate New York—I think Syracuse and Rochester—but this was the first time I could really see him.

What was most impressive to me was that he talked about the importance of prayer to his ministry, and the humility he showed as he talked to us.

I also heard George Beverly Shea that night at Moody. He sang "How Great Thou Art," which was still fairly new.

Thank you both for the encouragement you've been in my life.

GOD'S HUMBLE SERVANT

It seems as if Billy has always been with us. It is because he has spoken the Word of God with humility and power and brought God's Gospel and timeless truth wherever he has preached to any and all who would listen.

My family and I saw Billy twice in the mid-1990s, in Louisville and Indianapolis, and came forward both times to dedicate our lives to Jesus. Billy always gave the same message of saving grace, how we all are loved by God "just as we are," and how we can find salvation through faith in Jesus Christ!

Thank you, Billy and Ruth, and all those related to this wonderful man, for your many, many years of devoted service to God and the speaking of His glorious Good News throughout the world!

IT ALL STARTED WITH YOU!

Mr. Graham, when I heard you were coming to Cleveland to our "old" stadium, I asked my girlfriend Mary if she would go with me, and she agreed. At the time, my divorce had come full circle—meaning that the man I left my husband for had left me for another woman. Surprise, surprise. Well, I was, and I was devastated. When you made the call, I went forward. At the time, I was also drinking heavily and doing drugs to ease the pain—and because I thought I liked it. I was blessed by you through many tears.

I would love to tell you that I lived happily ever after. Unfortunately, Satan is alive and well and was living in my brain. So although I picked up my Bible after many years of not reading it, I was justifying my drinking because my drink of choice was wine and I would say that Jesus' first miracle was turning water to wine. I also found the passage about "enjoying the green herb of the earth" (and I'm sure you know what I did with that). So I was drinking and drugging for another nine years.

But on March 8, 2003, I went to the Glenbeigh treatment center, and I have been sober ever since. I then changed churches to my new, beautiful, small Baptist church, where I was baptized on December 26, 2003. I am still a very happy member today. Billy, it all started with you! Thank you, and God bless you!

Linda

EVERY TIME

Every time Billy Graham had a crusade on TV, I felt compelled to watch it. I knew I would hear the pure, unadulterated Word of God and that a change would come about from it.

He was pure, he was concise, he was clear, he was fresh, and he spoke flat-footed from the pulpit. And, as you know, people came in droves to accept Christ. . . . He will always be in the hearts of God's people.

Thank you, Billy Graham, for "Just As I Am." Rest now, for you have served your Master and the people of God well.

Karen

CALL CENTER WORKER

I was able to work in a call center for the Billy Graham television ministry. That experience was truly a blessing and a wonder. To be able to help lead callers to the Lord, or just listen and pray with them, was an amazing opportunity.

Billy made that possible, through his many TV ministries. Just to be a part was a blessing to me.

It was scary sometimes, to have that responsibility; but it's something I'm glad I did and will always treasure. Thank you, Billy.

TJ

FIRE IN YOUR EYES

In the mid 1960s, when I was approximately twenty, you came to the University of Houston. I wanted to see what all the fuss was about, so I went to your lecture. From my seat about one-third of the way back, I could see your eyes, and they looked like they had fire in them. They were very penetrating. I never forgot that. I feel very fortunate to have been able to see you live once. Years later, I understood and accepted salvation. Today, I enjoy your crusades, no matter what year is being shown. Thank you, Dr. Graham, for showing us how it's done.

Mary Margaret

THE HOLY SPIRIT AND THE TEENS

My wife and I sat in the nosebleed section of the Carrier Dome in Syracuse when Billy did his crusade there in the 1980s. We were in a sea of teens. Hundreds of local churches and churches from many miles away were represented, but the common denominator was that they were all teens. Well, you know how teens can be. . .lots of talking and passing notes and all that stuff. When Billy started to preach, my wife and I were somewhat distracted by all the commotion . . .when all of a sudden, about halfway through the sermon, a hush fell around us. I witnessed the power of the Holy Spirit like I've never seen it before. Weeping. . .lots of weeping. . .all around us, teens were crying and weeping. Then, just before the invitation, a lot more weeping. . .and it seemed that dozens of teens started to get up and go downstairs before the invitation was even given.

Hundreds left their seats to go forward to receive Christ that evening. It had a tremendous impact on my wife and me. That was the only time we saw Billy in person, but I look at the crusades in a different way now. I was amid the power of God, and I saw Him move. Thank you, Billy, for being faithful to your call!

I UNDERSTAND THE BIBLE SO MUCH BETTER

Dear Billy, thank you so much for being obedient to God! I accepted Jesus as my Savior when I was nine years old, was baptized, and later took several of your correspondence courses. After I was married, I sent for the paperback *Living Bible* that you published. It meant so much to me to be able to understand the Bible so much better. I read and reread that Bible. It helped me to grow further in the Lord. Blessings on you, thank you, and God bless you!

Mim

AMSTERDAM 2000

I had the privilege of being invited to attend the Amsterdam 2000 conference in the Netherlands. The messages were instrumental in renewing an evangelistic spirit within me. When Billy's daughter spoke, the Lord spoke to my heart and inspired me to begin a ministry online to point people to Christ. I knew nothing about the Internet, but God sent me a lady whose job is to build websites for churches and religious organizations. Rhonda offered to build a website for my ministry, His Love Extended Ministries International. She refused remuneration and offered it as a love gift to the ministry! Through the years, as God has been teaching me the ropes, the messages and challenges of Amsterdam 2000 always underlie the zeal with which I administer this ministry. Several (that I know of) had spiritual growth, and others have been saved! To God be the glory. Only eternity will reveal all that the Lord has done with this ministry. Thank you and Franklin and your daughter, Billy! God bless you, brother!

NOW I KNOW JESUS CHRIST PERSONALLY

I was raised in a Christian family and attended a traditional Anglican Sunday school and church. I learned about Jesus Christ, and when I was twenty-six, I made my decision to become a confirmed member of my local church. When I was invited to become a counselor at the Ipswich Billy Graham crusade, I attended the teaching sessions and still treasure the materials, which gave me solid teaching that I lacked from church.

When the great day arrived, it was one of the most awe-inspiring occasions I have ever had the privilege to attend. I clearly remember many of Billy Graham's words, and through his inspiration and teaching I came to know my Lord and Savior Jesus Christ personally. My heart is full of gratitude and admiration for the amazing work Billy Graham has carried out all over the world through the enabling of the Holy Spirit.

BUILDING FAITH

I grew up watching the Billy Graham crusades and have always received so much from them. I also remember the movies that Billy Graham produced in the late 1960s, and the wonderful messages that came with them. I'd love to have copies of those even now. I was raised Southern Baptist, but got away from the church for a while during my early married life. But even during this time, I continued to watch your crusades, and God always spoke to me and begged me to return to Him.

Thanks to you and the wonderful, God-inspired messages, I did. Thank you so much for your inspiration—and for the inspiration of those who have stood by you through it all. I have always felt that Billy Graham is one man whose eyes I can look into and truly see the face of God. God shines through you, Billy, like no other. I thank God for you and your wife, for Cliff Barrows, and for everyone else who has made your crusades what they are—a true inspiration to us all. God bless you all.

Nancy

Thank You, Billy Graham. . .
for Your Spiritual Legacy

GOD DID CHANGE HER

My mother died on May 12, 2007, just short of her nineti-
eth birthday. It was a day of celebration for her six children
because we knew she had gone to be with the Lord. About
ten years earlier, she had shared with me her decision to
follow Christ, based on one of Billy's TV crusades. She said,
"I prayed the sinner's prayer, and invited Christ into my
heart. . ."

Thank you, Billy, for presenting the Gospel in such a way
that, in the privacy of her own home, my mother could make
that decision. God did change her. Praise Him!

IN FRONT OF THE TV

In 1973, at the age of twenty-five, I assumed the pastorate of
a church in Panama City, Florida. I immediately met "Lot-
tie and Earl," an elderly couple who were the delight of the
church. The first time I talked with Earl, he told me how
he had come to faith in Christ, at the age of sixty-five, by
watching a Billy Graham television special. He showed me
the exact spot in his living room where he had prayed to receive Jesus as Billy led the prayer.

Over the next four years, I heard Earl tell that story scores
of times. Each time he told it, he did so with the same conviction and and enthusiasm as the first time. Earl was a great
encouragement to me as a young pastor. When I had a tough
day, I would go see Earl, knowing that somewhere in the

conversation he would tell me again about watching Billy Graham on TV and how it had changed his life forever. He said that when he got to heaven, he wanted to see Jesus and Billy Graham.

THROUGH FOUR GENERATIONS

I first heard of Billy Graham from my grandfather, who would sit by the radio and listen to Billy whenever he was on. When the crusades became televised, my mother used to watch, and she took me to the Philadelphia crusade to hear Mr. Graham. These were the years when God was calling me to Himself. I accepted Christ at the age of eleven. My children were raised on the televised crusades, and all have accepted Christ. God used Billy Graham through four generations of our family. I never miss a *Larry King Show* or other program where he's interviewed. I can't imagine a world without him. I am so thankful to God that He placed Billy Graham here in my lifetime. I'm so glad I could express my love and thanks.

Mary Jane

WHAT BILLY SHARED HAS BEEN PASSED ON TO OTHERS

I gave my life to Jesus at a Billy Graham crusade when I was ten. As a senior pastor for the last twenty-four years, I have had the privilege of seeing many also come to Christ, both here in America and around the world. What Billy shared with me has been passed on to others; Jesus saves.

MY MOTHER

I attended the first Billy Graham crusade in Sydney as a counselor. I also sang in the choir. I took my Mum one night, and she gave her life to the Lord there and continued serving Him till she went home to Him in 1975. Also, my older sister and her husband gave their lives to Christ during that crusade as well. I made a commitment to become a missionary. That didn't come about till 1996 when I went to live in an aboriginal community, where many came to the Lord. I am still working with them from my home here in Tennant Creek. Thank you, Dr. Graham.

ONCE UPON A TIME

My mother was an immigrant from Puerto Rico. We lived in Spanish Harlem, in Manhattan. My mother had five daughters and a son, and because she was a stay-at-home mom, she watched television throughout the day while her children were in school.

As the youngest of the daughters, I was too young to attend school. One day, I recall seeing my mother kneel in front of her television set with her hands lifted high as she repeated the sinner's prayer. . . . The preacher's name was Billy Graham.

As an adult, I have had the privilege of serving God by volunteering and singing with the choir during the Billy Graham crusade in Queens, New York. What a privilege and a blessing to serve God and Billy Graham, the man responsible for my mother's salvation.

Ana

THE RIPPLE EFFECT

My parents and my uncle took our youth group to the New York City crusade in 1959. When we walked in, I could feel the presence of the Lord. All of us went forward. (I was disappointed that Billy did not counsel me! Ha ha.)

My twin sister and I went on to get involved in InterVarsity Christian Fellowship in nursing school. Now, we both have sons who are preachers! Between us we have nine children, all trusting in the Lord. And the ripple effect continues. Thank you Billy (and Ruth) for your faithful example through the years. God bless you richly!

FROM RUSSIA TO FAITH IN JESUS

My parents escaped from Russia separately with their families into Iran in the 1930s, and later met and were married in Tehran. They emigrated to the US at the end of WWII. My mother was a believer, but my father was not, and we were members of the Russian Molokan Church. But God had his hand on my father.

My mother and maternal grandmother were praying for my father's salvation. In 1963, when I was in the eighth grade, Billy Graham came to the Los Angeles Coliseum for a crusade. I went every night with my father. One of the nights, my dad got out of his seat and made the long walk down to the field to acknowledge God's call on his life. What a glorious day that was. That same year, I was called by God at camp. My father's decision set off a series of events that changed our family's lives forever. The biggest deal was that my father decided to be baptized, and this decision made his family ostracize him and we were kicked out of the Molokan Church. Today, at eighty-four, my father is still actively serving the Lord.

In their seventies, my parents returned to Russia and started a Bible study, and then a church, in the village where some of their relatives still live. My father baptised many, and

God used him to bring God's hope and salvation to this little village. Billy Graham and his crusades hold a special place in my family's hearts. We thank God for Billy's faithfulness and the way he always brings Christ into any conversation he has with newspeople. Thank you, Billy, for your love for God and the good news of the Gospel of Christ!

MY GRANDMOTHER "HEARD FROM BILLY"

Our family has always watched the crusades on TV throughout the years and greatly benefited from them. My only grandmother, who is now in heaven, thought a great deal of Mr. Graham. She was on his mailing list and would tell us with great joy that she had "heard from Billy." She did not receive the mail as just a nonprofit organization sending a letter. She received the letters as if they were personally prepared for her. She really enjoyed them. She was a widow for many years, but she loved to send donations. She often sent a few dollars in cash, until her daughter realized this. (She then wrote checks for her.) My grandmother lived to be eighty-nine. She read her Bible through every year. Thank you, Mr. Graham, for blessing her and our whole family.

I JUST WANT TO SHOW MY APPRECIATION

I'm not even eighteen yet, but I'm so moved by the way Mr. Graham has touched so many people. Even though I haven't met him, I wish I could meet someone so brilliant, yet humble. I just want to thank you for doing so many positive things in this world. You truly have put a little slice of heaven on earth.

ESCORTED MY MOTHER-IN-LAW

I am so very grateful that Billy Graham was conducting a crusade in Philadelphia during the time my mother-in-law visited from Charleston. She was a mighty woman of God, and the crusade was the highlight of her visit. It was wonderful. Seeing all the people being saved and giving their lives to the Lord Jesus was almost unheard of at that time. May the Lord increase your greatness and comfort you on every side.

BILLY, DAD, AND ME

When I was a child, every time a Billy Graham program was on TV. . .it was on in our house. My dad was a great fan and follower of the Billy Graham crusades. He loved to listen to George Beverly Shea sing. To my knowledge, he never missed a telecast.

Some of my greatest memories of my dad are shared watching Billy Graham. Unfortunately, my dad has passed on, but he instilled Christian values in me that I cherish and live by to this day. Now my husband and I watch the telecasts whenever we can. (The other day, we watched one that originally aired a year or so before I was born!)

Because of great Christians like you and my dad, today I am an ordained minister and share the Word of God and the love of Jesus wherever I go. Billy, I want to thank you for helping to shape my life. You are truly a great Christian leader. . . . I always felt the presence of the Lord whenever you were in our living room.

YOU ARE AN INSPIRATION TO US, BILLY GRAHAM!

Thank you, Billy Graham, for your faithfulness in preaching the Gospel of Jesus Christ in such a way that *all* are able to understand. You've been a blessing in my life ever since your 1949 Los Angeles crusade.

In 1949, I was a freshman at BIOLA (6th and Hope Street campus). I was looking for a job after school hours and was sent to your office close to the school. (Up to this point, I had never heard about you.) What a joy it was to have a little part in helping by folding letters and stuffing envelopes for mailing. As a result of this, I was able to attend some of your meetings in Los Angeles. You were a real blessing in my life, and I thank you.

Now, fifty-eight years later, my husband of fifty-five years and I enjoy your taped TV shows of many of your crusades. We are both grateful for your ministry!

Lora Mae

A DIRECT LINK

I got saved from a very turbulent lifestyle. In 1968, my father died in a hail of bullets as he was attempting to rob a bank. I was only sixteen at the time. The oldest of four boys, I led them all into drug abuse and crime. In 1981, I befriended a Christian family that led me to the Lord.

So what's the connection to Billy Graham? Well, Mike, the friend who led me to Christ (and who is now with the Lord), told me that in 1957, in Madison Square Garden, he knelt down in the sawdust under the bleachers and trusted Christ while Billy was still giving the invitation down front. So, thank you, Billy! I feel as if my coming to Christ has a direct link to you and the ministry God has entrusted to you. I can only imagine how many people you have directly or indirectly influenced as a result of your ministry.

EASTERN EUROPE ENCOURAGED

Greetings from Romania! It's so wonderful to remember the time when our dear brother Billy Graham preached in our country during the time of deep and dark communism. I was just a little child at the time, but I remember how much it meant to my father, who was a Baptist pastor and had lots of trouble with communists because of his faith. That crusade was a renewing and lifting experience for all of us. We will always remember that time with thankful hearts. We love you and bless you, Brother Billy Graham, in Jesus' name.

Iren

A STONE DROPPED INTO A POOL

I never attended a crusade, but looking back on my life, I see that others who knew the Good News through Billy have consistently impacted my life and faith. A stone dropped into a pool produces ripples. The ripples from Billy Graham will spread far beyond his lifetime and into eternity. Thank you, Billy. I look forward to the end of my time on earth as a child looks toward Christmas.

A SICK LITTLE GIRL

I was ten years old. My dear grandmother had died the year before and my mom was still terribly sad. She started listening to Christian programs on our old radio and in 1950 gave her heart to the Lord. We lived in a very small house and the radio could be heard easily into my bedroom. It was February 14, 1950, and I was sick. The radio was on and Mom was listening to a new preacher everyone was talking about—Billy Graham. I listened, too, and through my fever and misery, the Lord touched my heart, and I gave my life to Him.

Fifty-eight years have passed, and I still love the Lord. I lost my husband and my father. My mother is still teaching a Bible study class every Tuesday at age ninety-three. I raised two beautiful daughters, and both accepted the Lord at early ages. One is married to a wonderful pastor; my other daughter and her husband love the Lord, and one of her jobs is at a Christian radio station. I thank God for Billy Graham and his uncompromising message.

THE WORLD STILL NEEDS A "BILLY GRAHAM"

My parents came to America in 1951, Ukrainian immigrants from Germany. Because the quota to America was full, we were delayed immigration for two years, during which time my parents became Christians. When I became a Christian at age thirteen, my parents began to listen to *The Hour of Decision* on the radio. When we heard that Billy Graham was going to have a crusade in Chicago, we were all excited. I signed up for counseling and singing in the choir. It felt like heaven. I got my first Bible training at the counseling meetings. I also met a godly woman who mentored me after the Billy Graham crusade was over at McCormick Place. My brother came forward at the crusade, and that completed our whole family.

Years later, I got married and had three sons. My family moved to Tampa, Florida. In the 1990s, Billy Graham "followed" us to Tampa and had a crusade. I sang in the choir again and brought a nonbeliever with me. I made her sit with me in the choir. I told her she had to mouth the words, even though she didn't know the songs, because the cameras would be on her at any given moment as the program was filmed and aired. It was very difficult for her, but she had no choice. I told her I would go spelunking with her if she came to the crusade. She liked her sinful lifestyle, but when Billy Graham spoke, she was convicted and gave her heart to Jesus.

As I grew older, my friends and family and I would talk about the method of preaching that Billy Graham used. We all agreed that it was very simple and unadulterated, yet it had you spellbound. . . . It was simple for the unsaved to grasp the truth, and convicting to the saved to grow further in Christ. . . . The world still needs a "Billy Graham."

ON SOLID GROUND

Billy, my father, who was born in Puerto Rico and had a second-grade education, began as an usher at the 1950s Bronx crusade. He always referred to you as the most truthful preacher he has ever heard. Your messages meant so much to him, and he passed his experiences to all of his four children. Today, my husband and I do the same with our children, and we thank God for your obedience and passion for God. . . . We believe we are on solid ground because of your obedience to sacrifice yourself to help families all over the world. Billy, we love you!

"LET'S GO HEAR WHAT THIS YANK HAS TO SAY"

It was right after World War II when Billy came to England for a crusade. My dad said, "Let's go hear what this Yank has to say." Well, they did hear, and hearing is believing, so both my parents came to know the Lord. Dad was drafted to the coal mines during the war; but when the war was over, he set out to work in a machine shop. Not long after that, my dad and mom came to the States to live and settled in Pennsylvania. Dad felt the Lord calling him to be a pastor, and he did. . .serving the Lord for thirty-five years till the Lord called him home. Both Dad and Mom are gone now, but through their conversions, my granddad and grandmom were saved, my sister and husband and three children, my brother and wife and four children (and my brother works with Wycliffe Bible Translators and has served on the mission field for thirty years), my wife and I and three children. . .and I could go on and on. All of these generations touched by the love of the Lord because of this one Yank who listened to the voice of God.

THE ONLY TELEVISION PROGRAM SHE WOULD EVER WATCH

My grandmother, born in 1883, was the finest Christian I ever knew. The *only* television program she would ever watch was when Billy Graham spoke. She was as strong and bold as he was in urging everyone of the necessity to give their life to Jesus. Thank God for these courageous people who lived by example. My grandmother did not see most of the fruits of her efforts, but she never gave up, and most of her family is serving the Lord now. The Graham family is loved and the most highly respected family in America.

A STANDARD AND A LIGHTHOUSE

Dear Mr. Graham, thank you for your faithfulness for all of these years. You are in my prayers regularly. Your ministry has been an integral thread that has been woven into the fabric of my family. Several of my great-aunts, great-uncles, great-grandparents, and grandparents were saved and/or participated in one of your crusades. As for me, your ministry has provided instruction, guidance, and sometimes correction. I thank God that you answered the call all those years ago—but most important, you have lived a life above reproach that has served as a standard and a lighthouse for this mighty nation of ours. God bless you richly in the coming years!

You Were His Hero

My grandparents watched you faithfully on TV as I was growing up. I continued the tradition, and when my son was four, you were his hero. He would stand outside and preach to the children in our neighbourhood, telling them that they "must be born again if they want to go to heaven to be with Jesus." Today, he is a mighty man of God, still preaching the Good News.

We are so grateful that our children grew up with a mighty man of God (you, Billy) as their inspiration. Thank you, Billy, for having been a part of four generations of our family. My father, who never went to church, wept while watching one of your crusades just days before he died suddenly. I often wonder if he made a commitment to Christ that day. May God bless you and keep you forever in the palm of His hand.

Billy Graham and Hershey's Chocolate

My father became a preacher in 1966, when I was seven years old. We moved to Wyoming from Nampa, Idaho, where my dad had been going to Northwest Nazarene College. The church, on a good day, had around twenty-five in attendance. We were there every time the doors opened.

We got a TV in 1968, and while we didn't get to watch it much, whenever Billy Graham was speaking we had to watch. Then, as soon as the service was over, we had to go to bed.

My mom used to like Hershey's chocolate bars, and she would buy the big, family-size bars and would give each of us kids a couple of squares of chocolate while we watched Billy Graham. There were five of us kids, and we all lined up in front of the TV. Mom would always tell us that she got to go see Billy Graham when he went to Iowa in the late 1940s or early 1950s.

I would dread when I knew that Billy Graham was on TV, as that meant we would have to sit still for hours. Now, looking back, it is a great memory that we did as a family. It was also a change of pace from listening to my dad the preacher—because most times, our family was half the audience for him. Thank you, Billy Graham, for all the years, memories, and truth you have given to us.

We All Stopped Whatever We Were Doing

I was raised in southeast Georgia on a big farm with five brothers and a Christian mom and dad. We went to the Baptist church. We got our first TV when I was about nine years old. Before that, however, I would hear my dad playing a Gospel station from Ohio on his bedside radio at night.

When the Rev. Billy Graham came on TV, we all stopped whatever we were doing and watched all the people he was preaching to. So many people were there, and his words were so interesting that I could not leave the TV. I loved it—from the beginning songs until the invitation at the end. And I loved watching all those people who came to know God! I would always get closer to the TV and wish I was there, too, praying in my heart that God would hear my prayers, too.

I have kept that faith all my life, and I will be sixty-four next month. I am forever grateful to this man God picked to preach His Holy Word in so many nations. If I could meet anyone, it would be him.

HAPPY BIRTHDAY AND THANK YOU, BROTHER GRAHAM!

Dearest Brother Graham, I was introduced to your ministry by my grandmother (via the television) when I was ten years old. My brother and I went to live with my grandparents for a short while, and I remember watching all of your crusades on television with my grandmother. I soon came to love you as much as she did. I wanted *so* badly to be able to go to one of your crusade revival meetings in person!

My children were invited to go with our dear neighbors and their church to one of your crusades in Fresno, California, in 2000. I threw proper manners to the wind and invited myself as well. I did not want my children to miss such a wonderful opportunity, and I wanted to see you in the *worst way*! Well, of course, my friends responded to my request with an immediate, "Certainly!" and I was afforded one of the most wonderful experiences of my lifetime!

I could barely make out your features. . .but, that was okay. I know your face by heart. I have always jumped at every opportunity to watch a rerun of one of your crusades on television. You are a beloved man of God, respected by many, and I know that we will meet one day face-to-face in heaven.

A FAMILY CHANGED

It was a Monday night under a starry sky—July 13, 1964. Billy Graham rose to the platform, and it was electrifying. In our fourteen years of life (we're triplets), it was the biggest crowd, the biggest event we had ever been a part of. Our whole family was there: our parents, the three of us, our younger sister, and two younger brothers. We were church attenders in a fairly liberal church, so we had never heard the plan of salvation before Dr. Graham came to the podium. That night, he made it clear, even for our young understanding, that we needed a Savior.

I'm not sure what text Dr. Graham used, but what I do know is that when "Just As I Am" began, the three of us and our twelve-year-old brother all went forward. I look back on that night and realize that I didn't completely understand all that took place. And still, almost fifty years later, I am awed and stand in wonder at the truths I learned that night. I am amazed at the complexity of a plan that offers forgiveness because of the death and resurrection of Jesus, but also the simplicity of a plan that says "whosoever calls on the name of the Lord will be saved." Again, I'm not sure what the counselor said, but I do remember that, later that evening driving home, I looked up to the sky from the car window, knowing, *knowing*, that if something should happen, I was going to heaven. I am still amazed by that.

Today, all of our siblings, our children, and our grandchildren who are old enough to make a decision for Christ, have done that. In our family, we have pastors, full- and part-time missionaries, Sunday school and Bible teachers, counselors, and soul winners. That night, we made the best decision any of us could have ever made. Not only were individuals changed but the legacy of an entire family, the direction of generations, was changed. Thank you, Dr. Graham, for being faithful on July 13, 1964, to share the plan of salvation. That night, our names were written in the Lamb's Book of Life, and we are eternally grateful.

Kris, Karen, and Kathie

HE READ *DECISION* MAGAZINE COVER TO COVER

I came to know Jesus Christ as my Lord and Savior in 1966 at the age of twenty-eight. It was the most important decision I ever made in my life. I started attending a Christ-centered church, taking my two little girls with me. My husband was not interested and would not go with us.

I had a very strong desire to share Jesus with my father, who lived almost two thousand miles away, clear across the United States. He was not a religious man and was an alcoholic. He and my mother were divorced. I decided to send him a subscription to *Decision* magazine, hoping he would read it and learn about the saving grace of my precious Lord. When I attended my father's funeral service four years later, his wife (he had remarried) told me that when *Decision* magazine was delivered each month, he read it cover to cover. That was all she told me.

A few weeks later, while sitting in church one Sunday morning during the worship service, I felt the Holy Spirit speaking to my heart, revealing to me that my father was with Him in heaven and I would see him again one day. I am so thankful to God for speaking to my father through His Holy Spirit. That thrilled my heart. *Decision* magazine had a great deal to do with that.

BILLY AND "BIG MAMA"

My grandfather (Big Daddy) died in 1963, leaving a grieving, lost widow. Big Mama didn't drive and had never written a check or bought groceries. She was a child bride at fifteen and a widow at sixty-nine. I was one of the youngest grandchildren, and as such was able to devote more time to my Big Mama. Over the next thirteen years, we bonded as loving family members, friends, and Christians.

Because Big Mama didn't drive, her church attendance was spotty. But she was the first person I knew who read the Bible from Genesis to Revelation as if it were a novel! And she achieved that goal several times in her lifetime. And, every time—I mean *every time*—there was a Billy Graham crusade on television, we sat and watched. In those days, the crusades might be on every evening for two weeks. Didn't matter! We were watching.

Big Mama would say, "Wow that Dr. Graham can really preach," and, "Doesn't he know the Bible?"

In those formative years of my life, I learned more about my Christian walk from my Big Mama and Dr. Graham than anybody else. For the rest of my days, I will cherish those evenings listening with Big Mama to the Billy Graham crusades. Thanks!

TOSSING TURTLES

In 1952, my mother divorced her first husband, an alcoholic, gambling womanizer. In Shreveport, Louisiana, in 1952, divorce was rare and socially unacceptable, but my mother took her one-year-old daughter, set out on her own, and became a working single mom. In 1953, she married my father, who, it turned out, also was an alcoholic, gambling man. I was born in 1954.

In 1955, Mom asked Christ into her heart at a Billy Graham crusade, and her life took a remarkable new direction. Her sins were forgiven, and she found new life. The change in her life was so dramatic that, within a year, my father accepted Christ into his life. As their faith in Christ grew over the following ten years, my father felt the call to be a pastor.

Despite pervasive financial hardships and health problems throughout her life, Mom had a joy and light that always shined brightly. The hallmark of her life was offering grace to everyone. She judged no one and treated strangers as lifelong friends. She brought soldiers stationed at a nearby army base to our home for Thanksgiving, because they had nowhere to go. When adulterous women were thrown out of their homes by their husbands, Mom brought them into our home and gave them refuge. One stranger that Mom brought home stole her diamond wedding ring from the windowsill over the kitchen sink, where she put it when she washed dishes. After she had fed this stranger breakfast, washed the dishes he'd dirtied, and changed the bed linens he'd used, he repaid her by lifting her ring. He then said his good-byes, never to be heard from again. Even losing her only prized jewelry didn't change Mom's behavior toward strangers. She never let anyone rob her of her joy and commitment to be like Christ.

Mom passed away in 2003 at the age of seventy-four. More so than anyone else, my mom was the most Christlike human I've ever known—and she was a spiritual offspring of Billy Graham!

When I think of the impact that Billy Graham had on my mom, I am reminded of the boy who was trying to rescue hundreds of sea turtles that had washed up onto the beach after a storm. A giant sandbar had formed and the turtles couldn't make it back to the water. They were dying from the heat and sun exposure. One at a time, the boy would pick up a turtle and carry it hundreds of yards across the sandbar to the water's edge and release it. A man came along and said, "Son, what are you doing?" After the boy explained the task, the man said, "Well, son, you're wasting your time. You're not going to be able to save all these turtles, and it really doesn't matter." The boy replied, "Well, mister, if this turtle was you, I bet it would matter."

I imagine there were times when the enormous task that Reverend Graham accepted from God's call seemed impossible. . .that he couldn't reach everyone who needed the good news of salvation through Jesus Christ. I want Billy Graham to know that he reached my mom. . .and it mattered.

Thank You, Billy Graham. . .
for Your Personal Touch on My Life

WORDS CANNOT DESCRIBE BILLY GRAHAM

Allow me to write these few words in the form of a personal letter to a man who has, for most of my life, occupied a unique place in my heart. As I humbly try to share why this is, I think many will understand.

I was born in the mountains of Switzerland and raised by two wonderful parents who gave me not only their love but also more than anybody needed in love, guidance, education, and comforts of all kinds. They worked very hard and sacrificially for many years.

We were taken to church and taught to pray. At times we were read the Bible. God was there, but not close or personal. As I reached my early teens, I grew restless in my heart, not knowing why. I had all the world could possibly offer, and yet no peace, no contentment, and no joy. Gradually, I realized that my need was a spiritual need. I had nowhere to go to find answers; I didn't even know the questions to ask. I knew down deep that neither my parents nor my Sunday school teachers had the answers—nor anyone in the church. At least, if they did, they didn't seem able to communicate it to me.

With a sense of quiet desperation, I pursued answers on my own but could never seem to hold the truth in my hand: it always seemed to slip through my fingers, leaving me frustrated and discouraged. There was no one to help, nowhere to turn. But in some way unknown to me, God had heard my cry. He had prepared a way and sent a messenger on his way to reach me.

Haerig, the Armenian word for "father", you were the one. You wrote a book—on your knees you said—called *Peace with God*. My father one day gathered us in the living room of our home on the shores of Lake Geneva and tried to tell us of a drastic change that had occurred in his life and in his relationship with God. I didn't quite understand what he was trying to tell us. I asked, "You always told us about God. What is different?" His answer stunned me. "I was searching," he said, "but now I have found."

"How?"

"I read this book, just translated in French, called *Peace with God*."

"Can I borrow it, Dad?" I said.

Haerig, this was the first time you spoke to me, through your book. You gave me the words that would forever quench the thirst in my soul. You told me how to be born again, according to the scriptures.

That night, a fifteen year-old boy knelt by his bed, alone with God and invited His Savior, Jesus Christ, to forgive his sins and live forever in his heart. Peace finally filled my soul. Thank you, Billy Graham.

Several years later, our relationship became more significant and more intimate. You and Ruth honored me by accepting my request for your daughter's hand in marriage. And there followed many years of happy memories as you became a friend with a father's heart to me. Your genuine commitment to Christ, your faithfulness to your call to proclaim the Gospel, and your love and kindness for the humblest person, as well as for the mighty and powerful of this world, inspired me time and again. You lived your faith, whether people saw it or not. As your son Franklin said one time, "There were not two people, one at home and one in public." I have witnessed this for more than forty years and will never forget it.

Thank you, Billy Graham. You have been a father to me, the grandfather to my children, and a friend who is—and forever will be—closer than a brother. Above all, you have introduced me to our God and showed what it means to honor Him and walk with Him.

I love you and thank you,
Dr. Stephan Tchividjian (1939–2010),
father of seven of Billy Graham's grandchildren

My Rememberance of Bill and Ruth

I was Rev. Graham's stylist for eleven years in Asheville, and I have the deepest respect for not only his spiritual dedication to his work but for his personal character as well. It was a treat to have him come in for an appointment, because he always shared wonderful stories of his life and his family. With Ruth also being a client for many years, I had the privilege of having them come in together a few times for their hair appointments. It was wonderful seeing them interact with one another, and even after many decades of marriage, the twinkle of love still sparkled in their eyes.

The one event that impressed me the most was the time Jim Bakker was removed from PTL. There was much ado in the news that day of Bakker's removal. . .blame and accusation were flying everywhere, especially from some other evangelists. That same afternoon, Dr. Graham came in for his haircut, and of course the Bakker scandal was the topic of the day in the salon. I was quite interested in hearing Dr. Graham's perspective on all the horrendous rumors. He looked at me and said, "All I blame Jim and Tammy for was not surrounding themselves with the right people. When people live their lives in the public eye, it's imperative that they know how to handle themselves properly and have a credible and competent support staff. That's where they went wrong." I was more than impressed with his understanding and compassion for what the Bakkers were going through. I gained an even greater respect and admiration for Dr. Graham that day and realized that he indeed was a great man sent of God.

I was blessed in getting to know Ruth even better. It was a joy seeing her each week for eleven years, because she wasn't just a client but also a dear, loving friend to me. She came in for an appointment the day one of my friends mysteriously disappeared, with foul play expected. Since the authorities had absolutely no leads or information to go on, we feared it would soon end up as a cold case. When Ruth saw my despair over Jaymie's disappearance, she picked up the phone and spoke to an agent she knew at the FBI. Within four days, Jaymie's body was found and the killer was captured. I always credit Ruth for being the catalyst in resolving the case and sparing Jaymie's family and friends years of not knowing what had happened to her. Through Ruth, I also met Bunny, Anne, Gigi, and many of the grandchildren. I feel so very privileged in having known Ruth. She was a remarkable, loving, and gracious lady. I knew Dr. Graham was right when he said there would be great fanfare in heaven when she entered the pearly gates. I also know that when the time comes and he approaches the heavenly gates, Ruth will be there to greet him with her warm, beautiful smile and outstretched arms. Then they will once again have that loving sparkle and gleam in their eyes.

Memories with My Great-Grandparents

Ever since I can remember, the names Billy and Ruth Graham have meant something to me. God has so richly blessed me in being one of their many great-grandchildren. I am so very thankful that I have gotten to know him and knew her. I have made so many memories up on the mountaintop in their house. I always enjoy hearing stories about him and Ruth. I really love the ones about her! She was, and still is, one of my role models. I loved her so much and am so happy that she is with Christ and she is healthy. I am also very sad, but God blessed me with knowing her for twelve wonderful years. Though I barely remember when she could walk, I will always remember the times I spent with her. One day we were at their house on the mountain and she said we could have one of the many stuffed animal mice she kept on the rails of the stairway near her room, and of course we did. When I grow up to be a mother and a wife, I want to be like Ruth. I also have had many great visits with Billy (or, as we call him, Daddy Bill). Recently, we visited him in Jacksonville. I loved that time because nobody was there except our family and we had a great visit. I also love visiting him on the mountain. As long as I can remember, their freezer has always been full of ice cream! So when any of the great-grandkids go there, we always end up leaving full of ice cream. Most famous people that you meet are different than the everyday person, but when you spend time with my great-grandfather, you feel like you're with a friend, not with somebody who is an evangelist known worldwide. I love Billy Graham as my great-grandfather, and I am so blessed that I have known him.

Hannah

DADDY BILL

In mid-September 1949, a young dairy farmer headlined what could be characterized as the greatest religious movement in the twentieth century. This man had a way of connecting with people. For over sixty years, he has preached the Gospel to more than 210 million people on six different continents, in eighty-five countries, and in all of America's fifty states—more than any other man or woman in history. There was something different about him. He is a man who has stayed humble, before both God and man. His motives have always been right before God; they have never been self-serving.

As Dr. Charles T. Cook once said, "It would seem to be God's purpose to choose a man. . .divinely gifted and empowered to interpret to his own generation their deepest needs, and to declare the remedy." He has counseled and become a mentor to every American president since Harry Truman. His true faith in Jesus Christ is what has kept him humble.

This man is known to the world as Rev. Billy Graham, but to me he is Daddy Bill. My mother is Billy and Ruth Graham's eldest child, and I am the youngest of seven and Billy and Ruth Graham's sixteenth grandchild. The most admirable thing that comes to my mind is, first, my granddad's humility. He truly believes that he is just a regular country preacher. He has told me on many occasions, "I am not a great preacher, and you know I don't claim to be one. I have heard great preaching many times and wished I was one of them. I am just an ordinary preacher communicating the Gospel the best way I know how."

My grandfather has accomplished more than most of us will in a lifetime, and he seriously believes he is just an ordinary preacher. The Bible verse that always comes to mind when I think of Daddy Bill is Titus 3:2: "To speak evil of no one, to be peaceable, gentle, showing all humility to all men." It is almost as if he read that verse and put it into practice wholeheartedly.

I can remember a time when my grandfather was in South Florida for a board meeting and he was getting lonely. So he took out his black phone book and began to look for friends who lived in the area. He found a younger couple and decided to give them a ring to invite them for dinner at the hotel. I will never forget what he said when he called, it was truly unbelievable. He said, "Hello? Hey how are you? This is Billy, Billy Graham. Do you remember me?" I couldn't believe that a man who has been listed number six in *Time* and *Life* magazines as the most respected man in the twentieth century was calling a couple he had not seen in a while and he truly thought that they might have forgotten who he was. Daddy Bill has reminded me what the whole journey of life is all about.

Daddy Bill has impacted my life most in showing me what it means to be truly humble, not to take myself too seriously, and to always remember that I am the creature created by the Creator. I am by no means satisfied at where I want to be spiritually, but I don't believe there will ever be a time that we are where we should be spiritually; we will always have to grow closer to the Lord in order to have a relationship with Him. So I want to say thank you, Daddy Bill, for being the loving, most wonderful grandfather anyone could ever wish for. I love you with all my heart, and I am always praying for you.

Antony Tchividjian

HIS FAVORITE GRANDCHILD

When I think of Billy Graham, I think of all the pictures I've seen over the years. His tall stature, deep voice, and the passion that flows through his face and hands. He has met many dignitaries, presidents, celebrities, down to the poorest of the poor. He treats them all the same, with kindness, tenderness, and love. He has preached to millions and brought millions to Christ. He has chosen to talk the talk and walk the walk, and he has done it to perfection. Billy Graham is truly a man of God.

This is the public man, but I have had the privilege to know Billy Graham as Daddy Bill all my life. I have been able to get that rare glimpse of a private man. I have watched him tenderly love my grandmother. He has taught all of his children and grandchildren how a man should love his wife. Every night before bed, Daddy Bill calls all the visitors to the living room to have devotions. He reads from the Bible and then prays. This has taught me the importance of devotions with your family. Even at home, he lights up when he reads the Word of God. I will never forget him calling me his favorite grandchild. After all my downs in life, I was so happy that he saw me favorably. (Much to my dismay, I later found out that he tells all the grandchildren that they are his favorite.) My favorite memory is when he went for a walk and I joined him. This wise man sometimes wanted to talk, and other times we walked in silence, holding hands. I learned more about him in the silences.

As I watch him growing older, I realize how fragile he is. He finally has to admit that he can't do the things he used to, and this makes me love him more. So, to my Daddy Bill, I love you and admire you more than you know. I can only hope to have a fraction of the faith you have.

Windsor Bauders

A GRANDSON'S TRIBUTE

*After greeting them, he related one by one the things that God
had done among the Gentiles through his ministry.*
ACTS 21:19 ESV

Ever since I can remember, I have called my grandparents
Daddy Bill and TaiTai. Regardless of their fame and noto-
riety throughout this world, they are first and foremost my
grandparents, and for that I am so very grateful. My earliest
memories of my grandparents are of spending summers and
holidays with them in Montreat, North Carolina, traveling
to various crusades around the country, their visits to our
home in south Florida, and eating at Daddy Bill's favorite restaurant. . .Morrison's Cafeteria! During our visits to
Montreat, TaiTai invited each sibling to take turns sleeping
at their log cabin home that sits near the top of a beautiful
mountain nestled in the Blue Ridge Mountains of western
North Carolina. During sleepovers I was spoiled by TaiTai,
who gave me as much ice cream and soda as I could consume
and allowed me to go to bed at whatever time I wished! Each
night, before my grandparents would go to bed, we would
gather in the kitchen area and get on our knees and pray
together. Those nights of us on our knees praying to our
heavenly Father are forever etched in my memory. What a
blessing.

As I grew older, I learned that Daddy Bill and I share a
common interest. . .the world of politics! We have had many
interesting political conversations over the past many years.
What always fascinates me is that he is friends with many of
the subjects of our conversations. Something else that always
stands out to me is that, while Daddy Bill enjoys discuss-

ing politics, he never becomes "political," and he is always respectful, regardless of political affiliation.

I will never forget when he invited me to the 1980 Reagan inauguration. I was only twelve years old! Shortly after arriving at our Washington hotel, I noticed out my room window that a large number of limousines had pulled up to the rear of the hotel. Upon doing some investigation, I learned that President-elect Ronald Reagan had just arrived to give a speech. I immediately convinced my grandfather's assistant to go with me to where the limousines were parked, so that I might be able to get a glimpse of Mr. Reagan as he left the hotel. I will never forget the moment when Reagan walked out and my grandfather's assistant introduced him to me and informed him I was a grandson of Billy Graham's. As soon as my grandfather's name was mentioned, I saw a smile on Reagan's face and he began to tell me how much he loved and admired Billy Graham. As a twelve-year-old kid, I was so impressed that the next president of the United States knew and loved my Daddy Bill!

Throughout the following years, I traveled with my grandfather to various other political events, such as the 1984 and 1988 presidential inaugurations. One incident I will never forget, and which has always been an encouragement to me, occurred during the 1988 Republican National Convention in New Orleans. One evening, a friend and I were looking for a car to borrow so we could drive around the city. As a twenty-year-old college sophomore, I was simply interested in getting out into the city to have some fun. Sadly, God was not a priority in my life at the time.

My grandfather's assistant had rented a car when we arrived, and I decided to go to Daddy Bill's hotel room to see if he would allow us to borrow the rental car. We arrived at his hotel at about nine p.m. Keep in mind, this was during the middle of a huge convention at which Billy Graham could have attended any number of political social gatherings. . .he probably could have had his pick of which ones to attend. Thus, I was a little surprised when he opened his hotel room door wearing his pajamas. As we entered the room, I noticed his Bible open on his bed. At that moment, God convicted my heart in a significant way. Here was Billy Graham, "America's Preacher," in New Orleans during a political convention attended by many influential and famous people, and he chose to spend his evening. . .sitting in his hotel room reading scripture while spending time with his heavenly Father. I left his room that evening forever impacted—and without the car keys!

Perhaps the greatest characteristic that stands out in my mind about both of my grandparents is their incredible humility, anointed to them by our Lord. The apostle Paul writes: "But far be it from me to boast except in the cross of our Lord Jesus Christ, by which the world has been crucified to me, and I to the world" (Galatians 6:14 ESV). This verse is given a very practical meaning to me when I think of Daddy Bill and TaiTai. I have been in the room when my grandfather has called and spoken to the president of the United States and then got up to pull the kitchen table chair out for the housekeeper, who was regularly invited to join them for dinner. This is just one small example of many. I have found that my grandparents are as sincerely interested and excited about having conversations with "everyday people," such as taxi drivers, housekeepers, waitresses, etc., as they are with presidents, queens, and popes. The only matter for which

Daddy Bill and TaiTai "boast" is the Gospel of Christ, and that is communicated to all persons equally, both in words and actions.

In many ways, Daddy Bill and TaiTai have been the "hands and feet of Christ" in my life—for which I give God the glory! Though the world knows and loves Billy and Ruth Graham, God has graciously allowed me to know Billy and Ruth Graham as Daddy Bill and TaiTai. Perhaps the greatest blessing is that there is absolutely no difference between the public life of Billy and Ruth Graham and the private lives of Daddy Bill and TaiTai. The authenticity of the Gospel lived out in the lives of my grandparents has been a gracious example given to me by our loving heavenly Father.

There are so many more blessed memories that I cannot share, due to the limited space provided. Memories of my wife and I spending weekends in Montreat with Daddy Bill and TaiTai while I was in law school, memories of my many afternoon visits with Daddy Bill when he visits the Mayo Clinic in Jacksonville, memories of my precious young children spending time with their great-grandparents during their summer breaks. I praise God for granting me such memories, and I am looking forward to many more with Daddy Bill and TaiTai.

Basyle "Boz" Tchividjian (grandson)

IT IS ALL ABOUT THE GOSPEL AND JESUS

I met Billy and Ruth about fifteen years ago, when I began to date their granddaughter Jerushah, who is their eldest daughter, Gigi's, youngest daughter. I was extremely nervous to meet them. *What should I say, or not say?* I wondered. *What should I wear? Should I hug them, shake their hands, bow down in humble submission?* I sincerely considered all of these options and more. This was the greatest evangelist the world had ever seen. *Will his face shine like Moses?* I thought to myself.

Upon meeting them, I realized that the revered Billy Graham and the radiant woman Ruth, who stood behind him while he so consistently and faithfully declared, "Come just as you are, come and receive Jesus. . ." seemed to be extending the same invitation to me. They treated me as one of their own from "hello." They were simple, kind, loving, and very thoughtful grandparents of the girl who captured my heart. What mattered to them was my heart, not my clothes or my carefully constructed words. From that day forward, I have learned more about God, life, and love from Billy and Ruth than from anyone or any book.

Daddy Bill has shown me humility like I never dreamed or imagined. It's as if he has never tried to be humble. He is not a product of "three steps to humility" or a well-practiced line of, "Oh, praise God, it was Him and not me." He sincerely does not seem to understand why someone would thank *him*, the messenger. He becomes uncomfortable when I share the compliments, love, and admiration for him of people I have spoken with. He has appeared confused and several times has responded, "Why would they want to thank me?" I have learned not to ask, "Are you serious?" anymore; he really does mean it.

It's as if he really knows and experiences God doing the work through him and understands that the tool doesn't have a place to boast while he is in the Maker's hand.

He has taught me that Jesus is the most important truth I will ever learn and proclaim. He has never swayed from that challenge—every time I sit and talk with him about ministry. Each time I see him, he says, "Hello, Chris, how is the church?" I respond with details that I am excited about, and he responds every time, no matter what, "It is all about the Gospel and Jesus." He is right, and he doesn't allow details, numbers, or program ideas to stand beside the place of Jesus, and he never lets me allow it either. Jesus is always the most important part of our conversation.

Lastly, and maybe equally important, he has taught me how to cherish my bride. He hasn't given me advice, like he has with preaching, writing, or leadership. Those spoken insights are things I have appreciated immensely. His love for Ruth has clearly been on display each time I have seen them together, heard him speak of her, and have watched and listened to him miss her when they are apart. His longing for Jesus seems to be closely rivaled only by his love for Ruth. What a beautiful picture he has given me of what it means to love one woman all of our days here. Watching him love Ruth has taught me how to love Jerushah.

He has given me the best picture I have ever seen of what it looks like to love God and love others. Thank You, Jesus, for teaching me to love You and love others through the life and love of Billy and Ruth Graham. Thank you, Daddy Bill.

Chris Armfield

Thank You, Billy Graham. . .
for the Time I Met You in Person

THE DAY I MET BILLY GRAHAM

In 1987, I was in my first year serving as youth pastor at Calvary Baptist Church, in Burbank, California. This was an interesting position, because at the time, Calvary Baptist was a church without any youth. So, our "youth group" was made up of non-churched teens from the neighborhoods, none of whom had yet professed Christ.

I received a call from a woman at Billy Graham's World Wide Pictures, telling me about an advance screening for their new movie, *Caught.* They were holding the screening at Universal Studios, and she wanted to know if I would bring my youth group to the screening. She told me they especially wanted the reactions of non-Christians to the movie, and she asked me to encourage my Christian youth to invite their non-Christian friends. I told her I didn't actually have any Christians in my youth group, but I would ask them to invite their friends anyway.

The night of the screening was a hoot. My friend Martin and I brought eight teen boys from the neighborhood to the screening. Other church youth groups were arriving by bus, dressed nicely for the occasion, walking quietly and politely in groups to the theater. Our guys were all over the place. They were loud and obnoxious, dressed for the street, running pell-mell here and there, excitedly checking out the grounds of Universal Studios after hours. We stuck out like sore thumbs in an elegant hand gallery.

After we finally gathered them all (and got them to put out their cigarettes), we made our way into the screening theater. It was a first-class theater, with high-backed chairs that reclined all the way back. Our guys naturally pushed their way to the front of the theater where they proudly sat down front and center in full view of everybody. One of them asked me where there was a water fountain. Instead of releasing him now that we finally had them all together and sitting, I told him I would check. I walked up to a man in the back of the theater who looked official to ask him about the water fountain. He turned out to be Bill Brown, the president of World Wide Pictures at the time.

He asked me my name and said, "I have someone I would like you to meet." Then he tapped the shoulder of a man who was standing with his back toward us and said, "Billy, I would like you to meet Ray."

"Billy" turned around, and sure enough, it was Billy Graham. I had no idea he was even going to be there that night and was caught totally off guard. I think I managed to squeak out something brilliant like, "Hello. Nice to meet you. I've heard you speak."

Billy shook my hand, smiled at me, and with a twinkle in his eye, nodded toward the front of the theater. "Are those your boys?"

I looked to the front of the theater where Martin was doing his best to contain eight overly exuberant boys, who were rocking all the way back and up again in their high-backed reclining chairs as fast as they could go. They looked like eight alternating levers in some wildly gyrating machine. I said, "Excuse me," and raced back to the front of the theater where we finally got the boys calmed down in time for the movie.

So that was the one and only time I got to meet Billy Graham in person. I got the impression he was glad that I had brought my wild "youth group" to the screening, and when he came up front after the movie to talk, he smiled at the whole lot of them. Of course, they were completely freaked out to see this man they had only seen on TV suddenly standing in front of them talking about Christ. All in all, it was a great night, and definitely one for the youth pastor books.

FROM A MONTREAT STUDENT

I was a student at Montreat-Anderson College in the early 1980s. I have such fond memories of Billy Graham showing up at Montreat Church every now and then and leading a prayer or just being a part of the congregation. One time my friend's parents had driven over from Arden to go to church with her at Montreat, and Billy Graham happened to be sitting near them in the congregation. They were amazed that Dr. Graham greeted them like he was any other worshipper. His humility is a credit to our Savior's name.

I also remember Ruth Graham coming over to do a Bible study with us in the lobby of the girl's dormitory. I remember going to the Billy Graham Association for a movie occasionally, too. The Grahams were hospitable to us students. Thanks for being authentic in your faith!

INSPIRATION TO YOUNG PASTORS. . .IN 1951

In 1951, my husband, Rev. Eddie King, and I were serving Asheville St. Baptist Church in Morganton, North Carolina. In April of that year, a simultaneous crusade was held in area churches. Two young men, Jim Blackwell and J. W. Magee, who had surrendered to the preaching ministry under our ministry in Mississippi, came to preach. One day, we toured points of interest in the mountains. We came near Montreat and pointed out your home. Someone suggested that we stop by to see if you were home. We did and you were. You graciously received us for a brief visit. As we have watched God work in your life, that visit has been a lifelong inspiration to us all. We returned to Morganton to see God work through these two young preachers to bring many to Christ. The crusade scheduled for one week lasted three weeks instead. All three of these pastors served the Lord faithfully for many years. I share your grief in the parting of your dear wife, Ruth, as I am learning to live without my Eddie, who went to be with the Lord in March 2006. Thank you for your hospitality, friendship, love, and concern for those you have met on this wonderful journey with our Lord and Savior, Jesus Christ.

HOW BGEA AFFECTED US

I want to thank you for your ministry and how you touched our lives. During the 1960s, when Wayne and I were in our late teen years, we were both chosen to work for you in the outgoing mail department, where we mailed 3.5 million *Decision* magazines a month. I worked as a secretary to the men who ran the department. To make a long story short, Wayne and I met and worked together at BGEA in Minneapolis, dated, and later married.

During the time we worked at BGEA, we had some wonderful times, which made for *great* memories—like the Christmas parties where George Beverly Shea would come and sing! Another time was a Sunday afternoon when

BGEA put on an afternoon tea for employees, and you were there.

I had a wonderful time sitting and talking with you as I would with a member of my family. This impressed my dad very much, as he was born the same year you were, and he would always say, "Billy and I are turning forty, fifty, sixty, etc." This is a great memory, as my dad went home to be with the Lord two years ago this month.

I just want to thank you for your ministry where Wayne and I met and married thirty-seven years ago. The work I did at BGEA prepared me for other jobs I have had since.

TAYLOR'S MIRACLE

My story starts back when my husband, Tim, and I were trying to have a child. We had infertility problems and struggled for eight years until God blessed us with a baby boy. When our son, Taylor, was born, he had medical problems. His esophagus was not connected to his stomach. If he ate or drank anything, it could aspirate into his lungs. We were sent to Minneapolis Children's Hospital, where he was to undergo surgery. My husband and I were so afraid, and we kept asking God why it would take us eight years to have a child and then for something to be so wrong.

Taylor underwent surgery and things were going well. Then, one morning, he got a blood clot in his kidney from having his catheter in too long. His body started to shut down and we were not sure whether he would make it. I remember crying out to God and asking, "Why?" We were at the hospital every waking moment. The nurses and a social worker told us we really needed to get out of the hospital for a break. We decided to go for a walk around Lake Calhoun.

We were walking and talking and not really noticing anyone that we were passing. Then Billy Graham walked by. He was incognito in a Twins baseball hat, but as soon as we passed him, my husband and I looked at each other and said, "That was Billy Graham." It was as if God spoke to us at the same time, telling us it was him.

We turned around and ran excitedly toward Billy's bodyguard. We asked him if we could meet Billy. He said it would be okay, and we approached Billy. He was such a gentleman. He took his hat off and greeted us. We shared with Billy about seeing him at a crusade in Fargo, North Dakota. We thanked him for his awesome work for the Lord, and we shared with him about our son. He wrote a get-well-soon note to Taylor and signed it. He gave us each a hug and we said our good-byes.

After that point, it was as if things turned around for Taylor. The really neat thing is that, the day before this, Tim had said that if there was anyone he could meet before he died, he wanted to meet Billy Graham. God works in mysterious ways. Tim got his wish. We both felt such peace after talking with Billy. We went back to the hospital and shared with everyone. We said to the nurses and family members, "I'll bet you can't guess who we just met." They all guessed Kirby Puckett. We said, "No, think bigger than that." When we told them it was Billy Graham, they couldn't believe it.

We have shared this story for the past fourteen years, and it still touches people in such a way. Everyone has such respect and awe for Billy Graham. Our son is doing very well—you would never guess he ever had anything wrong with him. God restored his health. God gave us hope by sending Billy Graham across our path on a sunny day in August 1993.

Billy was on the cover of *Time* magazine in November 1993. We have that magazine framed with the note he wrote to Taylor hanging on his bedroom wall as a constant reminder of how God works in wonderful and mysterious ways.

Tim, Gwen, and Taylor

I MET BILLY GRAHAM

I am so grateful to God for the opportunity to meet the Reverend Billy Graham in person. I had just completed nursing school, was a wife and mother of two, and had a brand-new job at Mercy Hospital in San Diego. My friend and I were on a lunch break from our orientation training and were just coming out of the elevators when. . .there he was! No posse or security guards with him, just one gentleman and Rev. Graham with a walking cane. I was so overjoyed I extended my hand, took his in a firm handshake, and asked, "What are you doing in San Diego?" as if it were any of my business. He so gently and kindly answered that he was visiting a friend.

I've always thought about what an incredible encounter I had that day with Rev. Graham. He was always such a huge influence on my life growing up. I grew up in El Paso, Texas, in a Spanish-speaking household, yet that didn't stop my grandmother or my mother from watching Billy Graham and the crusades on TV. I think the song "Just As I Am" will forever be engrained in me. I remember many times crying for joy just seeing all those people come forward to accept Christ as their Lord and Savior!

Since then, with God's help, I've followed wherever He has sent me. I now live in Tucson, Arizona, and am a member of a church with an incredible passion for mission work reaching the lost in the 10/40 window. This summer, I will be leading a team of doctors and nurses to Thailand. My first time leading, but my third time on a mission trip. God has absolutely revolutionized my life since I stepped out of my comfort zone and followed His lead in sharing His heart with His creation.

To think that what I have experienced these last three years is what Rev. Graham has experienced for his entire ministry career. Walking hand in hand with God! What an honor and a privilege. Thank you, Rev. Graham, for allowing yourself to be used by God to impact millions, including me. Thank you for taking the time to shake my hand and say hello. I rejoice knowing we will someday be in heaven, talking about all the Father did, is doing, and will continue to do!

Mary

My Encounter with Billy

I'm sure Billy Graham doesn't remember my encounter with him, but it was one of the most special moments of my life, and I will never forget it. No words were spoken between us, but the memory of his simple kindness can still today move me to tears.

I grew up watching the crusades on television. My favorite part of the telecast was the invitation to accept Jesus. When the choir began to sing "Just As I Am," something would leap in my spirit. Though I was a little girl at the time, I know now that it was the Holy Spirit prompting my heart.

As I grew up, I rebelled and turned away from God, but whenever I was surfing the television channels and one of the Billy Graham crusades was showing, I could not turn the station; I had to watch.

In 1988, when Billy Graham came to Rochester, New

York, I had out-of-town company and was not able to attend the crusade. But God did a marvelous thing. My guests and I decided to go to Red Lobster for dinner. As we were going in, my one-year-old daughter fell in the entrance of the restaurant. A tall, distinguished gentleman bent down, stood her up, placed his hand on top of her head, and smiled at me. It was Billy Graham! I was speechless, and even today could kick myself for not talking to him and telling him how much it meant to me to just see him. His simple, yet eloquent message that Jesus died for my sins and loved me and wanted to save me from hell did not fall on deaf ears.

I often tell my daughter, who is now twenty-one years old, that she is blessed because she was touched by Billy Graham. She says, "Mom, how many times are you going to tell that story?" I tell her, "I'll tell it until Jesus comes and I see him face-to-face, and then I'm going to find Billy and ask him all the things I was too awestruck to ask the first time I saw him."

PAYBACK

My father was an educational pioneer in the Southern Baptist Convention. We spent many summers at Ridgecrest, as a family, while he led conferences. During the summer of 1963, my father was invited to Montreat to visit with Dr. Graham (and my mother and I could meet him). My father declined the invitation because he had a conference to lead. As a ten-year-old, I was quite upset with my father. A year later, Dr. Graham spoke at the Southern Baptist Convention in Atlantic City, and we were there. After Dr. Graham's speech, my father took me to the front to meet him. My father told him that it was payback for missing dinner the year before. We all had a laugh over it. Growing up in our household, I knew many of the giants of the faith. They were my father's friends, and they knew me by my first name. Dr. Graham was very gracious and humble. I thank God that our paths crossed.

AMID GREATNESS

I have been inspired by Billy Graham for many years. I first heard him preach on television in the late 1980s when I was living in North Carolina. I was a military wife living far away from family and felt very alone. Listening to Billy preach reassured me that all is well and that there was a specific plan for my life. I rarely missed a televised crusade.

I later moved to Florida, where I attended the Tampa Bay crusade in the late 1990s. It was held in the brand-new football stadium. Not only was every seat in the house filled but there was an overflow into the parking lot where the faithful watched it on a big screen.

Perhaps the biggest thrill was when I met Billy Graham in person. I heard through a friend that he was staying on Marco Island, finishing up his book *Just As I Am*. I went into work the next day and told my boss, "I have a once-in-a-lifetime chance to meet someone who has significantly influenced my life. I have to go. I cannot work today. I am going to find Billy Graham."

I believed there was a plan for me to meet him. God presented an opportunity to me that day, and I took it. I found him, and not surprisingly he took the time to talk to me personally. Although it was brief, I could not help but think as he walked away, *I am amid greatness.*

My Prayers Answered on a Plane . . .

I was a flight attendant for many years. Usually on my drive to the airport, I spent time praying. One morning, the Holy Spirit led me to pray, "Of all the people in the whole world, Lord, would you please put Billy Graham on my flight?" I was working a flight that month that went to Atlanta and then on to Los Angeles. Within three weeks of that request, God answered my prayer. There is nothing impossible with God! Mr. Graham boarded the flight in Atlanta, and his seat was right where I was assigned to work! Thank You, Lord Jesus. Billy Graham was so polite, kind, and such a gentleman. It was an honor to serve him. He was a humble man and so very precious. I have never forgotten that day. Many times since then, I have prayed for Billy Graham. He touched my heart. I thank God for that divine appointment.

God and Show Business

Many years ago, in Washington, DC, I had the privilege of meeting Dr. Graham, and I told him that my husband wanted to go into show business and sing. I asked him if he thought a Christian could stay true to the Lord there. He told me it could be possible, but it had to be God's will. He also told me he would pray for me and to meet him in the same place the next day. When I went to meet him, I saw him coming up the hallway, and he told the many reporters to wait; he had to talk with me personally. The first thing he said to me was, "I prayed for you last night." I shall never forget that. He was so right in his counsel; my husband went into show business and on his separate way. Thank you for praying for me.

Thank You for Shaking My Hand

I met Billy Graham when I was a teenager and he was just starting his crusades. When he came to Pittsburgh, my friends and I were invited to sing one night in his choir. When the crusade started, we met in the Hunt Armory, which was a rather small place. By the time the two weeks were up, we were meeting in Forbes Field because the crowds had grown too large for the Armory. Notice that I said *we*. After hearing Billy just one night at the beginning of the crusade, my friends and I *had* to keep going back—not just to sing in the choir but to hear him. His message was very brief, loving, and much to the point. And I believe this man started changing my life for the better. Not that I have always followed God's teachings—far from it—but I have followed Billy Graham and his ministry since then. Whatever person I am today— and I know I am God's child—I owe to Billy Graham. Thank you for shaking my hand back in 1952 at the Hunt Armory in Pittsburgh. Thank you, too, for being such a wonderful influence in my life since then.

Role Model and Mentor

I was a Bible college student preparing for the ministry in North Carolina. On a Sunday afternoon in 1954, I heard the name Billy Graham for the first time while traveling in my car to visit my mother in the hospital. I was tuned to the *Hour of Decision* broadcast. I was so fascinated with his marvelous voice and powerful message that I've followed his ministry ever since.

I attended my first Billy Graham crusade in Richmond, Virginia, as a young pastor. His ministry so profoundly influenced me that I moved from being just a professed believer to a committed Christian. I learned the difference between allowing Christ to be *dominant* rather than merely *dormant* in my life. If I've ever had a role model and mentor that influenced my life and ministry above all others, it is evangelist Billy Graham.

Later, I was invited to begin a revival in Hawaii on the day that Billy concluded his crusade there. The main part of the crusade was in Honolulu, but Billy came to the island of Kauai to speak at the last service where one of his associate evangelists had been ministering.

After the sermon Billy delivered, I had the opportunity to meet him and have a few minutes to share. I consider it one of the most thrilling encounters with a fellow minister of my fifty-six years serving our Lord.

I love Billy Graham for his faithfulness to the central message of the Christian faith, for his honesty, integrity, and the crowning virtue of humility. I only wish he could be forty years old again and continue what he has been doing for more than half a century.

"BILLY, MAY I HAVE YOUR AUTOGRAPH?"

I have two special Billy Graham stories, twenty-five years apart.

I was twelve years old when Billy came to Pittsburgh, Pennsylvania in 1952. My mother, a faithful listener of *The Hour of Decision*, convinced our little church to charter a bus and attend one of the meetings. Growing up in a Christian home, I was aware of Billy Graham, and even in those days he was kind of an icon for believers.

We arrived early and found our seats, and I noticed Billy and the team checking out the stadium from the infield. As Billy and the team left, they went through the dugout right below us. Excited, I asked permission from my mom to go and see if I could get Billy's autograph. She approved, and I bounded over the fence before I realized that they were already in the dugout tunnel headed back up underneath the stands. I followed and called out to Billy from quite a distance in my young boy's voice: "Billy, may I have your autograph?" He immediately turned and came back toward me, met me halfway, and very humbly gave me what I wanted. At the time you'd have thought I had just gotten an autograph from Mickey Mantle.

Only years later, after seeing this wonderful servant of the Lord rise to prominence, did I realize how rare that little encounter was—that a person of his stature would take time for a snot-nosed kid and even give him the time of day, much less give that kid something to hold on to for life. Now I realize how Christ felt and acted when the "least of these" came to see him.

The second story occurred at a crusade in Nashville in the mid-1970s. Grown by this time, I had my family with me. Storms were predicted— and scary ones at that. As we settled into our seats, the clouds to the west were begining to rumble, and tornados were in the forecast. The blacker it got, the more concerned everyone became.

Just as we were thinking we would need to leave, Billy came out on the stage and lifted his hands, much like Moses must have done when God parted the Red Sea. Billy began to pray, asking for an immediate miracle. To everyone's pleasant surprise, the clouds parted, with half going north and the other half going south. The stadium stayed dry that day, and it's a good thing because that was the day my youngest daughter accepted the Lord. News reports later indicated that severe damage had occurred in the path of the storms.

So, not big stories of presidents and kings, but for me it was something to show that Billy was everyone's pastor and friend.

Thanksgiving Feast

While teaching at Coral Springs Christian Acadamy, I had Billy Graham's grandson Antony in my second-grade class. What a delightful experience to work with him and come to know his mother and dad. In November that year, we had a Thanksgiving feast and the Rev. and Mrs. Billy Graham came for our feast and I got to meet them in person. I was thrilled. So humble and gracious in person.

I have continued to follow Rev. Graham (and his son Franklin) through the media and his books. What a blessing he has been to so many people throughout the world.

The Highlight of My Dad's Capitol Hill Career

My father retired in 1995 from the US Capitol Police in Washington, DC. He was acting assistant chief of the entire department, protecting presidents, members of Congress and their staffs, the US Capitol building, and tourists who visited from around the globe on a daily basis.

Dad is a humble man, and integrity and discipline are two of the hallmarks of his life. He made everyone he met, known and unknown, feel important. My parents took me in person multiple times to watch Billy Graham preach.

My father had the pleasure to meet earthly kings, prime ministers, Hollywood celebrities, and Super Bowl champions, and he protected *seven* US presidents. But when asked at his retirement who was the most memorable and influential man he met while working in Washington, Dad said without hesitation, "The two times I met Dr. Billy Graham."

On one occasion, Rev. Graham was in a holding room at the US Capitol, getting ready to give the prayer for the inauguration. Dad had a picture of his childhood home, which is now on the grounds of the Billy Graham Library in Charlotte. The picture had been taken twenty years prior, and Dad found it and asked Dr. Graham if he would sign it. One of his aides politely said, "Dr. Graham doesn't sign autographs much anymore." But despite having Parkinson's disease, Billy Graham took Dad's photo and signed his name with a smile.

The other occasion was after President George H. W. Bush's last State of the Union address. That evening, Rev. Graham rode in the motorcade with the president to the US Capitol. My dad shook hands with the president and was pleasantly surprised to find Billy Graham right behind him. Dad shook hands with Dr. Graham, and the evangelist said, "God bless you." Dad later recalled that he had just shaken hands with "the most powerful person in the world" (President Bush), but when he shook hands with Dr. Graham it was almost as if lightning went through his body. Dad taught me twenty years ago that political power is temporal, but God's power is eternal.

Thank you, Billy Graham. After seventeen years working for Congress, I walked away by faith to follow God's call and your footsteps. Today, I am also an evangelist. You have inspired millions, and I thank you for inspiring my family. Well done, good and faithful servant.

MY HUSBAND AND I WORKED FOR BILLY GRAHAM

I am so grateful that I had the opportunity to work for the Billy Graham Evangelistic Association. What a blessing to work for such an honorable ministry and a man of such integrity.

I had the privilege of meeting you, Dr. Graham, at the annual BGEA picnic. You were so personable and genuinely friendly. What a man of God, who loved the Lord with all your heart, the Word of God, and people all over the world. The ministry that God called you to. . .what a tremendous responsibility, but God chose the right man, at the right time, to complete the assignment He had for you.

Thank You, Billy Graham. . .
for the Day I Got Saved

GRACE AND LOVE

In the summer of 1961, my husband, Bill, and I were asked by my cousin to go to a Billy Graham crusade at the State Fairgrounds in St. Paul, Minnesota. We went, and Bill and I went forward and received Christ as our Savior at the invitation. It was a wonderful experience. We also received the Bible study. Years later, my cousin told me they had been praying for us and knew we would go forward that night. We thank the Lord for His wonderful grace and love.

Marian and Bill

SAVED AT AGE TWELVE

At age twelve, new to this land of liberty and still learning to speak English, I got in trouble with the police in Cleveland, Ohio. I was hanging around with some friends my same age, when we were approach by the local police, who took us home. After the police explained to my parents what had happened, they decided to send me to New Jersey to spend that summer with my older brother. His wife had come to know the Lord, and she introduced me to Jesus. On Monday, August 23, 1976, while watching a Billy Graham crusade on a very small black-and-white TV, I accepted Christ. During the altar call, we knelt down and I received Jesus as my Savior. When I got up, my sister-in-law asked me, "How do you feel?" I answered, "Like a great burden has been lifted off my back." Since then, I have been serving the Lord, and today I am senior pastor of a church in Pennsylvania.

MY SON WAS ON LIFE SUPPORT

My name is Patricia, and I am from North Carolina. I can remember, as a child, my parents making remarks about Billy Graham and listening to him on television. I always trusted my parents, and I knew Billy Graham spoke the truth. When George Beverly Shea sang, my father would always break down and cry.

In the summer of 1997, I had the opportunity to go and hear Billy Graham speak in Charlotte. I took my husband and my three children, along with my oldest son's girlfriend, who was pregnant with his child. She was fourteen and my son was seventeen. My hope with the crusade was that it would open these two children's eyes. I was so touched by hearing the message. Unfortunately, when we returned home, my oldest son continued with his partying and trying not to accept responsibility for his unborn child.

Two months later, after my granddaughter had been born, my son was shot in the head. The sheriff came to give me the news that my son was on life support and I needed to go to the hospital. When I arrived, I was told he wasn't going to make it, and they asked if I would donate his organs.

While I was waiting for the paperwork, a nurse ran out of the ICU asking for my son's mother. When I said, "Here I am," she looked at me and said, "He's asking for you."

When I ran in to the ICU, my son asked me where he was, and I explained that there had been a terrible accident and he was in the hospital. He knew his name and how old he was, etc. The doctor told me he could not explain what had happened, but it was a miracle. Then the doctor told me my son would not walk again—but he did, and he came home after four weeks. . .walking.

I later found out what had happened to cause the incident. My son had gone to the house of a friend who was pregnant. She lived with her parents and her boyfriend. My son had been drinking. He went to the window and knocked on it, and to his surprise the boyfriend came outside and started fussing at him. My son left and returned shortly to throw a rock at the window. I'm not sure if he threw it, but the father ran out of the house with a gun. My son was already off his property, but the man was also drunk and he shot my son over his right eye. The bullet bounced around inside his head and exited out the back. The ambulance was called, and they said he'd lost a lot of his brain.

The district attorney came to talk with me, and I was struggling with the fact that if my son had not been in that man's yard, he would not have been shot. I was having so much distress over my son and the man who shot him, who was now in jail. This man's family and I went to the same church.

I finally wrote to the Billy Graham Evangelistic Association and gave them my story, asking what should I do—have him prosecuted, knowing he would probably go to prison, or drop the charges because both of them were wrong. I knew that if my son had not done this stupid thing, the shooting never would have happened.

Within a week, I received a reply. I was so touched and so grateful. I thank BGEA for taking the time to write me back. What a relief it gave me. Thank you from the bottom of my heart.

Here is the outcome: After my son came home and realized how his life had almost been snuffed away and that God had saved him, he went and dropped the charges. He also met with the man, and they asked one another for forgiveness. My son said he had to get on with his life and try and make himself a better person and set a better example for others.

BILLY GRAHAM'S MEDIA OUTREACH
HELPED LEAD ME TO CHRIST

I was brought up in a Catholic family in the Midwest. My parents were good people and practiced their faith seriously. Though I wouldn't say I was a seeker at the time, I remember watching the 1957 New York crusade on TV when I was a youngster. I was curious and certainly paid attention to what was being said. I don't remember very much, except that when he gave the invitation to make a commitment, I wondered exactly what it meant.

Years later, having gone through many of life's challenges, I was a seeker and adrift, dabbling in the occult and New Age thought. By then, I was living in Los Angeles and working in the media. A Christian coworker bought me a Bible and invited me to a breakfast meeting at an LA hotel, where Billy Graham was speaking. The devil didn't want me to attend, because we got caught in a traffic jam, and when we arrived at the hotel, we found the last two seats way in the back of the ballroom. My friend asked me if I was born again, and I said, "Sure." I wasn't, but he and others were praying for me.

A few years later, I fell for a graduate of the Moody Bible Institute. She asked me about my faith, and I said I was born again. I couldn't fool her, though, so to impress her, I purchased and read the Billy Graham book *How to Be Born Again.* Today, finally trusting Christ, I know that Billy Graham's ministry played an important part. I work in media and marvel at how different media played a part in bringing me to the truth. God used BGEA in a mighty way. I thank God for Billy Graham and his vision, and pray God's richest blessings for him, his ministry, and his family.

TRUTHS THAT I COULD EASILY UNDERSTAND

I come from a culturally Christian home in Madras, India. Growing up, my church attendance was regular, but I found no meaning in going to church. I just went because my parents took me along. Nevertheless, in my early teen years, I developed an interest in Jesus. I decided to read *How to Be Born Again* by Dr. Graham, which my father had bought. It was the first time I was exposed to the truth about God, Jesus, and myself. Dr. Graham presented these truths in such a manner that even a fifteen-year-old could easily understand. The Gospel was clear to me, and also the fact that I was not a Christian just because I came from a religious home. God used John 1:12, which Dr. Graham quoted, to drive home the fact that I needed to receive Christ as my Savior. I quietly slipped to my knees and prayed the sinner's prayer that was at the end of the book. I immediately knew that something had happened to me. God had adopted me into his family.

Life treated me quite badly, even after this life-changing episode. Space does not allow me tell everything, but I have to confess that I reacted in ungodly ways at times. But God has been faithful in restoring me to fellowship with Himself time and again.

I'm extremely thankful to Dr. Graham for not only leading me to Jesus Christ but also for being a role model for me ever since God saved me. His humility, integrity, and faithfulness are more attractive to me than his great accomplishments. His compassion for people, and his love for dear Mrs. Ruth Graham and their children, are so appealing to me that I want to emulate him. He'd be the third person I'd meet (and hug) in heaven, after my Savior and my mother. Once again, my heartfelt thanks to Dr. Graham for leading me to "the Way, the Truth, and the Life."

GOD IS SO GOOD

The crusade was shown on a huge screen at our local ice rink. When Billy Graham gave the invitation to follow Jesus, I could not stay in my seat. I had gone to church all my life, but I had never been told about Jesus in this way. The experience has changed my whole life and my family's life. Praise God for Billy and Ruth Graham.

In 2006, I went to North Carolina as part of the Scotland Connection group. We were blessed to be allowed to visit and tour the Billy Graham headquarters. Dr. Graham sent us a message, which his sister read to us. I felt this experience was so special in view of having been saved through his ministry.

SEARCHING

Unfortunately, I was too young to know anything about Billy Graham when he was doing his crusades. It wasn't until I was in my twenties that I heard him speak on TV. I thought he was a powerful speaker, and there was a warmth to him that was comforting. I remembered something he said that had me thinking for ten or fifteen years. He said he knew that if he died he was sure he was going to heaven—not because of what he had done but because of what Christ did for us. I thought, *How can he be so sure?* I wasn't sure whether I was going to heaven, yet I believed in Christ also. So I put that in the back of my mind for many years.

My dad got sick in 1999 and had a stroke due to many years of abusing alcohol. Even though he was a recovering alcoholic for twenty-five years, he struggled from time to time and went on drinking binges. As a result of the stroke, he was in a coma for four months, and then he died.

It really had me wondering what God's plan was for our lives. It seemed to me that we were just here to "live a good life" and then die. What was the purpose of that if we were to struggle our whole lives with problems or addictions? I read the book *Left Behind*, which made me wonder whether I was really going to go to heaven or would be left behind during the Tribulation. I thought, *How can I live a life pleasing to God so I would have a guarantee of going to heaven?*

I asked myself, "Who do I know who leads a life pleasing to God?" and Mr. Graham was the only person who came to mind. He was the only evangelist out there that you never heard anything questionable about. I also remembered what he had said about going to heaven, and I also wanted to be sure. I thought if I read something about him, I could find out where he was coming from, and then I would know what I should be doing.

I read Mr. Graham's autobiography, *Just As I Am*. It amazed me how he let God be in control of every aspect of his life. He opened up my eyes to a lot of things, but mostly that I needed to seek God and let Him work in my life. I also read *Peace with God*, *The Holy Spirit*, and *Facing Death and the Life After*, by Mr. Graham. I finally gave my life to Christ in March 2002, and now I know for sure that I will someday be in heaven for eternity with Christ.

THE BABY HAS GROWN!

How did I become a Christian? Well, I often say, "I am a Billy Graham baby!" I had just started my nursing career in 1966 and was beginning to wonder whether I would make the grade. An old school friend invited me to go with her to Earl's Court to hear Billy Graham. I had never been to such an event before, so I agreed to go.

As a very young child, I can remember an experience of something or someone bigger than I. As I grew up, I felt drawn to discovering God, and I had even asked my non-churchgoing parents if I could go to church. I later sang in the choir and helped in the Sunday school, but I did not know a personal God.

Earl's Court 1966 became a turning point in my life when I went forward to accept Jesus as my personal Savior. I have no idea what Billy Graham preached—all I know is the Holy Spirit convicted me of my need of Jesus. Thank you, Billy, for being obedient to God's call to come to the UK.

What since? Following Earls Court, I was referred to a Bible-believing church near the hospital where I was training. I had a great grounding in the foundation of God's Word, and after qualifying as a nurse and midwife, I moved to my current church, where the Holy Spirit is using me now in prayer ministry.

Billy, this "baby" of yours was not "stillborn," but is still growing in Christ. Thank you!

THANK GOD I'M SAVED!

I was sixteen when I attended the crusade with my cousins. It was the best thing that ever happened to me. In spite of all the bad decisions I've made, by far this is the best one. Please give my love to Brother Billy, for he is an inspiration to us all. We love him, and we need him. Peace be to you all!

CHANNEL SURFING

I was flipping through the TV channels to see what was on. I heard you speaking and decided to listen. I was raised in a Lutheran church but had never heard anything about the saving grace of our Lord and Savior Jesus Christ. I knelt before the TV and gave my heart to Jesus. I sent for your lessons that were available at that time. I have been to one of your crusades and have watched you on TV over the years. I also read *Decision* magazine for many years. I thank you for bringing me to the Lord; I love Him more than I can ever say. Again, may I say thank you, Billy, for your faithfulness to the Lord.

JOB WELL DONE, MY GOOD
AND FAITHFUL SERVANT!

I'm not sure of the exact year, but I will never forget the night Billy Graham allowed the Lord to reach through him and grab hold of my heart! I was asked to help a friend volunteer at a Billy Graham crusade to sell sodas in the stands of the stadium in Orlando, Florida. I agreed, not knowing that God had planned this entire event for me (and I am sure for many others). While selling sodas, I heard the message Rev. Graham delivered and was touched beyond control. The next thing I knew, I was in the middle of the field asking Jesus Christ to enter my heart. And He certainly did!

Though I did not surrender my entire life to Him at that time, He was faithful to remain in me, and the Holy Spirit continued to lovingly tug on my heart. I went through some very difficult times, including two divorces, before the Lord gently reminded me that all I needed was in Him and with Him, just as Rev. Graham had told me so many years before. I found myself in church that next Sunday and completely and totally gave my entire soul, mind, and body to Jesus! Besides the night when Rev. Graham allowed me to receive Jesus into my heart, this was the best day of my life! Since that time, the Lord has blessed me beyond belief. He has brought me a wonderful, God-fearing husband. My home and my family are serving the Lord.

At times, servanthood is difficult, and at times it would be easier to let others reach the lost. However, I am often reminded how a faithful servant by the name of Rev. Billy Graham touched my heart and was used to save me from an eternity in hell and allowed me to walk in the glory of all God has planned for me. How could I not push forward and do my utmost to touch at least one other person as Rev. Graham has touched millions.

Thank you, Rev. Graham, for being a faithful servant, for giving so much of yourself and your family to reach lost souls. Your reward will certainly be your entering heaven and being greeted by the Lord with, "Well done, my good and faithful servant!," which is so well deserved by you!

SALVATION!

I was only twelve or thirteen when I sang in the choir the year that the crusade came to Birmingham, Alabama. My mother had faithfully brought me to church every Sunday, and I loved Sunday school. However, it had not occurred to me that salvation was something I had to ask for! I loved singing and enjoyed being in the crusade choir. When Brother

Graham preached that night, I went forward and prayed the sinner's prayer. The ministry sent me some material after that to help me along my journey.

I will forever be grateful to my heavenly Father for the obedience of Dr. Billy Graham! My salvation has lasted through all of my ups and downs. I still remember the joy of my salvation as a young girl. Wow! God had spoken to me, and I loved being able to feel Him with me. I still feel the wonderful "knowing" that God is always with me! Thanks!

Walking the Sawdust Trail

I was a young teenager and at a church camp in Winona Lake, Indiana. There was a Billy Sunday tabernacle there, and this new evangelist was preaching. We got to go to see him, and I got saved that night. It took a lot of years for me to learn that I had to grow up and be an adult Christian, but by the grace of God I did. Years later, we saw Billy Graham again in Columbus, Ohio, but I forget the date. Thank you, Billy, for being the person you are. It says a lot when no one can dig up any "dirt" on you. I know that you had strict guidelines for yourself and your worship team. We praise God for that. By the way, my husband also got saved—at the Columbus crusade.

Linda

You Got Me When I Was Ready

My story is short and sweet. I watched you on your TV specials off and on. There was not a crusade that came near my hometown. One evening, I felt that you were looking at me through the camera, and I nervously called the phone number on the screen to accept Jesus Christ as my personal Savior and repent of my sins, to be born again. The operator was friendly and led me in prayer, just as you said. I received some literature in the mail soon afterward. I am saved because the Holy Spirit was working on me that evening, and I was open to your words of salvation and forgiveness. You got me when I was ready and willing to pick up the phone. Thank the Lord! I pray that many, many people will continue to come to Jesus before it's too late.

Carol

MY SPIRITUAL JOURNEY

Thank you, Dr. Graham, for faithfully preaching God's truth for decades. I watched you on TV growing up. My parents took me to Sunday school and church regularly as a child and teenager. I went through confirmation as a teen and became a member of my local church. In 1966, I entered the US Air Force. My parents gave me a small Bible to take with me as I left home. One Sunday evening, in the fall of 1967, I was alone in my barracks room at Sheppard Air Force Base in Wichita Falls, Texas, and I started reading my Bible. I didn't get very far in Genesis before I quit reading because I "wasn't getting anything out of it." I then turned on my radio and was tuning across the stations and heard a voice that I recognized as Billy Graham's, so I listened. As Dr. Graham was speaking from Matthew, he made a comment that just because a person goes to church and is a member of a church, it doesn't mean Jesus will automatically receive you into heaven. Those words laid heavy on me, and at the conclusion of the radio program, I knelt at my bunk as Dr. Graham prayed and extended the invitation. It was that night that Jesus entered my heart as my Lord and Savior, and someday He will receive me into His heaven. Praise God! I went on in my life to receive my ordination into the pastoral ministry and am still serving our Lord from a small church in Ohio. Thank you, Dr. Graham, for being an important part of my spiritual journey!

Ron

BECAUSE OF YOUR FAITHFULNESS

Because of your faithfulness, I found Jesus Christ in 1986, watching a crusade on TV. I had been curious and had gone to church as a child; but as I got into my teenage years, I took my own path, which led to alcohol, drugs, and an abusive marriage that just topped my life off. I didn't care whether I lived or died. Drugs and alcohol were a way to cope with life.

I got involved with someone I met in a bar and had a two-year relationship that ended when I became pregnant. I was now a single parent, working in bars and using drugs to get me through, until one night, out of curiosity, I began to watch your crusade on TV. At the end, I remember that you asked people to accept Jesus as their Savior, and right there I bowed my head and asked Jesus to come into my life. I felt the presence of God in that room that night and called my sister-in-law to let her know that I had gotten saved. Her question was "saved from what?" Hell, I explained. I just received Jesus as my Savior watching Billy Graham. That was twenty years ago, and there have been ups and downs during that time, but I have always known that, no matter what, God was with me.

Thank you, Billy Graham, for your faithfulness to God. Because of you, I was saved from the fires of hell, and one day I hope to be able to tell you in person what you have meant to me.

Twice Blessed

Billy Graham came to our town when I was a young girl. I went forward at the crusade, which was held at the Ratcliffe Stadium in Fresno, California. After years of mistakes and falling away from the Lord, I found myself going through a sad divorce. Thankfully, Billy Graham came back to Fresno again. It had been more than thirty years, and I went forward again, promising the Lord this time that he would be the center of my life. I have been filled with the Holy Spirit, and my walk with Christ has been a daily learning experience. I feel like I'm finally home. Thank you, Billy, for being His messenger all these years. God bless you.

"What about Me?"

My sons and I were watching Billy Graham on television when we were in Washington, DC. At the end, when Billy Graham was having the altar call and the number was put on the screen for people to call, my oldest son (who was six years old) asked me, "Mom, are you going to call?" I told him I was already saved, and he said, "What about me?" I told him you have to understand what accepting Christ means before you can give your life to Him. He replied, "I am ready." So I led him to the Lord after watching Billy Graham. My son is now serving in the US Navy, and I am very proud of him. I thank the Lord for you, Brother Graham, for all your wonderful work around the world. Also, I rededicated my life at one of your crusades here in Atlanta. May the blessings of the Lord continue to be with you and your family.

Thank You, Billy Graham. . .
for Reaching Me with Your Books

THANK YOU

I just want to thank you for the book offers you have. Your books have been such a blessing in my life. My finances never would have allowed me to purchase them, but the fact that you send them for free is so deeply appreciated. Each book has helped me in one situation or another in my walk with the Lord. Thank you for being Kingdom minded. All that you do is truly a blessing. I would think you will definitely hear, "Well done, good and faithful servant."

"BUY THAT BOOK"

I've loved reading since I was a small child, and so it was fitting that my difficulties in raising three little children virtually alone took me to a Christian bookstore, twenty-eight years ago, on a doctor's recommendation. I had avoided such stores in the past, but wanting to follow the full course of the doctor's "prescription," I went as he suggested. The doctor's recommended Christian counseling book was there, but more important was a table display I saw as I walked in the door. The book had a black cover and in large red letters said, "How to Be Born Again."

Boy, I thought, *that's what I need.* I moved past the display and picked up my assigned reading, but as I walked past that table again to check out, I felt a tremendous pressure in my mind and body: *Buy that book.*

I replied in my head, *I'm too embarrassed to buy that book.*

Too bad. There was no way I was going to get out of that store without that book. Eventually I picked it up and tried to laugh it off with the young girl at the counter. I remember how she looked at me like, "You're in for it." But she smiled sweetly throughout the transaction, and off I went.

The book went into my top drawer at home, but two days later, with the inner pressure building again, I called a sitter, grabbed the book, jumped in the car, found a great private parking place, and read *How to Be Born Again* cover to cover.

After I went through the steps in the final chapter (even though I wasn't sure about this "sin" thing), Jesus came into my heart. It didn't seem to matter to Him that I didn't completely "get it." Nevertheless, my cup runneth over. . .tears of joy, love, and gratefulness poured forth. And then Jesus spoke to me: *"Go home and do the best job you can."*

I couldn't wait to get back to the house. When the door opened, my two-, four-, and five-year-olds came running into my arms, and I could hardly believe the three gifts I held in my arms. No longer feeling overwhelmed by responsiblity, I was overwhelmed with gratefulness beyond measure. Absolute pure joy. My children had always been so wonderful, no terrible twos, no discipline problems, just loving; but the handling of the maintenance left me so tired. Their dad was not involved, but none of that mattered anymore. I floated, and the whole journey changed.

My kids are now in their thirties. They continue to be so wonderful. I can't imagine having raised them without Jesus. During those growing up years, I wrote Billy to thank him. He wrote back and said how much the note had meant to him, for he hadn't been feeling very well lately. Can you imagine?

I am now married to a wonderful born-again man, who is also another of God's gifts. He certainly knows the Billy Graham story, as do all my children. I owe my life to Jesus and to Billy Graham, whom Jesus used to change my life. Mr. Billy Graham, thank you, thank you, thank you. I am forever grateful.

Nancy

THE SECRET OF HAPPINESS

In 1969 or 1970, at the age of thirteen or fourteen, I read a book written by Billy Graham. As I read that book, I came to know Christ. The presence of God was so real that I knew without a doubt He was all He said He was. Unfortunately, I took a very wrong path in later years, becoming mixed up in the homosexual world, and I identified myself as a lesbian for nearly twenty-two years, until April 2000.

When it became clear to me that this life was simply not working, I again turned to a book by Billy Graham, *The Secret of Happiness*—with some skepticism, but needing answers and relief from my pain. I sat down to read that book, and the presence of God was again so strong that I knew I had come back to Him. I was filled with the love of Christ that night, and I rededicated my life to Him. I have now walked out of the lesbian-identified life and have remained alcohol-free for more than seven years and smoke-free for more than four years. I owe Billy Graham so much for his faithfulness to write and say the words given to him by God. God bless Billy Graham and all of his family!

I WAS A SUNDAY-ONLY CHRISTIAN

The year was 1985 and I was twenty-six years old. I had a husband, two children, and a nice home. But something was missing. I was raised Catholic and did not understand what a "personal relationship" with Christ meant. Someone gave me the book *Peace with God*. The question that Mr. Graham posed in his book was, "If you died today, would you go to heaven?" I didn't know for sure. I had been a Sunday-only Christian for many years. I prayed the sinner's prayer at the end of the book, accepted Christ in my life, and put Him on the throne of my heart. Immediately, my life began to change for the better! Praise God, and thank you, Mr. Graham, for that book. I truly have peace with God.

TOUCHED BY YOUR BOOKS

I am a disabled forty-four-year-old man, who has been a Christian since 1996 when I went to a Promise Keepers rally in Kansas City. Because I was disabled, out of work, and not receiving Social Security or any kind of disability payment yet, when I became a Christian I had a hard time getting things to read so I could grow.

I found the Billy Graham website and the Billy Graham Classics on TBN. These were really great for me as I was not raised in a Christian atmosphere and had not watched Mr. Graham at all when I was a kid. Not only did I continue to grow because of the Classics, but I got the free mailings from your organization, and I even sent you a letter asking for some of your past books for free (and you actually sent me three or four of these).

Together with Dr. Kennedy, your ministries have really helped me continue to grow when I wasn't able to make it to church, and I really want to thank you for that. In the past, I read my Christian books on and off, but now I have a real thirst for them and I am so glad I built up my library. Thank you all so much for your help. I really wanted to see Dr. Graham in one of his last crusades when he was in Kansas City, but I wasn't able to go because I was hurting, and it really got me down. Mostly, I just wanted to say thank you so much!

William

INSPIRED TO REACH OUT TO OTHERS

Dear Mr. Graham, I was reading your book *Just As I Am* and was so moved by it that I signed on to help with the Harvest crusades this year. What a blessing that was. You inspire me to reach out to others so that they might know the Lord the way I do. I truly love the Lord our God with all my heart and soul. Thank you so much for all your good work.

Kathy

IT WAS A DARK NIGHT!

I had been feeling blue for a while. I was having serious financial problems and was just feeling lonely, very lonely. I was at my wits' end, and praying wasn't helping anymore. I felt abondoned by God. That night, there was a Billy Graham crusade on TV, and I called the prayer line. A girl answered and talked to me extensively. Through my tears, I kept her on the phone for a good forty minutes. Afterward, I felt better, but nothing changed. Then I started receiving books and pamphlets in the mail, and I read them with an open heart. Soon, I got the job I was praying for, and I won an amazing trip—which lifted my spirits and made God's presence felt again in my life. I am not out of financial trouble yet, and I am still lonely, but I am not crippled by it. I have renewed my faith in God, and He helps me through every day. Come next spring, with the Lord's help, I will be on my way to financial recovery.

REACHED THROUGH ONE OF DR. GRAHAM'S BOOKS

Dearest Dr. Billy Graham, while reading your book *World Aflame*, I received the Lord Jesus Christ as my Savior. It happened in the summer after my high school graduation, in the midst of preparations for leaving home to attend university. Apprehensions of the unknown challenges and temptations with which I would be faced in that environment, far from home, put me on a path to resolve my long-held, and mostly unvoiced, doubts and misgivings about my faith.

Dr. Graham, while viewing your telecasts and listening to your radio broadcasts throughout my growing-up years, I was convicted about my disconnectedness from God. But since I had joined our small country church at a time when several other ten-year-old classmates were doing so, I was reluctant to now "out" myself as a fake Christian. Nor did I have confidence that the pastor or anyone in the church would understand or know how to deal with my dilemma.

Consequently, I suffered through many verses of "Just As I Am" during your telecasts. This silent agony lasted until that summer evening in my bedroom as I read your book.

I encountered the book providentially. While riding in the auto of a work supervisor, I spotted the words *Billy Graham Evangelistic Association* on the mailing label of a package lying in the seat between us. As I curiously fingered it, my supervisor suggested, "Would you like to borrow that book?" A voracious reader, I eagerly assented. And what a godsend the book was!

I had always wondered why I was so privileged to have been born in the Bible Belt of the United States and to have heard the Gospel all my life. Other world religions offered a path to God, too. In your book, you wrote that the world religion founder, Buddha, for example, on his deathbed indicated to his followers that he was still searching for the truth. You reiterated Jesus' words, "I am the Way, the Truth, and the Life. No one comes to the Father except through Me." I had known this passage since childhood. But at that time, the power of those words impacted me such that I was compelled to cry out to God with honest desperation about my lostness. No more, "If I'm not saved, save me," which I would silently utter at times whenever I heard guidance about receiving salvation.

There in my bedroom, Christ met me, revealing Himself as my loving and welcoming Savior, putting an end to my anguish and infusing me immediately with His peace. Best of all, it did not fade—instead my assurance grew.

Thank you, Billy Graham, for your giving to the Lord. You pointed me to Jesus Christ through effective methods of communication and faithful ministry. And thanks to those out there who supported the BGEA, through finanancial gifts, volunteerism, and prayer.

Elizabeth

THANK YOU, BILLY!

I first attended one of your crusades in New York City, in 1957 or 1958. This kind of set the tone for me as I always read your "Faith" article in the newspaper, which answers questions from people about many difficult situations that are bothering them. Your explanations using Bible passages as a basis are so honest, sincere, thought-provoking, and filled with the wisdom of Solomon, that they must be helping people all over the world. Since 2002, when your devotional book *Hope for Each Day* came out, I consider the day incomplete if I have not read it.

Ron

INSPIRED BY BILLY GRAHAM'S AUTOBIOGRAPHY

Dear Billy Graham, thank you for loving God and letting all of us see that. Your dedication to God has had a great impact on me through your autobiography. I read it along with my Bible each day and then began watching your crusades that are broadcast on Saturday evenings here in New Jersey. Your devotion and ministry have helped me reclaim my interest in serving God through ministry. I began preaching when I was fourteen, and I won many souls for God, but I left the ministry when I was twenty-four. I am now forty-three, and your godly influence has helped me return to God with a fervor and devotion that is truly phenomenal; the Lord has also opened doors for a return to the ministry.

Thank you for loving God and helping all of us with your clear and concise presentation of the Gospel. You could have done many other things in life, but you chose to obey God, and the fruit of your obedience will fill heaven with a myriad of thankful souls.

Jay

LOVE SAVED ME

One day back in 2002, I was awake in my bed late at night. I was watching TV, and Billy Graham came on preaching about Jesus. I was so moved by what he said that I made a decision right then and there to accept Jesus as my Lord and Savior, even though I was as messed up as any person could be. I'd had a problem with drugs on and off since I was thirteen years old. I am now forty-three. Brother Billy offered a book for free, called *Peace with God*. I was moved to order the book, so I did. Right then, I felt as if God had begun a good work in me, and He is well able to see it to full completion. I began to watch a Christian television network and learn more about my Lord and how I am supposed to live. I started reading the New Testament, and God started moving in my life. Now God is still moving in my life, and every day I get to spend with the Lord is my privilege. I give Him praise and glory, for today I am truly free. Today I thank the Lord for Billy and Ruth Graham for bringing me to the Lord. Love saved me.

Donna

MY ANSWER

When I was fifteen, a friend gave me a box of books that I promptly put away in the top of my closet. A few years later, I was searching for a change in my life. I found in that box a book by Billy Graham called *My Answer*. I was looking for an answer, so I started reading the letters that people had written to Billy Graham and his responses. On page fifty-seven, I read about a teenager who, like me, wanted to change. I took Billy Graham's advice to heart about reading the Gospel of John and a chapter of Proverbs each day. It wasn't too long before I knelt and prayed to be saved. More than thirty years ago, my life was changed forever.

THE JOURNEY

My name is Becky, and I would like to say how very much I love Mr. Graham. He saved me from giving up on Jesus.

It was about two years ago, when I was going through a bad bout of depression. All I did was cry and pray to God to just take me home. I was one step from suicide. Then the Lord performed a miracle. I went to the hospital for a sore shoulder, after a fall on the ice, and they discovered I had a broken neck, the same type of break that Christopher Reeve had. They told me that it had been broken for a while and that it was almost completely healed. It was being held together by one ligament; one sneeze could have killed me. I was told flat out that there was no medical reason for me to be alive. . .but I am. The night before surgery, as I was signing papers for guardianship of my children, I decided that I did want to live and be a better person. God wanted me here for something, and I didn't want to let Him down. The surgery was a success, and I went home to recover.

I was then told by my company that they were not going to hold my job for me while I recovered. I could not collect disability, unemployment, or welfare, I had only $600 a month to live on, and the bills just kept coming. Added to that now was an astronomical hospital bill, because I had no insurance. I was grateful to God for saving my life, but maybe the things I had done in the past were too much. I didn't feel like I was worth it. Why did He save me?

I was at Walmart one day (to get the pain pills I couldn't afford), and I happened to go to the book section while I waited. There I found a book called *The Journey*, by Billy Graham. I had always known who Billy Graham was but had never paid that much attention to him. The book called to me. I picked it up, knowing I couldn't afford it, opened it up, and read a passage. Mr. Graham told me that no matter what I had done or who I was, God loved me and wanted to be a part of my life. He wanted to be on this journey with me. I cried as I read it and am crying now as I remember. I bought the book and read it in two days. It was like he had written it just for me. Everything he said was my life. I laughed and cried, and at that time I gave my life to Christ.

I now get anything I can that has to do with Mr. Graham. I watch his crusades on TBN and absolutely give him the credit for making me see that even when times are hard, God loves me and will *never* leave my side. I am still over my head in debt, but the Lord pointed me to a new job, and people see the change in me. I always give first credit to God for saving me, but He also put me in front of that book and led me to one of my most favorite people in the world. I would not be the Christian I am today if not for Mr. Graham. I am reading *The Journey* for the fourth time. I read it whenever I get discouraged, and I have given copies to others to help them find the answers they need. It is by far the best book, next to the Bible (which I have also read!) that I will ever read. I just want to say that the song "Thank You, Billy Graham" says it all. Thank you, Mr. Graham, for saving my eternal life! I look forward to giving you a *huge* hug in heaven! I love you!

A Career Criminal Saved from the Pit

I was a career criminal for nineteen of my first twenty-nine years. A drug addict, thief, and drug dealer. On Christmas Eve 2006, I found myself in the same hole (a solitary confinement cell) I had been in two years prior to that, on my way back to the same prison for the same senseless crimes (drug dealing). All alone again, I wanted to die, but I knew I couldn't kill myself, so I started praying and reading *Peace With God* by the great Dr. Graham. I had known about God and even believed that Christ was His Son, but I had never known the Gospel or about having a relationship with Him. On Christmas Day, I got down on my knees and gave my life to Him, and I have never been the same. After that, I have watched every TV crusade that Dr. Graham and his ministry has played on TV, and read many of his books. I love Billy Graham and his ministry—they changed my life!

THE MAN WHO WOULD WAIT

Billy's writings have often been pivotal in my development as a Christian. I recall such books as *The Holy Spirit*, *World Aflame*, and *Approaching Hoofbeats*. I would always be eager to view telecasts throughout the year from various venues and featuring interesting celebrity testimonies. Billy's sermons were short, illustrative, current, sincere, and convicting. Ever the gentleman with his message, he would close, fold his arms, and tell the people that he would wait for them to respond. This same quiet and courtesy was always the style of Jesus. The waiting moments for me were always filled with awe.

Doug

Thank You, Billy Graham. . .
for Reaching Me with Your Movies

TIME TO RUN

One would think that because I was a churched Sunday school kid, I would know Jesus. I knew *about* Jesus as a person in history, but I had no idea that he wanted to be my Savior and have a relationship with me. I was lost.

Thank you, Billy Graham, for coming to our city by way of film! The year was 1973, and tickets were available at church to view *Time To Run*. I didn't know what we would see, but I took a carload of seekers.

The family in the film was experiencing conflicts in their relationships. I could really relate to that. There was a young girl in the film who knew and loved Jesus. I wanted what she had. My heart was open to your preaching that night. There was a call to come to the front of the theater. My heart was pounding: *Should I go? What would my sister-in-law think if I got up and went?* Well, I was going anyway!

When I got to the front of the theater, my sister-in-law was down there also! There were people there to pray with us and give us literature. Late that night, I read the little book that showed how God is holy and I am a sinner. I am separated from God by my sin. But Jesus, on the cross, closed the gap and made a way for me to come to a holy God. I prayed and I trusted in Jesus to take my sin away, and He did! All the weight of that sin was lifted off my shoulders, and I had amazing peace. Glory to God! The song of my heart was "Nearer, Draw Me Nearer, Precious Lord," and that is just what Jesus did and continues to do in my life.

Thank you also, Billy, for sending your book *Peace with God.* I had many questions, and it was so amazing how God brought books and people and Bible studies to help me. I know that God sent you by way of film to Reading, Pennsylvania, back in 1973, because I so desperately needed to receive Jesus as my Savior. Less than five years later, my husband also received Jesus as his Savior. He says in his testimony that he saw and knew that I was not the same. The Holy Spirit was at work inside of me. Praise to God! The gift of life goes on. Thank you, Billy Graham, for being faithful to God's call. God bless you!

HE IS REAL

For thirty-two years, I was in the world *and* of it. I always thought I was a good guy because I wasn't as bad as others. My parents took me to a small United Methodist Church during my school years, but I never really heard the good news of the Gospel. I was bound in sin, but I didn't know it. I was enjoying life but not content within. I was always looking for that job that would make everything all right. It never happened.

Several times, I caught the Billy Graham crusade on television. Billy, you always made sense to me, and God was speaking through you. In 1973, my dad was diagnosed with lung cancer, and it left me depressed. During his illness, my wife, Pat, and I went to Shea's Cinema West to see the movie *Time to Run.* Your preaching in the film led me to go forward that night with my wife to receive Jesus into my heart. We were led in the sinner's prayer—and *bang*, something went off inside of me. I've not been the same since.

Thank you, Billy, for being such a role model and a humble servant of our Lord Jesus Christ. Your dedication is such an inspiration and a breath of fresh air! I'm looking forward to seeing you in the Kingdom, along with your beautiful wife, Ruth. Keep pressing on; the best is yet to come!

Jerry

BILLY GRAHAM IS EVERYWHERE

My earliest remembrance of Billy Graham was in the early 1970s. My parents had banned film-going for their five kids, and yet one night our family walked into the "sin-ema" to watch a film called *Time to Run*. I was awestruck that Billy Graham could use this medium for God's glory!

God used World Wide Pictures again in my life at age fourteen when I had decided to toss God and my parents' beliefs out of my life. I was visiting a friend in New Jersey and he took me to see *The Prodigal*, about a rebellious man whose brother tries to love him back into the church. It was a very powerful film to a fourteen-year-old drug user who knew better. When I finally rededicated my life to Christ in 1985, at the age of seventeen, I chose to go into a Christian radio ministry near Detroit. I was able to honor Pastor Graham with a two-hour radio tribute on his seventieth birthday. The show featured George Beverly Shea, Cliff Barrows, Chuck Swindoll, Harold Lindsell, Gigi and Franklin Graham, John Pollack, Ernie Harwell (voice of the Detroit Tigers), and many, many more. . .giving honor to one to whom honor is due.

I now work for ABC Radio in Detroit. Just a few years ago, I heard that Billy Graham was coming to President Ford's museum in Grand Rapids. My wife and I drove up there, and at the press conference I stood up and asked, "Dr. Graham, how have you been able to hang on to your integrity as a televangelist?" He replied, "I didn't know I was just hanging on!"

I know it sounds corny, but one of the reasons I have kept my faith in Christ all these years is due to the consistency of Billy Graham. He has given me an example that it can be done—you can live the life you tell others about. Dr. Graham was never politically motivated or financially motivated; He was always just *heart* motivated.

JESUS SAVES!

My parents were born in Puerto Rico and went to New York City as young folks, where they got married and had four daughters. They both came from very poor circumstances and had hard, difficult lives, especially during the Depression.

My father was an alcoholic and an abuser. He had an extremely violent temper. When he was angry, or provoked for any reason, he beat his wife and he beat his children. He hurt or damaged anything in his path. I was the youngest of the daughters, so I had not only one person abusing me, but five. I was verbally and physically abused by my father, my mother, and three sisters, though not so much the older ones. Whenever anyone had a quarrel, I took the brunt of it. One of my sisters was three years older than me, and she abused me every day, even more than my parents.

But I was even more special than that. When I was born, and just a few weeks old, they put me in an orphanage. I'm not sure if they intended to give me up for good. However, at one year of age, on my birthday, they took me home from the orphanage. The story is that, when I was born, my father had abused my mother so badly that she was very ill and unable to care for me. Even though my sisters were from three to eleven years older than I was, I was sent to the orphanage. None of these things spoke well of me as far as the family was concerned. I not only had to endure my father's abuse (he started beating me when I was still in the crib, apparently because some of the manners I had learned at the orphanage were not to his liking), but I had to endure my siblings' abuse as well, because I had made my mother ill by the mere fact of being born. Lucky for me, they decided to take me home from the orphanage after a year!

We lived in a five-story tenement, and I was the errand child for every member of my family. I went up and down the five flights for milk, bread, magazines, cosmetics, the newspaper, the cigarettes, the "you name it." If they would sell it to a child, I had to run for it. Many times every day, I went running up and down five flights of steps. There's a great deal more to that story, but for the purpose of this testimony, suffice to say I had a broken heart to bring to the Lord. I had been raised by a father who called his children every evil name that one could possibly think of, regardless of age or condition. He called us all whores, scum, evil, stupid, of no account, whatever came to his mind. Whatever evil thing he could think of at the time came out of his mouth. He threatened us all the time. It was a horrible way to grow up.

Then when I was about seven years old, I was sexually abused by my brother-in-law. You know I didn't tell anyone about that. It's a strange thing to live in an environment where the only example you have is of cheating, lying, deceitfulness, abuse, alcoholism, adultery, and on and on, but everyone tells you to be good! How can you be good when you have a completely evil example all around you? It isn't possible. But while I was trying to be good I was being bad! Very bad! While I didn't know what the answer was, I wanted to know God, I wanted to please God. But I was spiraling out of control. I hated myself and I hated everything around me. I just didn't know how to put a stop to it.

I tried many times to commit suicide. I had lost all hope. I had no desire to live, but after I'd had two sons of my own, I couldn't find an easy way out.

I was one of the hundreds of thousands who tuned in to the Billy Graham televised crusades in 1975 and 1976 to learn about the love of God. I can remember that I'd watch sometimes with my husband and two boys. If there was anyone present with me, then I would not respond to the call. Finally, one day I was alone for a moment, and I quickly got on my knees to repeat the salvation prayer with Billy. I didn't understand spiritual things, so I thought nothing happened. However, I know now that it did; I was just not fully aware of those things at the time.

In 1976, a Billy Graham movie came to our area. I went to the movie with my family. I had great expectations by this time. After the movie was shown, the audience was addressed, probably by ministers of the local church. I had never heard an altar call before in my life. I didn't really know that's what Billy was doing in the crusades. I asked everyone in my family to go forward with me; I was ashamed to go by myself. My husband and my sons refused to go. My husband said, "If you feel you should go, go! You don't need us to go with you."

Well, that gave me the last push I needed. I went forward. The speaker asked us to face the stage curtain. My heart was pounding so terribly hard, and the blood had rushed to my head. It was so intense for me that I could not hear the speaker. The speaker asked the audience to leave the theater and wait outside for anyone who had responded to the altar call. Well, crazy thing. . .when I saw everyone leaving, I left too. I felt so silly. I thought, *Why did they ask us to go up to the stage if no one was going to talk to us?*

I did not realize that they didn't want the respondents to leave, just the remaining audience. When I got outside and found my family, my husband said, "What are you doing out here? You're supposed to be in there. The minister was going to speak to all of you."

Oh my! I thought to myself all the way home. *That was it! I lost my only opportunity to come to God. I'm going to hell!*

I did not understand the grace of God or the mercy of God. Thanks be to God that He had a hold of me and never let me go. Thank God, I've been walking with our great and wonderful God ever since.

As a result of my coming to Christ, my whole family and many friends and acquaintances in my community turned to the Lord!

Thank you, Billy, for your commitment, for your suffering, for your giving, for your family, for your tears, for your endurance, for your prayers, for all your family, for your energy, for your love of God, for your ministry, for your dear wife, now with the Lord, for all that you are and have ever been in the hands of God!

First Step on the Journey

Dear Billy, when I was four, maybe five, years old, I went to see a movie. I don't remember what it was or why the Gospel was presented at the movie theater, but I made a decision right after. I wanted to say that I believed in Jesus, and I wanted Him to come into my heart. Afterward, I remember receiving little comic books in the mail that helped me know more about Jesus. Now, thirty years later, I want to say thank you for introducing me to the Lord. I belong to Him, and I can't imagine my life without faith. Thank you for lifting up Jesus, the one who draws all people to Himself.

THANKS FOR THE MOVIES!

I knew about the crusades but never could sit through one. I went to see a movie with friends during my freshman year of college in 1973. I believe it was called *Run for Your Life.* I was yielding my heart to God but didn't understand enough to go forward. I wanted to stay and talk to people. My friends didn't. I still didn't "get" the Gospel, but my name was on a list, and three years later, I received tickets to *The Hiding Place.* I cried through most of the movie and went home asking every Christian I knew if they had faith like Betsie ten Boom. Still, I didn't understand. My intellect was in the way. Finally, in a discussion with a Christian counselor, he called Jesus his Master. Everything fell into place for me, and I gave myself, body and soul, to Jesus. Later, the movie *Joni* had a profound impact on my life. I'm happy to say that now I love to listen to sermons and read books, but it was your movies that were the bridge that reached me where I was. Thank you so very much!

THE GOD-SHAPED VOID

Billy Graham, borrowing from St. Augustine, frequently refers to a "God-shaped void" in the human heart. For as long as I could remember, I had experienced this void in two forms. One was an intense need to be sure. The grandson of Southern Baptist missionaries to Cuba, I'd grown up in a good home with a Christian atmosphere, but one where God was only occasionally acknowledged. From an early age, I was fully aware that the Lord desired a personal relationship. My problem was the question of truth. As I look back now from the perspective of an adult, I think I can say that, as early as age eleven, I was desperately anxious to be sure that whatever I ended up committing my life to reflected the central truth of reality, not some fragment I'd have to discard and then start over.

My other experience of the God-shaped void was what C. S. Lewis describes as "a homesickness for a place we've never been." He calls this "joy," although it's more like grief, because it's a yearning for something we lack. For me, this grief was so intense, it was positively painful. A paradoxical feature of joy is that its only satisfaction in this life is to feel it yet more intensely. I compare it to a photo of his family that a soldier takes with him on a tour of duty. The picture lacks the substance of his family and awakens homesickness, but it's a kind of pain he wants to feel. This seems to be the function of the God-shaped void in my life. By virtue of its resemblance to the thing missing in my life, it suggested the direction to go to fill that void.

As it was for Lewis, the quest to fill this emptiness became the central theme of my life. Outside of school, I chose every book to read based on how it reawakened this longing. For me, it was evoked most strongly by myth, fantasy, and science fiction. Ironically, I never met anyone else who ever expressed this longing, and for many years I suspected I might be the only one who felt this way. I was an adult before

I realized that this is a universal longing.

My family was part of a good Southern Baptist church, and I heard an evangelistic sermon every Sunday morning and evening. By the age of eleven, I was under strong conviction. However, my decision to come to Christ was delayed for several years after I was offended by an attempt by my pastor to coerce uncommitted children of my age group to "join the church." I finally responded to a call for salvation at age thirteen. Within hours of my decision, I found that the joy of yearning had been replaced by what Paul calls "the joy of the Lord," a sense of inner containment, contentment, and a sense of being in the presence of a person. As I've said, I had known the basic facts of scripture since early childhood, but now these truths took on the weight of reality. My God-shaped void had been filled. Joy in Lewis's sense is still important to me, but now it serves as an interior evidence of God's existence.

You'd think that after all this, I could now relax and settle into a contented routine of building a Christian life. But I soon ran into obstacles. At this point, the ministries of Billy Graham played a crucial role. Within about six months of my conversion, I'd begun to ask questions about issues that were never explicitly addressed in the life of my church. The pulpit ministry was so dedicated to evangelism that every sermon, including Christmas and Easter, was focused on winning the one or two unconverted visitors who might have sneaked in the back, rather than discipling the hundreds of committed believers who sat in the pews. I also was at fault, because I failed to begin studying the Bible; I'd known most of the stories since birth, but I had never read the Old Testament or the epistles as complete books. Although I had become active in the various youth ministries of the church, by about a year after my conversion the glow of my experience was fading, and I was losing the sense of the Lord's presence. I began to be lukewarm in my devotion.

At this key juncture, I was saved in my downhill slide through an invitation to go see the Billy Graham movie *The Restless Ones*. This film met several of my needs at once. It gave me a glimpse of what a Christian life is supposed to be like—not a resting on the embalmed memory of a conversion experience in the past, but an ongoing story of growth from one degree of glory to the next. Ralph Carmichael's film score also introduced me to my ongoing hobby of what we now know as contemporary Christian music. This led me to learn the guitar, which over the last forty years has opened the door for more ministry opportunities than I can remember.

The film also forced me to realize that I needed to learn the Bible systematically in order to grow. Eventually, this interest led me to a seminary degree in Christian education and a PhD in humanities, focusing on the spread of Christianity through cultural expressions.

During my teenage years, I sorely needed an example of a mature Christian man of humility, integrity, and stature. I read and reread John Pollack's authorized biography of Mr. Graham many times. Mr. Graham's popular apologetic books were also very important to my growth during those years.

One blessing I've prayed for many times is a chance to express my gratitude to Mr. Graham in person. Although it seems unlikely that I'll get a chance to do so face-to-face this side of heaven, I am grateful for this opportunity to tell my story and say, "Thank you, Billy Graham, for your faithfulness and your role in so many important influences on my life."

Robert

FOR PETE'S SAKE

I was born and raised in Gadsden, Alabama, and I can rarely remember a Sunday morning or Sunday night that our family wasn't worshipping at our local, downtown church. My older siblings were very involved in church youth activities, and I followed in their footsteps. Choir, Boy Scouts, church basketball, vacation Bible school, and weekend retreats throughout the year. . .you name it, and I did it. I had great training in discipleship classes and Sunday school. I was happy growing up. I had great friends. I stayed out of trouble. I lived a "good life."

But it was in a movie theater, of all places, that I exchanged this "good life" growing up in Gadsden for a greater life in Jesus Christ. On a Sunday afternoon in December 1968, at the Pitman Theatre in downtown Gadsden, our church youth group went to see a movie called *For Pete's Sake*, produced by the Billy Graham Evangelistic Association. I was thirteen years old at the time.

I guess sometimes you have to go "outside" church walls to fully appreciate what you've been exposed to "inside" the church. In a way that only God could have orchestrated, after watching *For Pete's Sake* I accepted Jesus Christ as my Lord and Savior. Although I was exposed to biblical teachings from birth, for some reason I had never actually made a public decision for Christ.

So, even though I never attended a Billy Graham crusade in person, through the magic of movies I was able to hear, and respond to, a Billy Graham invitation. As a physical and eternal reminder of that day, I still possess my ticket from that movie. On that day, on the back of the ticket, I wrote, "On Sunday, December 8, 1968, by seeing this movie, I accepted Christ into my heart."

In 2002, I was asked to share my testimony at my church, which of course included my *For Pete's Sake* story. A few weeks later, a package came in the mail. Much to my surprise, one of my church friends had found a VHS copy of *For Pete's Sake* at a store closeout sale and thought I would want it. That night, while watching *For Pete's Sake* again, I was taken back to that day some thirty-five years earlier when I saw the movie for the first time, and because of Billy Graham's invitation, accepted Christ into my heart. Despite the fact that I had grown up in the church, God used Billy Graham and World Wide Pictures to save a lost soul. Thank you, Billy!

SAVED IN A MOVIE THEATER

When I was seventeen, I was going through a very traumatic time in my life. My parents took me to see the movie *The Restless Ones*, and I sat glued to my seat! Once the movie concluded, the Rev. Billy Graham presented the Lord to us and led us all through the sinner's prayer. I instantly felt a humongous load being lifted from my heart and an inexplicable and overwhelming peace come over me. I was also filled with an immense joy that made me just shout to everyone (literally) that I felt so *great*! I kept telling my parents that I couldn't believe how good and happy I felt. I hadn't felt that good since the day I was born, although I was raised in a Christian home.

I haven't looked back since, and I now serve the Lord as minister of music for my church, as a youth counselor—and what I love to do the most, as armor bearer for my daughter, who is the youth pastor for our church. I love Jesus dearly and have always wanted the opportunity to let Billy know how much I love him for leading me to my Lord and Savior. I still watch his old campaigns—I love them all and still get ministered to by them. Thank you so very much for this precious opportunity to express my gratitude to God's servant, and a man whom I love very much. May God continue blessing him and all of you as you continue doing God's work. I wish I could speak to Billy myself, but I know he's feeling a little weak and cannot do so now. But I will talk to him when I see him in heaven, and then I can hug him and thank him in person—though I know there will be a long line of other saints feeling the same way!

Liz

TWO A PENNY

I was saved as a ten-year-old child after watching the Billy Graham movie *Two a Penny* at a movie theater in Marion, Illinois. I can't remember the exact date, but I can pinpoint it to the summer of 1968. While I had my problems and struggles over the years, and felt far from God for many years due to harboring an unforgiving spirit toward certain people, God hung in there with me. In 1989, I had the honor of singing in the choir during the Billy Graham crusade. More recently, I purchased the video of *Two a Penny* and watched it as an adult. The salvation message is simple and clear. I was reassured that I really did understand it as a child. About a year and a half ago, I began participating in a Christian recovery program at my church. It has helped me along my journey to spiritual healing and wholeness—God has held my hand every step of the way! Thank you, Billy Graham, for being obedient to God's calling for your life. I'm looking forward to meeting you in heaven so I can shake your hand and thank you personally.

OUR FOUNDATION

In 1973, I was a very immature, confused Christian. I picked up a copy of Billy Graham's book *Peace with God*, and it gave me the confidence to know in my heart that I was saved and going to heaven when I died. It clearly explained the basics about God and being a Christian. It gave me a firm foundation to build on.

In 1975, we were living in Idaho with our four young children. My husband and I volunteered to be counselors at the showing of a Billy Graham film. Our eight-year-old son was in the audience, and when the invitation was given, he walked right up to one of the other counselors and gave his heart to the Lord. We were thrilled.

Today, I can confidently say that all six of my grown children have accepted Jesus Christ as their Lord and Savior, and we can have the peace and joy of knowing we will be together in eternity.

OIL TOWN USA

Dear Mr. Graham, I was born into a loving Christian family on May 24, 1946, in Binghamton, New York. My dad had just come back from overseas, having been drafted into the US Navy. When I was eight years old, our family attended a Billy Graham Association film entitled *Oil Town USA*. Red Harper was the main character, and though I don't remember a lot of details about the film, I do know that when the invitation was given, I received Christ as my Savior.

Billy Graham has had a significant influence on my life since that film. I have seen numerous crusades on TV, attended one in St. Paul, Minnesota, and read many books and articles depicting Billy's life and telling his stories. My brother was a professor at Wheaton College, and two of our sons are graduates of that school. So we have had several opportunities to tour the Billy Graham Center and learn more about his life.

I want to thank Billy and Ruth Graham and their families for the sacrifices you all made because of this call to ministry. Your steadfast faithfulness to our Lord, and your influence on my Christian journey, are deeply and divinely appreciated by all. Blessings to all of you.

Mel

MY TESTIMONY

In February 1953, my parents took all six of us kids to the Bowling Green High School auditorium to see either *Oil Town USA* or *Mr. Texas.* I was eight years old. I had never heard a Gospel presentation before, even though we went to church regularly. At the conclusion of the film, an invitation was given for those who wanted to receive Jesus Christ as their Savior to come forward. When my oldest brother jumped up and headed down the aisle, I followed close behind. I remember a man prayed with me and gave me a red paperback Gospel of John. I remember walking out of that building with my feet barely touching the ground. I did not know what happened, but I knew something good had begun in my life.

In junior high and high school, I participated in Youth for Christ clubs, often leading them. I knew God was calling me into some form of ministry. The four years of college confirmed that call. In FWBC, I met my future wife. We graduated in 1967 and began our thirty-eight years of pastoral ministry in the Missionary Church the day after our wedding, August 5, 1967.

My life and ministry have been greatly enriched by the magazine *Christianity Today*, which Billy Graham had a hand in beginning. We have encouraged our people to participate in crusades and watch the TV broadcasts. The popularity of these broadcasts has given me many open doors to share my faith and explain the Gospel to the people I've met over the years. I want to thank Mr. Graham and our Lord for the long and faithful witness he has given. His example has encouraged me many times.

John

Thank You, Billy Graham. . .
for Setting Such a Good Example

A MAN OF INTEGRITY
I have the utmost respect for Billy, as he is a man who has had no "incidents" in his life. Thank you, Billy, for setting an example that shows us that it's possible to live a life of integrity.

THANK YOU FOR BEING
AN EXAMPLE TO NON-CHRISTIANS
Thank you, Billy, for being an example to all of us who have ever ministered in the US over the past sixty years. You have ministered to presidents but stayed out of politics. You and Ruth were honest about your marriage yet were never involved in a scandal. You pointed evangelicals toward outreach, toward assisting the poor, toward love and a hearable message. You brought together churches in your crusades that would refuse to speak to each other. You have been a powerful force for God and yet remained humble, gentle, and meek. For those of us who have never met you or even attended more than a couple of your crusades, you have still been the best and brightest of the evangelical church, the one we could point our non-Christian friends to. Thank you, Billy, for just being you, and for all the sacrifices you made so that you could be who you became.

Steve

THE CALL

Dear Dr. Graham, I have watched you throughout the years after becoming a Christian at twenty-six years of age. I would like to say thank you for being a man of integrity. You have been a man of example in doing what God called you to do and not going beyond that. Thank you for wearing the mantle of humility tightly and being the great example that we as humans should portray.

Rosalie

A CHRISTLIKE EXAMPLE

I have never been to one of your crusades, nor did I come to know my Savior through one of your crusades. I write this letter to tell you what you have meant to me because of how you have lived your life and because of your honesty.

With so many scandals within the ministry, locally and on television, you have always stood with integrity. You have managed to maintain a flawless image, which in turn has set a Christlike example for the nonbelieving world. This has been such an encouragement to me. I have stumbled so many times, yet I think about it and bet that you too have stumbled, but you have lived a life of service and with such perseverance. In this day and age, that is not a easy task to live, day in and day out.

When I look at your life and how you have lived, served, and continued on, I am in awe. I know you have had problems of your own, as I have read in your books, but this did not keep you from moving forward with the Lord's work. So many times, people let setbacks, whether large or small, keep them from doing what God has called all of us to do. Yet, when I look at your life, you have set an example no one could keep up with without the help of our Lord. I admire you, respect you, and love you for all you strive to be and are. I know your life is getting closer to being with the Lord, and what an exciting day that will be for you. I know through the reading of the scripture that your rewards will be great. But for you, I know your foremost reward will be seeing our Savior. I really want to say thank you, Billy and Ruth. I thank you, Mrs. Graham, for being a godly wife to your husband and supporting him all these years. I know that has not been easy being a minister's wife, but I applaud you for how you have done it. Thank you so very much for both of your obedience to the Lord's calling for your lives.

Thank You for Your Life of Commitment

I came to know the Lord because of the faithful sharing of God's love and His Word by my parents, who were missionaries in India. As a young person, I was able to attend the New York crusade when we were home on furlough. I was only nine years old at the time, and I remember it. But more important than that, your life has been a challenge to me to be faithful in ministry. I appreciate so much how you have been true to your word and have lived a life of integrity. You are one of the few in ministry on a large scale who have done better at withstanding the temptations that so many have fallen into, such as sex, money, or power. My ex-husband also appreciated this, as he had been almost disillusioned by so many who had fallen prey to the forces of Satan to bring down their ministries. So, mostly I want to say thank you for your life of commitment to the Lord and His leading, and the example that has been to many of us.

Your Exemplary "Christ Walk"

When I was eighteen, I decided I wanted to give my life to Christ. By my nineteenth birthday, I had decided that being a Christian was too hard and I was too scared. I kinda drifted away from it, but it was still heavy on my heart.

When Billy Graham came to Baltimore in 2006, I didn't even know who he was. I just knew he was bringing along Newsboys and Israel Houghton. Before I went to Camden Yards Stadium, I read up on Billy Graham, and I was more than impressed. I read how at such a young age he devoted and turned over his life for Christ. I said to myself, "This man has been following Christ forever," and I decided that I wanted to do the same. His "Christ walk" made me want a Christ walk of my own. When I read how he went out of his way to protect the reputation of his ministry by making a rule that his male employees weren't to interact with females alone, I thought it was extreme, but it showed how serious he was about his walk. Now, with so many church scandals, I always say, "They should have used Billy's method."

Billy Graham's example made me want a real walk with Christ, and it opened my eyes to the fact that being a Christian isn't so bad after all. Thank you, Billy Graham, for being an exemplary brother in Christ.

Huge Impact

When I was nine years old, I accepted Christ while watching Billy Graham on TV. Mama said that, after that, I tugged on the pastor's coattail until he agreed for me to be baptized. I requested and received the new believer's packet and also received *Decision* magazines. All of this helped me in my Christian growth. I was privileged to sing with the choir at the crusade held in Whiteville, North Carolina, in the 1990s. Billy Graham, you and your team have been an example and light, pointing so many to a wonderful, loving Savior. Now, almost forty years after watching that crusade on TV, I'm loving God and striving to serve Him and be an example also. Thank you, Billy, family, and staff.

AN EXAMPLE

He taught us how to live a constant, consistent life. To stand for the Word of God no matter what. His message was always the same: salvation by faith through grace. He taught me that, if I stand for Christ, the road will not be easy, but in the end I will receive a blessing. He was a rebel for God. Thank you, Billy Graham!

A MAN AFTER GOD'S HEART

I just wanted to say what an inspiration Billy Graham has been. From a young age, I was skeptical that anyone who was on television preaching to so many could be after anything more than money and recognition. I was also bored when I was younger and did not yet have a personal relationship with Jesus, nor did I really know what salvation was. When I accepted Jesus as my personal Savior at the age of eighteen, I continued to follow Billy Graham's career and his televised evangelism shows. The more I followed, the more I learned that this was a true man of God, a pure believer, and one who taught only from the Word of God and taught us of His love and our need for salvation.

I learned that Billy Graham's salary did not at all come from these appearances and that he was really a fairly simple man with a mighty message. He has withstood the scrutiny, and he has led a life that has focused the Light of the World on God and not on himself. I can only imagine the crown of glory that God has for him and the special place in heaven that will be his reward. Thank you, Mr. Graham, for your years of service and devotion to our Lord and for the many lives you have touched in His name. God bless you and your family.

No One Ever Says Anything Bad About You

I just wanted to thank you for all of the work you have done around the world. I have gone to two of your crusades in Montreal, Canada, and was a counselor both times. I was in awe to see how many people came forward on those nights. What impresses me the most is that when your name is mentioned, no one ever says anything bad about you at all. Even if those who are talking about you are not believers, the statement usually goes, "I have nothing bad to say about him, whereas some of the others. . ." I know that you are a man of humility and a deep love for our Lord Jesus Christ. Know that you have been used by God in a mighty way. Thank you, Mr. Graham, for your obedience, character, and godly example. It helps us to know that we, too, can be the people that God wants us to be, even amid trials and tribulations.

You Lived the Christian Life

Dear Billy, you have been a household name since I was a child. You are so loved by all. Thank you for sharing your life, love, your books, sense of humor, and most of all the Gospel, which has saved millions around the globe.

I have never heard a negative word about you. I only hear how grateful everyone is to know there is a true man of

God who shared his time with us preaching God's salvation. You never compromised or wavered, but you lived the Christian life. A real man of God and an example to all men of what they should be and how they should live. Our Lord will say one day, "Well done, my faithful servant." We know you from your videos, tent meetings, TV shows, and gatherings. Unfortunately, we have never met in person; but when we all get to heaven—what a celebration that will be!

My late mother had all your books, so I now enjoy them—what wonderful keepsakes. You have a wonderful legacy in your family, all serving God—what a blessing. May God continue to bless you and keep you healthy. Remember, your name is known all over the world, and is so respected by all. Even those still lost recognize the name Billy Graham as a true man of God, and they know who you are. Your reputation has never changed. You are so loved and respected. Thank you, Billy.

You Have Inspired Me

I have never personally met Billy Graham, and I have never been to one of his great crusades. But I have seen him and his family through the years on TV, leading thousands to Jesus Christ. I personally thank you, Billy and Ruth Graham, that you have kept the faith and been people of impeccable integrity through all these years of ministry. You have not sheared God's flock by asking for huge offerings to buy mansions and airplanes. You have always been accountable to other Christian men and women of integrity. You have never been found unfaithful to each other or to the evangelical call of God. Your message has been one of purity and the simplicity of the Gospel. You have inspired me and helped me to stay in the race to glory. I now preach an evangelical message at the county jail here in Georgia. I have had the privilege of leading many women to Jesus Christ. You are a part of what I do because of your example of faithfulness and perseverance through the years. God bless you. Love, in Jesus Christ our Lord!

Ongoing Legacy

Dearest Reverend Graham, I really want to pass on my heartfelt thanks and gratitude for your lifelong work in God's Kingdom. I am forty-four years old and my life has been touched by you through my father, who gave his life to Jesus at one of your crusades in Adelaide when he was about seventeen. Through this, I have become a disciple, and so have my children. Your impact will resonate throughout time eternal. Thank you for your dedication and perseverance. What a wonderfully prosperous and blessed life you are leading. You are a shining example and a light to the path of truth. Bless you, Rev. Billy Graham, and all your family, as you have surely blessed mine.

Staying the Course

In the mid-1970s, I attended the twenty-fifth anniversary celebration of Billy's ministry. In addition to the crusade at the Hollywood Bowl, I attended a special dinner and heard Billy's vision for the next century. It was moving, and inspired me to seek out what God had in store for me as a new Christian. Now, more than thirty years later, I credit Billy's message as the inspiration to stay the course with my business studies and work in Christian publishing. What a blessing it's been to have been working just where God planned.

And I have Billy to thank for pointing me in the right direction. God bless you, Billy, and thanks for staying your course.

GRATEFUL FOR YOUR EXAMPLE

My husband was saved at one of your crusades in New York when he was young. That must have been around 1958. He met me and led me to the Lord a few years later when we were in our mid-teens. We have been married for almost forty years now. If it had not been for the foundation the Lord laid in our lives through your ministry, I seriously doubt we would have known how to serve Him as a married couple. We are forever grateful to you and Ruth for the example you have set for us as husband and wife, and as parents. And not only for us, but for millions around the world. God bless you! Thank you, Billy!

A STANDARD OF EXCELLENCE

Billy Graham has set a standard of excellence for evangelistic crusades. He has taught me that preaching an evangelistic message is only the beginning. If new converts are to grow in Christ, they must be received into Christian fellowship and discipled by Bible-believing churches. This means that the evangelist must develop a relationship with, and enlist the cooperation of, local ministries. I still use the discipleship training manual I received when I was a counselor supervisor at a Graham crusade. Billy always cared about the new converts' growth and life even after the crusade was long over. Thank you, Billy.

THANK YOU, BILLY!

I just finished watching one of your telecasts from 1985. The crusade messages then are just as meaningful in today's world! I've not had a chance to see or hear you in person, but I would have loved the opportunity. I try to catch as many past crusades as I can find on my local cable channel. The messages are always very helpful in my life. As a result, I have requested and gotten many books from BGEA, for which I will always be grateful. I often read them and then pass them along to others to enjoy. You have led an incredible life, and millions around the world have been saved because of the sacrifices you have made of your time, talents, and resources. God has raised you up to be a mighty spokesperson in our time. You are the one minister of God who has never disappointed me. So many others have ended up proving to have led unspiritual lives (even in my own church), but you are a real exception to that. Thank you for your message. . .keep on proclaiming it, because the world is in desperate need of our Savior. Thank you so much for your ministry and your example. You, Ruth, and your entire family have been such an inspiration! Thank you, Billy. You have changed my life with your ministry.

Passing Down the Baton

What an amazing journey you've had. I remember, as a toddler, watching some of your crusades on television. I knew your name but didn't really understand how your work would affect me. I now see that you were an instrument of God to spread the Gospel, and an example to young Christians of how to impact the culture. I thank you on behalf of my generation for being obedient to the calling of God to the ministry and for passing down the baton.

Leo

A PASTOR'S VIEW

I had the privilege of serving as a pastor and counselor supervisor at the 1987 Denver crusade, my first time to see Dr. Graham in person. The first night, being on the field near the stage, where Dr. Graham was giving instructions to those who had responded to the invitation, was one of the most inspiring moments of my life. I saw scores and scores of people all around me, many of them weeping, as they gave their hearts to Christ. Dr. Graham, thank you for your simple obedience to Christ's call—your life has been, and continues to be, an inspiration to me personally and to the call on my life, which now takes me to Africa to train African pastors.

AN EXAMPLE OF GOD'S LOVE AND FORGIVENESS

Dr. Graham, thank you for being an unchanging, constant, humble servant of God, and an example of God's love and forgiveness in a world void of it. My family rededicated our lives to Christ in your Seattle crusade in the 1980s, and most memorable forever to me is that I had the honor of singing in the choir.

I often watched your TV crusades for the simple comfort they brought, knowing you were always there with the same unwavering message to us all. The earth is a much better place because of you, and heaven's population greater than ever.

Thank you for everything. I can't wait to see you in heaven and talk to you.

GOD CALLED ME BY RADIO

My story of how Billy Graham's ministry affected my life is simple. I came to the Lord during 1967, at the age of fifteen, while listening to the weekly radio broadcasts of the Billy Graham Evangelistic Association. Several years prior to that, our family—living in Calgary, Alberta, at the time—had drifted from the church, following the death of my younger brother (a protracted medical event that tested my parents' beliefs beyond their faith at the time). God definitely had His hand on my life, as the Holy Spirit later convicted me and drew me back to Him. It was providential; I had made a crystal radio from a kit, and listened to it on Sunday evenings as I went to sleep. God reached me through radio programs during that period, and I remember Billy Graham's ministry in particular as influential in my becoming a Christian. I have been a fond supporter ever since. Billy Graham has always struck me as a man of real integrity, uncompromising in his humility, in spite of the high profile God gave his Christian ministry. He has served God faithfully and sacrificially over the years, with a simple, consistent message and altar-call format in his crusades. My greeting to Dr. Graham and his family is one of respect and appreciation.

How a Christian Is Supposed to Live

I've watched Billy Graham all my life and have learned from him how a Christian is supposed to live and how a person is supposed to love God and family. Thanks for showing the masses and leading by example. Thank you, Billy!

Impact in My Life and Ministry

I thank God for Dr. Billy Graham, for his concern to preach the Gospel with simplicity, authority, and clarity. I happened to read his messages in *Decision* magazine and heard his sermons through the *Hour of Decision* radio programmes, and then later through electronic media. His messages motivated me to keep my evangelistic ministry focused without diluting the theology or deviating from presenting the Gospel with simplicity and clarity. Dr. Graham's life and ministry influenced me and my ministry to the extent that I strongly believe that the preaching of the Cross is the power of God unto salvation. His ministry taught me to appeal for a verdict whenever I preach the Gospel. I thank God for the impact of Dr. Graham in my life and ministry.

THANK YOU, BILLY GRAM-HAM!

When our youngest daughter was only six, she knew who you were. Just learning to read, she called you "Billy Gram-ham." Many smiles and many miles later, you remain Billy Gram-ham in our family.

Thank you for being on TV in the early 1970s, when I knelt and prayed and waited expectantly for your literature, which included a Bible. Having been raised Catholic, I had no idea what a Bible should be like, and (can I say this?) I was a little disappointed! But thank God, and thank you for having a BGEA table at a small fair in Florida a couple of years later. The only thing I remember about that night is purchasing a lovely black leather Bible. I still have it thirty-four years later—tattered and torn and no longer so black and shiny—but it has been a lifeline.

Though you won't accept much credit, you also have been a "strong rope of hope" when it felt like all hell was breaking loose and I didn't know what I believed or if I could hold on. Many times you would come to mind, bringing a sense of stability and peace. Thank you for the 1969 crusade at Madison Square Garden. (I saw the rerun tonight, and your gift of preaching is *still* nourishment to eyes, ears, heart, soul, and spirit.)

Thank you for being you. Please just let us love you. Though you don't seem to think you deserve all this attention. . .trust that we've heard you give God all the credit over these many years. But Mr. Graham, you are one of the closest things we have of showing the reality of that scripture, "Christ in you, the hope of glory." Thank you, Billy Gram-ham for stepping aside as God showed himself strong through you, being the best example of Christ walking this earth in this generation.

BILLY GRAHAM PRAYS

It was a rainy, foggy night in Nashville, Tennessee, when two youth workers were heading back to their hotel after leading seminars at a youth convention. As they passed by the building called The Parthenon which sits high on a hill overlooking the city, they noticed someone who appeared to be a homeless man sitting on the steps of that impressive building. His raincoat was pulled up high and his head was buried in his arms. He looked so pathetic that the two young men stopped their car, ran up the steps, and said to this pitiful figure, "Mister, you don't have to sit out here in this drizzle. We'd like to take you to the hotel where we are staying and pay for a room for you to have a good night's sleep."

The man looked up and when the young men saw his face, they recognized that it was Billy Graham. Billy was conducting a crusade in Nashville, and there he was at 11:30 at night, sitting in the rain, praying over the city. Billy said, "Thank you, but I want to stay here a little longer, and I really do have a place to stay tonight. Thank you for your kindness," and he went back to praying. Those two young men walked down the steps, got into their car, and before they drove away one said to the other, "So that's what he's all about. Here we thought he was just a great preacher, but his power comes through prayer."

Tony Campolo

Thank You, Billy Graham. . .
for Your Classic Crusades

SAVED ON THE FORTY YARD LINE

I accepted Jesus Christ as my savior at Alamo Stadium in June 1968. I remember it as if it were yesterday. My knees were on the forty yard line when Christ came into my heart. Thank you, Billy, for sharing Christ with me. You have made a difference in my life. I was seventeen years old at the time. I am now fifty-six and have been working in full-time Christian service for twenty-eight years. Following Christ was the most important decision I ever made. Jeremiah 29:11 says, "For I know the plans that I have for you, declares the LORD, plans to give you hope and a future." God bless you, Billy Graham, for touching my life. By the way, I was watching Billy Graham Classics on TV the other night and I saw the crusade in San Antonio. I was blessed to see myself walking forward during the invitation and accepting Christ.

THANK YOU, BILLY GRAHAM

A crusade was held in Miami Beach back in the late 1960s or early '70s. Our entire family attended, and it was such a privilege and blessing for us. I am now eighty-seven years old, a widow, and reside in a retirement community. I no longer attend Sunday church services but instead record the Graham Classic shows during the week and watch them on Sunday mornings. This gives me the opportunity to worship along with these inspirational programs, for which I am truly grateful. Thank you, Billy Graham!

BILLY CLASSICS

I am the mother of two boys, ten and seven, and a military wife to a soldier deployed in Afghanistan. I am currently living in Georgia and watch the TBN and CBN networks every day. I was watching a crusade in black-and-white (that, right there, was fascinating) and saw a young and handsome Rev. Billy Graham. I have always enjoyed the times when I have seen glimpses of his preaching.

Tonight, I was flipping numbly through the channels and found Rev. Graham preaching to thousands of people of Florida who had gone to hear him. Well, I stopped and let my ears hear. He spoke of real conversion, of how many "Christians" have never really converted.

I was thirteen years old when I gave my life to Christ in a small church in the Bronx. I have lived my life "my way," married my husband at twenty, and after our first son was born, went off to experience the military life. I had a good ol' time "doing my thang," which often involved my slipping away and leaving the church until the next deployment. I have done this now for ten years. Today, in watching the crusade, I truly converted. It was not a loud wail or a sudden change. In fact, I feel no different, but I believe what Rev. Graham said that I must humble myself, confess my sins (which include breaking all of the Ten Commandments), and accept Christ into my heart. God knows it isn't easy for me to change my ways, yet He will help me by giving me the strength I need to say no to sin.

Well, this is my thank you. . .I love you. . .God bless you and all your lovely family.

JUST ANOTHER SATURDAY NIGHT

In March 2002, I was sitting on my couch in Fort Lauderdale, on an ordinary Saturday night. As I was channel surfing, I ran across your Billy Graham Classic on TV. I was mesmerized by your words, and you forever grabbed my heart. The Lord used you as His vessel that night to forever change me, and I gave my life to Christ and entered His Lamb's Book of Life. As a result, I was baptized in the Gulf of Mexico in October 2003.

I now reside in Louisville, where the Lord has placed me to minister to my unsaved family and plant seeds in their hearts. As I minister here in this place, I am forever indebted to you. God be with you, and I pray that I will attend your great harvest of revival in November 2013. Thank you, Dr. Graham, for your faithfulness to advance the Gospel all over the world. The greatest thing is that I will be able to sit and have a conversation with you in the Kingdom, where we will reign for eternity with our great King, the Lord Jesus Christ. Praise be His holy name!

ONE OF MY FONDEST CHILDHOOD MEMORIES

One of my fondest childhood memories was when all the family would stop and gather around the TV set (it was in black-and-white then) to listen to Billy Graham bring us the Word of God. (I grew up in the 1950s.) My parents and our family loved the televised messages. . .it gave us all such great encouragement.

My parents and two of my brothers have now gone on to be with the Lord. In 1998, my mother came down with Alzheimer's. That was the same year I lost my dad, and also one of my brothers. But, as usual, Dr. Graham would have a word of hope and encouragement for us. God used you in so many ways to help us keep our eyes on Jesus. In our area, we receive the Classic Billy Graham crusades. What a word of hope and encouragement those have been, as well as bringing back those fond childhood memories of when the family was all together.

Thank you, Dr. Graham, for your faithfulness in preaching God's Word and for giving us hope when we went through some very dark days. To your family, I want to say, thank you for sharing Billy with us. He is truly America's pastor. Thank you, Billy, for teaching me how to love Jesus. May God always richly bless you!

Linda

I ONCE WAS LOST, BUT NOW AM FOUND. . .

I have battled depression all my life. I had parents who told me I was a loser and useless despite my almost perfect grades and outwardly perfect existence. I always longed for love, friendship, acceptance, and just a sense that I mattered in this world. I was "raised Catholic" and made all my sacraments, because that's what all the other children in my school did; but after those rituals were over, I never attended church other than for a wedding or a funeral. I was never taught about God or His love or salvation or anything of that nature, other than the punishment I would receive if I "continued to be bad."

I rebelled in my teens and early twenties, as most children do—drinking, partying, and the like—wandering through this world, wondering why I was still here on earth if no one wanted me around. Sure I had good grades in college, but I had been through a bout with cancer when I was eighteen, had eloped the same year, and two years later was left for dead on the hospital steps with my "I told you so" parents picking me up. I was the prodigal daughter they didn't want to welcome back home with open arms—just with hate and condemnation and finger pointing. Finally, in the middle of the night one night, I decided that if no one wanted me around, and if there was no real purpose for me here other than to be used, abused, and taken advantage of, then I didn't want any part of this world and figured hell couldn't be much worse than what I dealt with on a daily basis by living.

With tears in my eyes and a sense of complete hopelessness and uselessness—that no matter how hard I tried, I would never be good enough for anyone—I got up from my parents' couch planning to go and drive off a bridge, knowing that no one would notice I was even gone. As I got up off the couch, I stepped on the remote and it turned the channel to TBN, which had a Billy Graham Classic on. I can't remember specifically every word Billy Graham was saying, but I do remember him saying, "God loves you, just as you are, right now." And I thought to myself, *No, no one loves me.* And he just talked so convincingly about love, hope, and forgiveness, and I thought to myself, *If this man can give up everything to tell all these people this message, then maybe God has a purpose for me, too.* As I watched all those people come forward to accept Christ, my heart went forward with them. The next day, I went into a local Christian church, newly bought $5 Bible in hand, and said that I had just accepted Christ. *Now what?*

That was several years ago, and I am now getting ready to graduate from college. I am cancer free and engaged to a wonderful, godly man. I am also a teacher at a Christian church, where I work with the children's ministry, and I am the chapter leader of Bound4LIFE New Jersey, a Christian organization committed to taking an intercessory stand to end abortion and bring revival to America. I have found joy, peace, forgiveness—and, most of all, a knowledge that I *do* matter in this world and that God *does* have a plan for me, as his daughter, and has a seat prepared for me in His eternal Kingdom. Thank you, Billy, for answering His call so that all of us around the world could come to hear it and answer it as well. God bless you always!

THANKS FOR THE MEMORIES—KEEP THEM COMING

When the Internet was first starting and my pastor was very ill, I e-mailed numerous places for prayer. The BGEA was one of the few places that e-mailed back to express prayer, and even e-mailed back later to check on my pastor's progress. And when he went to heaven, they sent yet another message of symapathy and care. That means a great deal. How genuine and real this ministry is. We love the Billy Graham Classic crusade rebroadcast specials on Saturday night on TBN. What a great idea. Please keep up the great work. You have a great reward of loved ones you've never met here on earth but will consider you family in heaven.

BILLY. . .YOU INSPIRED ME

I have been a Christian for quite a long time. I'm twenty-one years old and have been listening and watching the Billy Graham Classic crusades on television. As I was watching a crusade several years ago, I became convicted about my lack of effort in reaching the lost for Jesus Christ. I became convicted about the fact that I had so many simple opportunities to share, and yet I would not. Yet, here on the television was

133

a man named Billy Graham, whom I believed if given the chance to deliver the message of Christ to the millions watching on TV would do anything. I have seen that Billy was willing to do anything to make Christ known to as many of the millions watching as possible, even if it inconvenienced him at the time.

I want to commend Billy for his service, and also to tell you that Billy has inspired me to reach the lost for Jesus Christ, just as Billy Sunday inspired a young Billy Graham. I now share my faith whenever and wherever I am able. I don't know if I will follow in the footsteps of Billy Graham, but I know one thing, I want my entire life from beginning to end to be devoted to nothing less than Jesus Christ. Thank you, Billy, you have inspired me by your messages, put a smile on my face, and encouraged and exalted me to do God's will whenever and wherever.

I Still Watch the Classics

Now a grown man of forty-four, I have been involved with Billy Graham since I was a kid. My parents had us watch his crusades on TV, and we read his books, too. I still watch the Classics, and so does my mom. It is good to see the old ones, since I understand things better now. I am glad and am reminded of my walk with the Lord, and the sermons and songs have helped me every week. Thanks for your kind words of encouragement and for your love! May the good Lord continue to bless you in your work

The Lasting Difference

I want to say thank you for your ministry to my life. About a year ago, I first started watching the Billy Graham Classics on TBN. I watched the first one, then the second one, then the third one, and started crying. I prayed and asked God to forgive me for forgetting about the tremendous impact that you, Dr. Graham, have had on my life. Ever since I was a little girl, I've had a love for God that burned in my heart from the preaching I heard from you and from the letters I received and the encouragement you sent to me to go to church. I know that God's message reached me early in life, and I am so very thankful to you, Dr. Graham, for your obedience to preach the Gospel.

Whenever the Billy Graham Classics come on TV, I always call my mother to see if she is watching. The programs continue to inspire me—much to my amazement. When I watch them, God speaks to me so much, and I remember so many of them as if it were yesterday. Your message on wholeheartedly following God forever changed my life, and that message has a continuing effect on my life today—in my thinking, emotions, and heart, and in what I say and do. I'm so challenged by it, and as I stay in prayer, God so directs my life in the most amazing ways.

Thank You, Billy Graham. . .
for Helping Me Deal with Death

Eternally Thankful

I was saved by grace and childlike faith at a church camp when I was ten years old. I never really understood the meaning of being saved, or why Christ took my sins to the cross and died the physical death that was truly what I deserved, but I believed. I longed to understand what the pastors were preaching.

Years later, after I was married and became a young mom of three girls, I joined an in-depth Bible study. I would watch your crusades and cry when people went down to confess Christ. I knew by experience that their lives would not be an easy journey but that God would always make a way, even when there seemed to be no way. Dr. Graham, thank you for being the voice and the living role model for my husband and me. We've been through many difficult, impossible situations, but you never changed. For my husband and me, seeing a Christian who walked the talk made a huge difference in our journey of choices. Your excitement and never-ending energy gave us so much strength.

When your book *Just As I Am* came out, I gave it to my husband "just because," and I wrote inside the cover: "Dear Dave, I thank God everyday for you! I hope you enjoy Dr. Graham's life story. The Lord has used him in a mighty way, as I know He is using you. Psalm 91."

One night in 2003, Dave came into the kitchen for a dish of chocolate ice cream and saw the Billy Graham crusade I was watching on TV. Your longtime friend George Beverly Shea was singing and Dave could not believe his amazing voice, still so good at his age. Dave loved music and especially Mr. Shea. Then he said jokingly, "He will probably outlive me!"

Dave went to the den, eating his chocolate ice cream and thinking about Billy Graham and George Beverly Shea—and then he suddenly went to heaven. I have found comfort in knowing what his last thoughts were before seeing Jesus and that I will see my Dave again someday.

My Grandmother Is in Heaven because of Billy

You know the Lord puts a desire in your heart and then brings it forward to glorify God. A month ago, my grandmother was blessed at ninety-two years of age to go home. I was sitting watching the sunset on the beach, thinking of her, her life, and the things you do when you get word that someone has passed on, and I rejoiced in my heart for Billy Graham. You see, my grandmother had been exposed to different faiths and was still seeking truth when she began watching a Billy Graham crusade. It took three years of watching every crusade that was televised before she would yield and ask Jesus to be her Savior. Several years ago, I was able to spend some uninterrupted time with her. It was during this time that I wanted to know if she knew what awaited her when she died. She shared her story with me and I rejoiced with her.

I am so blessed to know that I will see her again, which has made such a difference in how I deal with her passing. Thank you, Billy Graham, for being obedient to your call, for being willing to follow God's direction for your life, preaching the truth and sharing Jesus. . . . Great is your reward in heaven, and I know you will hear from our Father, "Well done, my faithful servant!"

WALKING WITH MY GRANDFATHER
THROUGH THE SHADOW OF DEATH

In June 2006, my grandmother went to be with the Lord after being diagnosed with melanoma with bone mets. She said, "What is so bad about being eighty-three and going to heaven to be with Jesus?" She was an amazing witness. When she died, and even now, my grandfather struggled a lot. They were married for sixty-four years. They were childhood sweethearts, who grew up on the same street and never dated anyone else. A wonderful grace for my grandpa was your book *The Journey: Living by Faith in an Uncertain World.* I am thankful for the comfort he received through reading the book. The chapters about Ruth's illness were particularly meaningful to him. Thank you for putting your experiences on paper and sharing the love and peace of God with him through this terrible time. I love him, and he has been a model of Christ's love for me. It is nice that he has someone to look to, even through the pages of a book. May God bless you and comfort you as well.

Melissa

HIS PRESENCE

My dear husband and I, a young mother at the age of twenty, lost our firstborn after only eight days. We were completely bewildered as to why we had to suffer this loss. I could not find peace in anybody's words. I was so lost and spent a lot of time alone. One day, it was raining, and I felt my baby was in the rain. I fell to the floor and asked God to please help me. I felt God's presence right there in my heart. Then I began watching a Billy Graham crusade on television. I feel his teachings led me in my Christian walk.

I have had a life with many blessings, and a share of losing loved ones. However, I now know life is a journey we all walk, and being a Christian is the answer to how we witness for God. Thank you, Billy, for all of the messages I've heard over the past fifty years. I still watch the older reruns and live that era again and see that the world is closer to the coming of our Savior. Thank you for the witness of your family, and for your son Franklin for carrying on the message of God's love.

My Sonya

It was September 21, 1980, a day much like today here in North Carolina, when I heard a loud knock on my back door. My neighbor was pale and frantic as she told me about an automobile accident down the street from my house. My only daughter, Sonya, sixteen years old, was killed in that accident. That was the worst day of my life.

Through the years, I had listened to you on television, had read your writings, and felt a deep respect for you, but I never knew you like I would get to know you over the next years ahead. You taught me that it was okay to be honest with God, that He already knows my thoughts and feelings. It was because of your teachings that Jesus Christ became my personal friend.

I had been a Christian since 1958, but I did not really know Him until I began that journey. I remember thinking, *Where was God when my daughter died?*, and I heard the answer—the same place He was when His Son died. My faith was tested over and over as I hungered for your sermons on television and your writings, including *Decision* magazine. I dwelled on your message of salvation and forgiveness. I had to forgive the person who had caused my daughter's death, and it was not easy. During this time, I received her death settlement, and I wanted to tithe the money. I asked God to give me the wisdom to know where I should give it. He spoke to my heart, and I have never regretted tithing it to the Billy Graham Evangelistic Association. God has richly blessed me just by knowing that my gift was used to promote the Gospel of Jesus Christ around the world.

Without you and Jesus Christ in my life, I never would have survived. Everyone knows how much I admire you. For the past five years, I have had a large picture of you on my refrigerator. The Christmas cards of you, Ruth, and your family decorate my refrigerator. You are like family, because you have inspired me to survive a lot of lonely, low times in my life. You are a reflection of the love of Jesus Christ. Seeing your picture on my refrigerator every day has given me strength when I was at my weakest point. I thank God for you.

GOD IS GOOD, SO GOOD

My name is Angela, and I am thirty-two years old. I went to the Billy Graham crusade at the Carrier Dome at Syracuse when I was twelve years old. God used Billy Graham to save me, and after that day I was never the same. I had blocked off my past because it was full of abuse by my parents. But God used Billy to touch me and help me remember the things I had survived by the grace of God. My mother died, and I had been praying and standing in faith that she would be healed from cancer and live longer, but God had other plans that He carries out for a reason. When my mother died, I got angry at God for a while. However, I ended up reading an article that Billy wrote in the newspaper, and God helped me understand her death. After that, I started attending church again, and I was at peace with my mom's death. Billy is a man filled with the Spirit of God, who has touched and changed my life. Thank you, Billy Graham!

MY HUSBAND IS IN HEAVEN BECAUSE OF BILLY GRAHAM'S TV CRUSADE

My first husband and I were married for twenty-five years and four months before he passed away from cancer. When we first got married in 1965, I was a Christian, but my husband was not. In 1968, when our second child was six weeks old, we watched Billy Graham on TV, and he was on several nights in a row. At the end, my husband knelt down in our living room and gave his heart to the Lord. He was later baptized. He went on to serve the Lord all his days on earth. He was a leader in our church and had Bible studies in our home.

A few days before he went to be with Jesus, he saw Jesus. He asked me if I had seen Him, too, and I said no. My husband told me to look hard, but I still didn't see anything. It was about midnight, and a friend who was staying with me came into the room and wanted to know what was the matter. I told her, and then she said, "I came into the room because I thought you turned the light on." I looked around and the room was bright and my husband's face was glowing. He saw Jesus, but we saw the Light. He died a few days later, but we will never forget the presence of the Lord.

My husband kept saying he needed to fight and win over cancer to take care of me. A couple of days before he died, he told our son that he wanted to know when his chemo was. My son said, "Where are you going, Dad?" When my husband replied that he was going to be with the Lord, my son asked, "How do you feel about that, Dad?" He told him that he was happy and wanted to go.

Sometime after he saw the Lord, he found peace about me, and that I would be all right. As a widow in my forties, I saw God do many miracles for me. I felt my husband prayed for me, even on his deathbed. Then God brought me a Boaz, and I remarried. God has given me another incredible marriage. I have now been married twenty-one years to my Boaz.

I will always be grateful for God's gift of Billy Graham in our lives. My first husband is in heaven because Billy preached the Gospel through the TV in our living room, and my husband was saved for all eternity! Thank you, Rev. Graham!

MY SISTER-IN-LAW JUDY

Dear Billy, what a great treat and honor to be able to tell you my story. However, my story is not really mine, but it belongs to my husband's family. You see, my mother- and father-in-law were Christians a few years before any of their children were, and they were and still are prayer warriors. My husband and I came to the Lord in January 1981. My husband's three sisters knew we had changed, but they did not desire to follow in our footsteps—that is, until 1983. You see, my sister-in-law Judy was watching one of your crusades on TV in December 1983. We had a five-month-old son at the time, and Judy and her husband had a one-year-old. My husband, David, and I were watching your crusade also, and stringing popcorn for the Christmas tree. Well, the phone rang and it was Judy. She was crying and pouring her heart out to David. She had just accepted the Lord while watching you on TV. From that day forward, our lives were never the same.

Judy lived about ten miles down the road from us, and when she passed our trailer she would either toot her horn or stop in to see us. We saw her more in that one month than we had for a long time. Well, Judy had a birthday on January 3, and three days after her birthday, on January 6, she was brutally murdered in her home. It was a tragic event, and our lives have been shaped by that awful night. But there is good news. We have the comfort of knowing that Judy is with the Lord, in part from your ministry.

Through Judy's tragic death, David's two other sisters came to know the Lord. Two other brothers-in-law did also, but have backslidden since. Many people heard the Gospel through this event. The murderer wasn't caught until October 2006. The man is in jail, and at the time of this writing, we are still waiting for a trial. The trial is expected to start after the first of the year. It will be a tough time, because most of the family are witnesses of that day in 1983, but it will be good to put this to rest. Thank you for your years of faithfulness and answering the call that God has put on your life. Our lives have been changed for eternity, as I'm sure many others have also. Blessings to you and your family.

Jackie

My Son Is Waiting for Me in Heaven

My son, Clayton, was fourteen years old when he was watching a Billy Graham crusade in his bedroom. He later came out and told me and his dad that he had just accepted Christ as his personal Lord and Savior. I cried and told him (as I had many times before) that accepting Jesus was the most important decision he would ever make in his lifetime. Little did I know that only three years later he would be home with the Lord. You see, on January 1, 1997, Clayton died protecting me from his father. (They both died on my bedroom floor—an unbelievable story.) Today, I am still as crushed and as brokenhearted as I was on that day, for losing a child is the worst possible thing that could ever happen to a mother. The only thing that gets me through each day is that I rest on God's promise that one day Clayton and I will be reunited, never to be separated again. Praise the Lord! Thank you, Jesus, for shedding your precious blood at Calvary, so that Christians don't have to say "good-bye," but, "See you later." Thank you, Billy Graham. Because of your message that night, Clayton is waiting for me in heaven.

Fear of Death Gone

For almost thirty-two years of my life, I was afraid of death and dying. I had been sent to Sunday school by a moral and religious mother, so I knew the popular stories from the Bible. From my earliest years, I believed there was a God and that Jesus Christ, His only begotten Son, had died on the cross for the sins of the whole world. Yet, when I prayed, I had no sense that God was really hearing me. And when I read the Bible, I understood the words on the page but none of the spiritual truths in it. So, through my growing-up years, and twelve years into my marriage, I was continually seeking peace of mind and heart.

By 1970, I had a wonderful husband and was the mother of four beautiful children. We lived in the suburbs of Washington, DC, and had a "good life" filled with things that are supposed to make one happy. Yet I was empty and continually searching for satisfaction in life and assurance that I would end up in heaven when I died.

And then Dr. Billy Graham came on the scene for me! As I had done often, I watched one of his telecasts in August 1970. In it, he asked the question, "If you should die tonight, do you know for sure that you would go to heaven?" He went on to say that he had absolute assurance of heaven and that anyone can. *How?* For the next two months, I searched diligently for the answer. Finally, on October 20, 1970, after I had listened to a Gospel program on the radio, the truth suddenly dawned on me. I was a sinner. This was something I had never seen before. And when Jesus shed His innocent blood on the cross, it was not just for "the world," it was for me! The radio preacher shared that "as many as received Him, to them gave He the power to become the sons (and daughters) of God." So, in childlike faith, I got down on my knees, confessed my sin, and invited the Lord Jesus Christ into my life. That was the beginning of a new life for me!

Assurance of my salvation was immediate and has never left. Awareness of God's hearing and answering my prayers began and has never left. And His book became a love letter to me! Since that time, my husband has been saved, and all five children (we had one more in 1972), and now we have twenty-one grandchildren who are all saved as well! My "religious" mother got saved on her deathbed in October

2005, and my dad just two months before his death in October 1980. To tell the continuing story would take a book, but I thank you and praise God, Dr. Graham, for your faithful preaching of the saving Gospel of the Lord Jesus Christ. I met you once in person some years later at a crusade, and I look forward to meeting you again in heaven!

Thank You, Billy Graham. . .
for *Helping My Marriage*

You Saved My Parents' Marriage

I am telling this story for my mother. My mom and dad were
going through a difficult time. My dad had been unfaithful
to my mother and they were split up. One evening, my mom
was watching a Billy Graham special on TV. My mom loves
Billy Graham and always has. I know it is a dream of hers
to see Billy Graham in person. Well, after the TV program
was over, Mom shut off the TV and was getting ready to go
to bed. As she got up and headed out of the living room,
she said Mr. Graham showed up on the TV and told her
not to give up, to stay in there, and hang on. Her marriage
was going to survive and all would be okay. Mom walked
back to the television to make sure she had turned it off, and
sure enough she had. She knew that message was for her! She
trusted what Mr. Graham told her because she knows he is a
mighty man of God. That was probably five or six years ago.
My mom and dad have since mended things and are back
together. It has not been easy; in fact, she has had to truly
grow in the Lord to forgive my dad for what he did and to be
with him. I don't know what happened with my dad during
that time, but he began to go to church with my mom, and
I know that he found God during that time. I want to thank
God for using Mr. Graham on that lonely night to speak to
my mom, and also thank God for my dad finding his way
into God's presence. I have heard that Mr. Graham is hoping
to put together one more crusade. I pray that God will be

merciful and gracious enough to make a way for my mom to go to that crusade to thank Mr. Graham and God in person. Thank you, Mr. Graham, for saving my mom and dad!

ONE NIGHT CHANGED OUR LIVES FOREVER

Dear Billy, I hope it's okay to call you Billy. Although we've never met, I feel like you are a great friend. Through you, God offered my husband and me the most precious gift we will ever own—a treasured possession—our dear Lord and Savior, Jesus Christ. We are forever grateful to you, Billy, for that one night, when darkness surrounded our souls.

Back in the winter of 1979, my husband and I were in the process of a divorce. We were like two passing ships in the wind, waving and yelling hi to each other but never docking so that we could experience an intimate relationship.

After serving ten years with the US Navy, my husband decided to leave the military and begin a new career as a civilian. We both rushed to find jobs so that we could pay our bills, find a home to live in, and provide food for our family. Tim became a dedicated police officer working different shifts, and I worked whatever hours I could get at Safeway as a checker/stocker.

One evening, Tim had a night off, while I had a four-hour shift at Safeway. On this special night, ordained of the Lord, God chose you, Billy Graham, to give a message that changed our lives forever. A night we'll never forget that caused the angels in heaven to rejoice over this one man, my husband, who humbled himself before God in front of the television and wept.

Billy, you preached a salvation message as you always do, that Jesus Christ is the only way to salvation, and God reached in and grabbed my husband's heart right through that TV screen. The message pierced Tim's soul as he listened to every word coming from your mouth, explaining what Jesus had done for him—how He suffered, poured out His blood, and died for him, a sinner.

That night, Tim was born again. He was a brand-new man. The heaviness left his heart, and he stood tall, shoulders back, knowing that God would work in our marriage. The following day, he told me, "God told me you aren't going anywhere."

I looked at him so strangely. I wondered if he was losing it upstairs. A few seconds passed as I thought about what he'd said. I placed a soft touch on his arm and said, "Don't be too sure." I tried to be gentle. We were both trying to be careful of each other's feelings while traveling this rough road that was leading to living separate lives. We didn't want our kids to suffer more than necessary. Our daughter was only four, and our son was six. When we did argue, it was over our kids. We both wanted them.

One day, a comment slipped from Tim that caught me off guard. He said it was a sin to divorce. For some reason, that really bothered me. I didn't have a religious background, but I did belong to a book club, had ordered a Bible once, and kept it in my drawer. I took it out, and though it was difficult, I found scriptures that talked about how God hates divorce.

Tim asked me one day if I would be willing to go to church with him. I said okay, just to keep the peace. The first time he brought the kids to Sunday school he came right back. "Hey," he said. "They have Sunday school for adults, too. Want to go?"

I gave Tim a puzzled look. "They actually have Sunday

school for adults?"

Again to keep the peace, I said I'd go. When we arrived, a nice elderly couple took us under their wing.

The Holy Spirit touched my heart ever so slightly, gently, but persistently. He wouldn't let go of me. He wooed me; He showed me the Savior, and the heart of our heavenly Father, leading me to the path of righteousness.

One Sunday, there was a song being sung while the pastor gave the invitation: *"The Savior is waiting to enter your heart, why don't you let Him come in. There's nothing in this world to keep you apart, why don't you let him come in."*

Tim nudged me as the song was sung. I was on the end of the pew, and he wanted to go up to the front. I thought he was nudging me to go up with him. Fear gripped my heart, and I strong-armed the pew and wouldn't let him pass. No way was I going up to the front. Tim said, "No, not you, *me*—I want to go up."

I sighed relief and immediately released my arms, dropping them to my side and allowing him an exit to the front. He always teases me that right when the song came to the line, "There's nothing in the world to keep you apart," was when I forbade him passage. We still laugh at that.

I wasn't ready to make a public declaration yet. It was difficult for me to surrender my life to the Lord. I was having the hardest time praying out loud and confessing my sin. I wanted to clean up my act before I accepted Jesus as my Savior and Lord. I knew what a sinner I was and thought I could clean myself up. I laugh at that now.

The couple that helped to disciple us explained to me that I didn't have to clean up my life. They said I just had to surrender to the Lord, confess my sin, and repent, and I would be saved. They said that God takes you just as you are. I finally got up the courage to speak a prayer out loud, and the following Sunday I walked up front to the pastor. All I could do was cry. I couldn't say a word. The pastor, so kind and patient, asked me all the necessary things I should have said. Between sobs and tears, I nodded my head. I joined the congregation of the saints, I was a part of God's family, and the angels rejoiced in heaven over this sinner, too.

Billy, I want to say thank you so much. May the God of Abraham, Isaac, and Jacob richly bless you for the years you've been obedient to Him and His Word. Because you answered His call, my husband and I have a new life in Christ and a restored marriage. Saved from the pain of losing one or the other parent as a result of divorce, our children avoided much suffering. Thank you, Billy, for serving God with a humble heart and a willing spirit.

SCRAMBLED EGGS

After divorce and remarriage to an unbeliever, I was suffering from the guilt of divorce and being unequally yoked. I had asked for forgiveness but struggled with the sin. One evening, while I was watching a Billy Graham crusade, Dr. Graham commented on those who have divorced and remarried. He said, "You can't unscramble scrambled eggs, but the Lord can make a wonderful meal, which will feed many." It spoke right to my heart, and I never looked back. Realizing that God could use me freed me from the guilt. I was determined to become an example to my husband. Thank you, Dr. Graham; that was twenty-six years ago. A few years later, my husband was saved, and we have been serving the Lord ever since.

I Have a Future Now

I grew up in a middle-class family. We weren't a Christian home, but we followed morals in many areas of our lives. Growing up brought some painful situations, including some abuse (not by my parents, but others) and my parents' eventual divorce. I always felt responsible to make sure everyone was okay. That isn't something that a person should take upon themselves, but I didn't know that until later.

Long story short, I felt a lot of pressure and didn't know where to go with it, so I started to drink at the age of sixteen. I was able to drink large amounts of alcohol without ever getting sick or hungover later. That was a very bad thing, because I blacked out more times than I can count, and put myself in some very vulnerable and bad situations. I made some very poor personal decisions and soon found myself pregnant, at nineteen, with my boyfriend's child. He did not want to marry at first, so we just lived together. (We ended up getting married after our daughter was born.)

Being a parent caused me to look at life differently. I wanted to change. I wanted to go back to the person I used to be. . .the innocent one. But I thought I had already done too much, too publicly, and that it just wasn't possible. Even going to church, I felt ashamed of how I'd lived. None of it ever seemed to reach where I was, yet I continued to go. I became pregnant with our second child in 1991. One night, while I was riding my exercise bike, I turned to a Billy Graham crusade. Normally, I would have turned the channel, but this day was different. I had always figured it was just for "religious people," but this day, I was curious. Maybe I would hear something that would give me some hope. I felt like my life was all over, as far as success was concerned, because of the poor decisions I had made.

As I watched and Billy began to preach, I couldn't believe what I was hearing: there was hope for me. I was reluctant to even believe that I could really start over. It seemed too good to be true! But I called a phone counselor and explained my life situation, and they prayed with me. I couldn't believe that God would still accept me! I could not remember ever hearing about being "born again," but I wanted it! My life began to turn around that night. In short, after a few years, my husband was also saved, and God restored our marriage. We now have three beautiful girls who know the Lord and are beginning to serve Him on their own. God has revealed Himself to me in so many ways, and I am so very grateful. I never could have hoped for the life that He has given me!

Thank you, Billy Graham, for living a life of integrity and leading hopeless people to the God who is more than enough for them to begin again!

I HEARD GOD SPEAK TO ME

I was going through a very difficult time in my marriage. As I put my five children to bed early one night, I was wondering what was going to become of us. I turned on the TV, and Billy Graham was on. I listened to him, and when he gave the invitation to receive Christ, I prayed with him. I really didn't know that anything had happened to me, but the next morning as I woke up, I heard God speak to me, telling me to take my husband back. I did, and it eventually led to his getting saved. He died the next year, but I know where he is! How God worked with me and my children these past thirty years is so like our great God! I thank you, Billy, for your faithfulness to His calling. You truly are God's messenger to the lost and hopeless of this world.

FROM DARKNESS INTO LIGHT

I am an American currently living in the country of Croatia. I would like to share my testimony of how I came to know Jesus Christ as my Lord and Savior through a Billy Graham telecast.

It was the autumn of 1973. My husband and I had been married fourteen months and were the proud parents of a beautiful seven-month-old baby girl. However, our marriage, our family, and our lives were in horrible disarray. We desired a change in our hippie lifestyle. We tried to stop drinking, smoking pot, occasionally using drugs, and going to parties because we wanted to have a healthy lifestyle for our precious little baby. We were also doing Transcendental Meditation, with hopes that this would wean us off of the use of drugs, but everything we tried didn't work. There was still a lot of stress between my husband and me and a huge empty spot in my heart.

Although I had no religious background and seldom went to church, I remember many times kneeling in the bathroom of our home and crying out, "God help me!" as dark depression, anxiousness, and desperation closed in around me. I remember calling a priest one time to ask if my husband and I could come in to see him and talk about our problems. He said, "Of course," but there was a fee to pay. We didn't have the money to pay the fee, so we never went to him for help.

I was so unhappy that I eventually called my father, who lived seven hundred miles away, and told him I wanted to leave my husband. He said he would put a check in the mail for me to use to purchase a bus ticket for my daughter and me to come to where he lived and try to figure out what I wanted to do. I didn't tell my husband about the phone call to my dad.

My husband came home from work that night and immediately switched on the television. Billy Graham was speaking to a large crowd somewhere. Usually, if anything religious came on television, we would quickly turn the channel as we had no interest in watching TV preachers. However, this time it was different as Billy Graham was telling the story of a young man who had a lifestyle very similar to the one my husband and I were living. He was lost out in a forest and cried out to God for help. The story immediately captured my husband's and my attention. After listening to Reverend Graham tell the story, my husband turned off the television, looked right at me and said, "Maybe that is what we need. Maybe we need God in our lives."

As soon as he said that, I knew he was right. Although I didn't accept Jesus that night, the next day I called a friend from my high school years, who I knew "went to church and was religious." She immediately came to see me and brought the *Living New Testament* to give to me. I was amazed that she knew I wanted to talk to her about God. She led me in the sinner's prayer and gave me the Bible, encouraging me to read it every day. I immediately felt a warmth and peace descend upon me.

I didn't really understand what had happened, but I knew that asking Jesus into my heart was exactly what I needed. My husband came home from work that evening to a different woman! I told him everything that had happened. He observed me closely, and we talked a lot about God for the next three weeks, and he then gave his heart to the Lord as well. Over the course of about six months, we stopped doing drugs, drinking, and partying. By the time the check arrived in the mail from my father, I had decided not to leave my husband and to allow God to build our marriage the way He wanted it to be. We surrendered our marriage to the Lord, which God has totally transformed over the years. That was thirty-four years ago.

God has been so faithful to us. There is no telling where my husband and I would be today if the Billy Graham crusade had not been telecast that evening in the fall of 1973. It is because of that Billy Graham telecast that my husband and I are serving the Lord today. Billy Graham has always been a tremendous inspiration to us and a man we deeply respect and admire because of his integrity and lifestyle. Thank you, Reverend Graham, for your faithfulness to God and for sharing the good news of Jesus Christ with us. We love you!

Lynne

Thank You, Billy Graham. . .
for Touching My Life When I Was a Child

GAVE MY LIFE TO JESUS

I was just seven years old when Billy had his crusade at the State Fair in Minnesota. I was raised in a Christian home but hadn't made the decision to follow Jesus until that night. They started playing "Just As I Am," and I started walking toward the stage. Thank you, Billy Graham, for pointing me to Jesus as the Savior of my soul. God bless you.

HONOR

Dear Rev. Graham, as a child growing up in Minneapolis, I heard your name often. My sweet, precious little Baptist grandma and aunt were wonderful Christian women. They were both consistent supporters of your ministry, which was then located in Minneapolis. They didn't have much, but what they had they gave to the work of the Lord.

As I was growing up in the 1950s, televisions were becoming part of almost every household, but not in my grandma's home. But around 1960 or so, she and my aunt decided they were going to buy a television set for one thing—to watch the Billy Graham crusades.

I grew up in an alcoholic household, and it affected me as I grew older. My dad often beat and abused my mother and us kids, and as a result, I had a lot of issues to deal with. Not a lot of happy memories growing up, except for those times with my grandma. I would think of her and my aunt watching you on their little black-and-white TV, and I would smile.

My grandma always prayed for her family. It was because of her prayers—and you—that I yielded my life to Jesus when I was eight years old. So I just want to say thank you. If it hadn't been for my little Baptist grandma and aunt and their devotion to your ministry, I don't think I would have ever heard about Jesus. I can't imagine how my life would have gone without Him in it. You have touched so many lives, and I know that God has a special place for you. Your integrity and honor are something to be admired. Few people in history have walked with the Lord and been so consistent in every way. Thank you for being such a man of honor.

Carol

He Put the Fear of God in Me

As a child, I was very active, and a lot of times I got into trouble and found myself sent to my room without any privileges. I did not know that God was using this time to train me. I usually found myself reading the Bible. One particular summer, during one of my punishments, the crusade was on TV. It was a natural process for me to watch, because we were trained by my grandmother to watch the crusade. So I started watching him on my own. I was about ten years old, and something about this message was so interesting. He was talking about going to hell, and I realized that I did not want to go there. I remember crying, and then I accepted the Lord when he offered the plan of salvation. The next day, I told one of my brothers, and he accepted the Lord himself. Since then, I have been growing in the grace and knowledge of Jesus and God's love for us through Him. I still make mistakes, but I know that if I go to 1 John 1:9, I can confess my faults to God and He will forgive me, for I am covered by Jesus' blood. Now I am a minister of the Gospel and I have a PhD in social work. One of my greatest desires is to meet the man who led me to Christ and to thank him for extending his life for the purpose of Christ. His ministry is still sprouting new roots. May God bless him, for I am better because God put him in my life when I was a sapling.

MY FIRST FAITH WALK

In September 1957, when I was eight years old, I attended your entire crusade in Louisville with my church. During that week, I gave my heart to the Lord Jesus. I remember in the following months that your association would send me letters of encouragement, and my mom was so proud of those. She'd put them on the refrigerator and think they came directly from *you.*

I have swayed many times in the working world, trying to please everybody else. But now I'm very happy to say that I have a wonderful relationship with my precious Lord, and it grows more precious every day. I'm learning to tell my Lord every day to "take over the day," like I've heard you say so often. One of the most amazing things of my fifty-year walk with the Lord is that He has never taken His hand off of me, no matter what. It's amazing what a *great Lord we serve!* Thank you so much for all of your years of encouragement, teaching, and steadfastness for our Lord.

A SEED PLANTED

I would like to say thank you to Billy Graham, a wonderful teacher and a truly godly man. As a child, I watched him on TV. I know that helped plant a seed in me. Billy's compassion, humble nature, and authority while speaking of the love of God was such a blessing to me. At such a young age, I understood that salvation through Jesus Christ was so very important. Now, about twenty-five years later, I know that watching the TV programs helped plant the seed of the importance of living my life for the Lord. Thank you, Billy, for all you have done.

FAITH AND TRUST

I grew up in Logan Square, inner city of Chicago. When I was about eight years old, I came to know my Lord. I remember Billy Graham working with the Moody Bible Institute in those years. I remember Youth for Christ. I remember coming forward at the church service to accept Jesus as my Savior. It was my "other birthday," and birthdays were very special. I grew up in a home filled with abuse and neglect yet at a very young age learned about God and Jesus. I knew that I would never be alone, that God promised, "I will never leave you or forsake you, I will be with you to the end of the age." That promise sustained me throughout my life, and still does.

Today, I am so incredibly blessed, and I pray that I am an example of a Christian mom, grandma, and person. Billy Graham truly influenced me from a very young age and continues to influence me today. Thank you for the Classic programs—truly a wonderful time to remember those special moments with Billy and all of his gifted people. God has richly blessed my life. I am humbled.

Lyn

AFTER THIRTY-FIVE YEARS, THANK YOU, BILLY

I received the Lord as my Savior at a young age and was baptized at age nine. Not unusual, considering I come from a long line of ministers of the Gospel, going back many generations. But I got drawn away by worldly pursuits. At age thirty, when I finally had everything I thought would make me happy, I felt empty and unfulfilled. Every Sunday, I watched a Billy Graham crusade on television, and when Billy gave the invitation to come forward and they played "Just As I Am," I'd begin to weep and feel such remorse and longing in my heart. I had received my Savior but had never made Him Lord of my life. Billy's message to give Him my all was really hitting home. One Sunday night, on my bed after hearing Billy preach, I truly made Jesus Lord of my life. That was more than thirty-five years ago, and I've never stopped testifying of the change Billy Graham made in my life. But I have never once personally thanked the man myself. While listening to Graham, Billy's grandson, on TBN, I was deeply moved to write and say thank you, Billy Graham.

MY FUTURE HUSBAND

In the 1960s, my family attended the Billy Graham crusade at the Miami Beach Convention Center. It was one of the most wonderful experiences of my life. I am always inspired by Billy Graham's messages and his sharing of God's love for us. Even though we are so undeserving of it, it is still so freely given to us. Also, that the power of prayer is in the One who hears our prayers!

After more than thirty-five years of marriage, my husband and I started talking about the Billy Graham crusades one day. I asked him if he had attended with his family. I told him I thought my family had gone at least one or two nights, and he said that, knowing his mother, his family had gone every single night!

I got to thinking that, many years before I had met my husband, God had placed us both at the same Billy Graham crusade at the same time—we could have been sitting in the same row. Little did I know at the time that God was preparing me to be a godly wife and my husband to be a godly man for someone at that same convention center.

It wasn't until, after thirty-five years of marriage, we discovered that we had been there at the same time, that I realized how awesome God's plan is for our lives, and how many more of those experiences we will know of fully when we reach heaven.

I ALWAYS WANTED TO ATTEND YOUR CRUSADE

I was a little girl from the small island of Dominica in the West Indies. I used to listen to your preaching on the radio; we had no television at the time. I always admired you and your faith and hoped that one day I would be able to attend at least one of your crusades. I was blessed to attend your last crusade in New York, in (I think) 2005. I attended all three days, and it was such a blessing and an honor to be in your presence. I thank God for someone like you who has been such an obedient servant. I pray God's blessings and wisdom will be with you and family forever.

Veronica

RIGHT THERE IN OUR SEATS

In 1957, I went to New York City with my mother, my brother, and my grandmother. My grandmother was having a cancer operation, and since my aunt lived in New York, she was certain she knew all the best doctors. While Gramma was in the hospital, we attended the Billy Graham crusade in June of that year. I was seven years old, but I heard Billy Graham enough on the radio to know that he was a special man preaching the Word of God. I was young enough at the Madison Square Garden crusade not to remember much about his sermon but that it had something to do with the heart, and that mine needed to be fixed. My brother and I wanted to go forward when Billy Graham gave the invitation, but my aunt said that we didn't have time for all that stuff, and that it was way too crowded, and that we might get separated from her and my mother in all of the pushing and shoving. So we had to stay seated. My brother and I decided to accept Christ as our Savior right there in our seats. It didn't matter if we were closer to Billy Graham or not. We had gotten his clear message, even as young as we were, and our lives were changed forever. Thank you, Billy.

A Broken Heart

I was only about six years old when I was hospitalized for mental illness. At five years old, I had decided I wanted to die. I remember standing in a dark kitchen with a knife to my heart, thinking how painful it might be, but how quickly it could end. My young mind seemed to be so full of grown-up anger and hurt. I had a loving mom, who chose to leave my abusive father and struggled to care for me and my younger sister all alone. I guess the separation was too much, or maybe my little mind couldn't understand the abuse I had seen inflicted on my mother. So there I sat, alone, sad, and depressed in an ugly, uncaring, and cruel place. The doctors told my mom it would be the best place for me, considering the circumstances. It was more than she could bear when I had confessed my desire to die. When a Billy Graham crusade would air, my mom, my sister, and I would sit in front of the TV and listen to every word. On a lonely night in the hospital, the other kids had asked to watch a specific show, one very popular during that time. But in the midst of changing the channels, I noticed Billy Graham was on TV. I begged the nurse to turn it back to Billy Graham. The other kids begged not to, but I refused to give up. Well, that night, I watched Billy Graham from that cold and lonely place. He brought the warmth of the Lord right where I was, and at the young age of six I gave my life to the Lord. I cried and cried in front of that television set. My little heart ached, and the more I cried, the more I was comforted by the words spoken by a great man. My life was changed after that night. A couple of days later, my mom had me removed from the hospital and brought me home. I never contemplated suicide again. Billy Graham touched my life that very day. I know that one day in heaven, as I stand before my Lord and Savior, I will also stand in the presence of a godly man, and I can then say, "Thank you, Mr. Graham, for being there to help save my life."

Your Crusades in Panama City

When I was a little girl growing up in the Republic of Panama, my father always attended your crusades. I grew up hearing certain songs that were played during your crusades, such as "How Great Thou Art" and "He Lives, He Lives, Christ Jesus Lives Today." Every time I hear these songs, I remember your crusades in Panama City. Thank you, Billy Graham, for your humble ways and your dedication to spreading the Gospel. May the Lord continue to richly bless you and your ministry.

THE RESPONSE

When I was about ten years old, I wrote a letter to the Billy Graham Association. I was puzzled by a certain story in the New Testament, which seemed spiritually inconsistent to me, and I wrote Mr. Graham to ask about it. Much to my surprise, he wrote me back. He did not discount my confusion or my age, but instead gave a thoughtful and serious response to my inquiry. I am forty years old now, and I still have that letter. Thank you.

"I NEVER HEARD BILLY GRAHAM SAY THAT"

The Billy Graham crusade televised program was always special to Mama and Daddy. In the late 1950s, my family would gather in our den to watch the program on our small black-and-white television. This was considered church time. A time to worship. And my parents believed we should behave exactly as if we were attending the crusade in person. Mama said it would be sacrilegious to shell butter beans while Billy Graham told us what God had directed him to tell us. That was fine by me—Lord knows I hated shelling butter beans. If I ever sat down in our home for at least three minutes, Mama would plop a big mess of butter beans in my lap. A country girl like me knew that meant two things: shut up and shell. There was only one possible way that Mama would change her mind. And that would be if Pastor Billy Graham walked to the stadium podium and said, "Good evening ladies and gentlemen, we're coming to you live from California, and before I announce our guest singer, I'd like to take a moment and say to all who are watching by way of television that now is a great time to get all those butter beans shelled. So, as our guest comes and ministers to us in song, I urge you to pile up all the butter beans your lap will hold. Get an old empty bucket for the hulls; don't scatter them all over the linoleum rug, because you'll have an awful mess to clean up later. Don't worry about those sore, rough, and raw fingertips you will have from all that butter bean shelling. I might not know what it's like to shell butter beans and get rough fingers and split nails, but I'm going to be sharing with you tonight about someone who does. And besides, tonight's message is about how doing nothing and just being idle could lead you into sin."

Thank goodness, I never heard Billy Graham say that! It was wonderful just to sit and relax and enjoy myself while watching TV.

I was always delighted and excited to discover a Billy Graham telecast was scheduled. But my Uncle Bob was always more excited. Uncle Bob, my daddy's brother and a unique bachelor, didn't own a TV, but he never missed a televised crusade. He loved all of us, Jesus, and the Billy Graham crusade ministry. "Thought we would all watch the crusade together tonight," he would say as he opened our front door, asking if we were up. His early morning arrival had become expected if it was the day of the crusade. "Thought I would come a little bit early, because time has a way of sneaking up on you and I never want to miss one bit of the program," he would say. I knew Mama's hot homemade biscuits and perked coffee were another reason my Uncle Bob rose early and came for a visit before the sun.

Late in the evening, we would finish our chores and take

a bath before the program aired. My older brother suggested to Mama that he would "just wait until the program was over to get a bath." His suggestion was not received well by Mama. She reminded him that we always took a bath before we went to church, and tonight would not be any different. Brother told Mama it would be all right to wait, since Pastor Billy Graham could not smell him all the way through the television. Mama got the broom and whipped Brother all the way through the house. He bathed, and it was a long time before he suggested anything else to Mama.

Finally, we gathered in front of the family television set, which worked only if the mop handle was holding down the channel selector. There was no feet shuffling, no fingernail filing, no gum chewing.

We listening as Pastor Billy Graham commented on the weather, saying the clouds were gathering and there was a good chance for rain. My fifth-grade mind became distracted when a yellow jacket flew into the house and buzzed around my head, but I remember Pastor Billy Graham speaking about living a life that was pleasing to the Lord. Reluctantly, I said to myself, "Oops! I have messed up." I was sure glad I didn't have to start making a list of my mess-up times and turn it in for a school assignment. I didn't dare voice my thoughts out loud for several reasons. One, I knew better than to interrupt you in the middle of your sermon. (Mama would have whipped me with the broom.) Two, Mama and Daddy and Jesus already knew I had many "oops" times. Three, I did not want you to hear me. I just knew this would be the miraculous moment when Jesus would zoom supernatural hearing into your ears. Then you just might announce on television, "I interrupt this message to say, 'Sylvia, you said a mouthful when you said you messed up. Shame on you! I am telling you to quit complaining about shelling butter beans. You should not be complaining about anything—you have plenty of food to eat and someone to cook it for you.'"

The telecast ended. I wanted to jump into the TV and say to you, "Listen, my hands have not been idle for the past eleven years—just look at these rough and split nails I have from shelling butter beans. In the summertime, why don't you come on TV at least once a week." Immediately, my heart talked to my head and I knew I needed to really work on my "oops" times. So, I said to myself, "Jesus talks to Billy Graham more than he does to me; or maybe he listens to Jesus more than I do. So, I'll take Pastor Billy Graham's advice. No more complaining for me." *No sir,* I thought, complaining about shelling butter beans was certainly not pleasing to the Lord. I knew my Daddy and Mama had to work hard in our garden to raise those butter beans.

I have many memories of watching your telecast in front of the old television, and how we believed in a pastor who believed in God.

Uncle Bob was right: time has a way of sneaking up on you. I'm not an eleven-year-old anymore, and I now buy shelled butter beans in a package. But sometimes I still complain. At these times I remember the nights you ministered to us through God's Word. So, I say thank you. And I know my parents are looking down from heaven and saying, "Yes, we thank you for helping us raise Sylvia—Lord knows we needed all the help we could get."

GOOD AND FAITHFUL SERVANT

As an eight-year-old girl, I remember walking the sidewalk to the 1959 Indianapolis Billy Graham crusade, through the cold wind, with my parents and my six-year-old sister. That was the first time in my life I had encountered such a mass of people, and it was a bit overwhelming. As always in worship settings, we joined in the singing of the hymns, bowing for prayer, and listening to the special music and testimony. You see, my dad had recently surrendered his life to full-time ministry and planned to enter college for preparation. I had the privilege of having Christian parents, so I was accustomed to attending church services. But when Billy Graham started speaking that evening, it was if he was speaking directly to me, and the throngs of people disappeared from my attention. I listened to each word that Billy Graham spoke and heard the Word of God speaking to my heart. At the time of the invitation, I wanted to affirm my decision to accept Jesus as God's only Son and show that I now understood the full meaning of John 3:16, but the crowds of people responding to the invitation were again intimidating, and I had no time to share all of this process with my parents. However, the seed was planted. At home, I saw my mother on her knees and overheard her prayer for me. I told my mother of my decision. My parents arranged for the pastor to visit and confirm my understanding of this important step. I made my decision public at that church and was baptized the following Easter Sunday in 1960.

I have followed Billy Graham's ministry throughout the years since, and compared the obedience, focus, and sacrifices of his family to mine. The hope for every Christian is to hear these words from God: "Well done, thou good and faithful servant." My heart tells me that Billy and Ruth Graham and family have been good servants of God's.

I AM NO LONGER AFRAID

Dear Dr. Graham, thank you for being such a gift to the Body of Christ for all these years. When I was a child, my mother and I watched you on TV. When you would give the invitation for people to come to Christ and you would say, "If you died tonight, do you know where you would go?," I would get scared. But, today, I am saved, and when I hear these words now, I am no longer afraid, but I am excited. Your words put a longing in my heart, even as a child, to know Jesus. Thank you for your devotion to the work of the Lord. May God continue to bless you and keep you.

THE PLAYING FIELD LOOKED A LOT DIFFERENT

As a little girl growing up in a small town in Tennessee, I remember sitting in front of the television and looking at a huge football stadium full of people. The playing field just looked a lot different this time. No players in uniforms, no cheerleaders, no coaches, no scoreboards. Yet, I was drawn to keep watching the activity in this stadium with a sea of people. My friends were outside playing games, but not me—this game was much more appealing.

I found myself listening to singing that grabbed my heart. I always went to church with my mom, but the singing wasn't quite like what I was hearing at this game. I began to sing along and actually learned the hymn "Just As I Am" while watching Billy Graham on television. I could always understand his teaching, and I truly thank God for his worldwide ministry.

The ministry of Billy Graham made a difference in my life when I was a little girl. Now grown and married with two beautiful children of my own, I am still singing the songs of Zion. Yes, the playing field again looks different for me. The uniforms are choir robes, the cheerleaders are worshippers and praisers, the coaches are preachers and teachers, and Jesus Christ is keeping score! I love to sing, and when I get in the heavenly choir, I will sing with high praise "Just As I Am." Thank you, Billy Graham, for being there when I turned on the television in Tennessee.

Johnna

THANKS FROM CHARLOTTE

I first found out about Billy Graham when I was six years old. My parents were, and still are, devout Christians, and back in 1996 my family went to Billy's crusade in Charlotte, at the Bank of America Stadium. I forget how we ended up with the tickets, but we had seats in one of the luxury suites. I don't remember much about the crusade, but this I do remember: it was the very first time I felt the Spirit move in my life. Thanks to Billy's preaching and a Spirit-led series of events, I ended up giving my life to Christ about a year later. Thank you, Billy!

GOD USED TELEVISION

In the early 1950s, there were very few families in England who owned a television set, so you can imagine the great excitement my brother and sister and I felt when my father bought a television in 1953. I can well remember how full the front room was with friends and neighbours as we watched the coronation of Queen Elizabeth on the little eight-inch TV screen.

Billy Graham came to England in 1954, and in those days the service was broadcast in its entirety by the BBC. (Sadly, that would not be allowed today.) As Billy preached the Gospel, the Lord in His sovereign mercy and grace opened my heart to the good tidings that my sins could be washed away if I would believe in the Lord Jesus Christ and ask Him to come into my life. Billy Graham then made the appeal to all those people who wanted to be Christians to come forward right there and then. I could not go forward, because I was at home looking at a TV screen. However, an amazing thing happened as Billy prayed the prayer for the Lord Jesus to come into the hearts and lives of those there in London. That evening, the Lord came into my heart, and He has never left me. I know that I will praise God around His throne with all the people of God, including dear Billy Graham. Sanctification is a lifelong process. One of the marks that a person is truly saved is that the Lord will save that person but also will keep that man, woman, boy, or girl from falling away. So I say, "Thank you, Billy, for telling me about my wonderful Lord and Savior, the Lord Jesus Christ."

Phillip

STONE OF REMEMBRANCE

This is such a privilege to share a precious memory of the first Billy Graham crusade I attended as a young girl in Jackson, Mississipppi. I remember the huge crowd, the beautiful music, and the flow of people from all over the stadium, who made a public profession of faith. That has been repeated over and over again at the crusades I have seen on television, and every time, in my heart, I return to that first crusade.

The greatest impact, however, was the power of the spoken word from the authoritative voice of Billy Graham. It was at this first crusade that I was introduced to the power of the Holy Spirit, the majesty and holiness of God and His plans for the world's salvation, and the willing sacrifice of Jesus on the cross.

Several years ago, when World Changers came to our church, there was only one way to describe that morning worship service when hundreds of people came from every entrance into the sanctuary after the regular membership had been seated and the music began. I turned to my neighbor and said, "This reminds me of a Billy Graham crusade." The power of the Holy Spirit was there.

Thank you for your obedience and faithfulness in proclaiming the love of God and salvation through the shed blood of Jesus. Your witness has made the Word so alive and so believable to me and to others. I still have the *Singing Evangelism* songbook compiled by Cliff Barrows, copyrighted in 1950!

Charlene

YOU PAVED THE WAY

When I was eleven years old, my church went to the Billy Graham crusade. I was excited and had never been to the stadium before. I listened with all I had to Mr. Graham. When the altar call came, my dad took my hand and asked me if I was ready to give my life to Christ. I knew at that moment that it was the time. I received prayer and encouragement, as well as the study guide. I studied hard, and when I completed the course, my pastor came to the house and talked to me. He agreed that I was ready, and two weeks later I was baptized in the Lord.

Over the years, I strayed and sometimes made the same mistakes over and over. I may have forgotten that Christ was there, especially after I lost my mom when I was a teenager. When I found my way back to the Lord and His promises, I realized that although I had pulled away from Him, He had never left my side.

When I think about all the wrong turns I made, and Christ redirecting me, I thank Him and always remember that Billy Graham brought me to my faith stronger than I even knew. He was a blessing brought to my life, and I pray that he will know he was loved by those he never knew. May God bless him with all of His glories, and he will be a strong soldier in God's army when he goes home.

Betty

WORLD LEADER

My daughter was in sixth grade in 2001, and her teacher assigned her a project. She had to write about four world leaders (alive or dead). Of course, you know everyone was writing about Osama bin Laden and Pope John Paul II. She couldn't think of a fourth one to write about. I told her, "Why not Billy Graham? He's a spiritual leader." She wrote about Billy Graham and completed her project, and she got an A! She was the only student in her class to use Billy Graham as a world leader. God bless you, Mr. Graham.

MR. GRAHAM'S FEAR OF PRIDE

I believe it was in 1949 when I heard Mr. Graham speak at the Maranatha Bible Conference campgrounds. I can remember him standing with organist Howard Skinner, one of the directors of the camp, and talking to him in front of a big flower bed. Mr. Graham wore a red leather billed cap. That evening, he spoke in the tabernacle, but before the service he came back to where I was sitting and addressed the pastors sitting behind me. As a thirteen-year-old boy, I was interested to hear what he had to say. He made a request of those pastors that they pray for him, because he was tempted with pride. That showed me an insight into this man's cautious walk with God. I went on to become a pastor myself, and I often remembered these words of concern. Incidentally, the first year he spoke in the tabernacle, it was not filled; but after the Los Angeles crusade, he spoke again and people were standing outside and sitting on cars. Thanks for a wonderful example of a man of God and for some most pleasant memories.

Harold

MEMORIES

I just want to thank you, Rev. Graham, for your unquestionable faith and service to our Lord Jesus Christ. All glory to our Father God for giving to this world such a devout follower and messenger of the good news of our Savior! One of the most memorable memories of my life was listening to and watching Rev. Graham on the television, with my mother and father. Daddy always knew when Rev. Graham would be on TV, so all homework, chores, and supper were finished in time to watch the crusade. It was a special occasion to gather around and listen to the message. My father was a God-loving man who read his Bible morning and evening, who taught his children about trusting and loving Jesus and how to be honest and hardworking. My father has since gone on to be with the Lord, twenty-four years now, and about the only times I recall my dad crying were when he read his Bible, talked of Jesus, and listened to Billy Graham. This has followed me all my life, and to this day I still watch reruns of the Rev. Graham crusades. I thank God for saving my soul through His only begotten Son, Jesus! I also thank God for Rev. Graham, who spoke the truth and led thousands to Jesus.

TEN YEARS OLD IN 1962. . .
THE BEGINNING OF A JOURNEY

I was sitting in front of our television set one afternoon in 1962. I remember I had just come home from school (I was only about ten years old), and being a very sensitive child, I had just had one more difficult day and needed something to lift my spirits. I didn't know what lay in store for me when I turned on the TV; all I knew was that I was lonely and needed cheering up.

As it happened, a Billy Graham crusade was being televised, and I sat and listened to Billy Graham preach. Somehow, by the grace of God, the Holy Spirit spoke to my heart, and I thought to myself, *He looks different from most grownups. He looks kind and loving.* Well, after Billy Graham stopped preaching and gave the invitation to accept Jesus as my personal Savior, I remember thinking that maybe Jesus had the kind of twinkle in his eye that Rev. Graham had. I thought, *If Christians are anything like he is, then I want to become a Christian, too.* I also remember secretly wishing that Billy Graham could be my father (in addition to my real father).

I was basically a very shy and lonely child, but I knew

one thing for sure: I needed Jesus and Christian friends more than anything else in the world. But because of a yet-undiagnosed mental illness, I still struggled socially and had only a few close Christian friends all the way through junior and senior high school. By the time I reached college age, I was really in trouble mentally and emotionally, as my condition grew worse and I had to take more and more medication to soothe the ache in my heart and spirit.

Finally, when I was about thirty-one, I read a book about emotional healing and I *knew* that God had an answer for me. My mother and I signed up for a Christian conference. I heard a woman speak about prayer for emotional healing, and I signed up for an emotional healing prayer in her home. To make a long story short, when I finished praying the prayer and forgiving every person who had ever hurt me, my whole world turned upside down. For the first time since I first heard Billy Graham preach, I began to have that same familiar peace that passeth all understanding that the Bible talks about, and I thanked and thanked and thanked Jesus for healing me.

I have had a difficult walk with God since that time. . .the devil is alive and well. . .but I believe I have finally gotten the victory, and I am going to stay very close to Jesus for the rest of my life. Thank you, Billy Graham, for showing me what Christians are supposed to be like. Thank you for leading me to Jesus! God bless you!

A Testimony a Child Can Understand

The Astrodome was a few years old, and it was my first time inside. But what thrilled me was the simple message of Billy Graham. He said that I needed Jesus. My little brother went forward quickly, and I followed him down to the arena. I got to stand very close to the stage and look up at Billy Graham. I was amazed to see a glow around his face. I told my mother, and she said she saw that, too. I have listened to Billy Graham so many times over the years and want to continue to hear him preach. He puts the Gospel in such a simple way that a child can understand and such a compelling way that an adult is drawn to the Savior. Thank you, Billy Graham, for living your life as a testimony in front of millions of people, young and old alike.

GOD BLESS MY GRANDMOTHER AND BILLY GRAHAM

Billy, I grew up watching you on TV. My grandmother would insist on watching you every time you were on TV, from the 1960s through the 1980s, until her death in 1984. She was never able to attend a crusade, but I did. I attended one in Atlanta sometime between 1994 and 1996. I went with a youth group as one of the adult chaperones. Your message and the Christian rock bands that performed that night were awesome for the youth who attended this crusade, as well as the adults. You have had a tremendous impact on my life through your preaching of God's Word. May God bless you and keep you.

Elizabeth

DEAR MR. GRAHAM. . .

It is an honor to be able to send you a personal note. I have watched your crusades on television since I was a young boy. God blessed me with Christian parents, and we watched your crusades and presentations as strictly as we attended our church. I did not get saved until later in life—1996, to be exact, at a truck stop ministry in Hebron, Ohio. You have been a great testimony for Jesus Christ and have been an inspiration for me. I never tire of hearing your sermons and watching your crusades. Each one I hear makes me walk away with a newfound dedication to living a Christlike life. I am now disabled partly from some of the hard living I did before accepting Christ, and another from a recent truck wreck. But the Lord has been good to me in spite of my life. My only two regrets in life are not giving my life to Jesus as a young man and not ever being able to shake your hand. God bless you, Mr. Graham, for bringing the world closer to God and Jesus Christ.

Pal

MAMA MADE ME; NOW NOTHING STOPS ME!

I don't remember the exact year, but it was probably in the late 1950s or early '60s. I was in my room when my mother came and got me. She told me there was a man on TV that she wanted me to hear. The man was Billy Graham. I listened to his message, and even at that early age, I realized something was missing from my life. Later that year, I accepted Jesus as my Lord and felt then I was called to be a preacher. For the next few years, I told everyone I spoke to that I was going to be a preacher. Then, in November 1963, my dad died. I became somewhat angry with God. I had asked that my dad be healed, and I fully believed that God could and would heal him.

When Dad died, I no longer wanted to be a preacher. I continued attending church and listened to every crusade that Billy televised. Now grown, and the father of two sons, I would still feel that call to preach. I would even fill in for pastors who were sick or on vacation. Then, in 1985, I became ill with the same symptoms that began my father's illness. I was diagnosed with hepatitis. I turned as yellow as a pumpkin. I was reexamined and was given a very bad report. That night, as I lay in my hospital bed, I apologized to God. I told him I wished I could back up time and never be infected with this illness. I was sorry I had never preached with a sincere heart.

The next morning, my doctor came in and told me he could not understand what had happened, but my blood test from last night had come back negative for the hepatitis virus. I regained my natural color and was back at work in a few days. But I did not forget my talk with God. I began studying and reading the Bible, later attended Bible college, and then took a full-time church assignment. In September 2006, I received my doctorate of divinity. This past September, my wife of thirty-seven years and I attended the BGEA training at The Cove. It was the most enjoyable three days I have known. My church is growing, and God is blessing, I think, because a young boy heard a great message from a great man of God almost fifty years ago. Thank you, Billy.

Praise God!

On January 19, 1948, at the Roseland Temple Baptist Church in Roseland (south Chicago), you, Billy, were the guest speaker in the evening service. I had just turned seven. Later that same evening, alone in my room, I knelt at my bedside and received Jesus into my heart, just as I had been invited to do by you. I grew in wisdom and stature in the years following, having the wonderful blessing of a Christian physician as my Sunday school teacher for a time. I myself began to teach Sunday school during my high school years.

Oberlin College, founded by Charles Finney, had morphed into a bastion of liberalism in the late 1950s, coinciding with the time of my study there. My faith was challenged, even shaken, during those years, which were generally not productive for the Kingdom of God. However, God used even those years.

I headed on to medical school at Northwestern, in downtown Chicago. The Christian Medical Society (now the Christian Medical and Dental Associations) was used powerfully by God to bring me to my senses and to Himself. In 1965, the last year of medical school, I served my first short-term mission. . .in Swaziland, Africa, for six months. That experience changed my heart and my life's direction. It became clear during my time overseas, and it has become increasingly clear, that God's inclining me into medical missions is a movement of His Spirit, which comes before me almost daily in my walk with Him. Even though I am not in full-time overseas medical missions efforts, my heart certainly is.

God has used me, and thus blessed me, in ways most remarkable. My life's aim aligns with that of the Navigators: "To know Christ and to make Him known." The locus does not matter. Soul-winning is my passion. My life verse is Philippians 3:10: "That I may know Him." May I be found faithful in His service, by His Spirit's power.

As I head into the final stages of living in this body, my only prayer is that I remain faithful to the high calling of God in Christ Jesus! I am a medical educator, now having taught over the past thirteen years, in sixty-four nations. I do not intend to "retire" from Kingdom work. Perhaps God will continue to bless my ministry among medical professors around the globe. My focus in particular has been, and remains, China, where I have served in more than a dozen major medical centers, bringing education and healing to the body and soul and spirit.

Billy, it's *all* of God. Boasting has no place. Only glorying in Him matters! Thank you, and praise God for bringing you into my life almost sixty years ago!

Doug

TOO YOUNG?

When you came to Boise, Idaho, years ago, I attended with a friend and my two-and-a-half-year-old daughter. While waiting in line, an elderly man behind me asked if my daughter was three years old. He continued to tell me that children are closer to God at that age than at any other. His final comment puzzled me: "I attend every crusade that Billy Graham conducts." As I turned to respond, he was nowhere to be seen. Could he have been an angel sent to prepare me for what was about to occur?

When you invited people to accept the Lord as Savior, my daughter turned to me and said, "I want to ask Jesus in my heart." The people nearby quickly turned and stared at me to see how I would respond. Looking at the great distance from the rafters where we were seated all the way to the ground floor, I decided it would be best just to pray with her quietly where we were. Since she knew nothing about sin, I just asked Jesus to come and be her very best Friend. She was satisfied and we returned home.

My daughter has never departed from that defining moment in her life. I learned to never underestimate what God can do in a small child, even one not even three years of age. Thank you, Billy Graham, for a lifetime of being faithful to His Word.

BILLY GRAHAM, GREATEST PREACHER EVER!

I can remember growing up and never missing Billy Graham on TV. My mom was a big Billy Graham fan. And to this day, I watch it whenever it is on TV. I just finished reading the book *The Preacher and the Presidents*. Billy Graham was a tremendous influence to every president and to our country. I appreciate all that he has done over the years. I mostly appreciate that he does not have a judgemental spirit like so many preachers you see on television. Billy Graham leaves the judging to God. I am proud that Billy Graham lived and preached in my generation. He is the example for all men and for all preachers.

MY GRANDMOTHER AND BILLY GRAHAM

When I grew up in Alexandria, Louisiana, we had one channel on television. My family watched Billy Graham crusades on that one channel. I loved to watch my grandmother watch Billy Graham. It was a sight to see. She was not able to read the Bible, but she eagerly waited for the next Billy Graham telecast. I watched her as she sat on the edge of the sofa, getting as close to the television as she could, so as to not miss a word that Dr. Graham was saying. Whatever she heard Dr. Graham say, she would pass on to her grandchildren or anyone who would listen to her. She never missed a day talking about the Lord. She was such a loving and caring force in my life. I thank Dr. Graham very much for ministering to my grandmother, who could not read but who understood perfectly what you had to say to all of us. We greatly appreciate your ministry.

Watching you on TV as a child will be forever imprinted in my mind. Your influence was major in my family. I attended a crusade in Baton Rouge, long after those telecasts at home, and I walked down to publicly announce my walk with the Lord. I watch the Classics now whenever they are shown, and the loving memories of my grandmother come again to visit. She died at the age of 103. Dr. Billy Graham, thank you so very much for your sacrifice, hard work, and dedication to the Lord. We see Jesus in you! God bless you!

Vivian

Thank You, Billy Graham...
for How You Explained the Gospel

I Didn't Have to Be a Rocket Scientist

Thank you, Pastor Graham, for preaching with such simplicity that even a child could understand. Every time I watched one of your broadcasts, my mind would immediately go back to the time when you taught about the Father, Son, and Holy Spirit. You talked about how they are three entities, but all in one. Who could imagine that using three paper cups would clarify the union of the Father, Son, and Holy Spirit as one? But that is exactly what it did for me, because it was explained with love and with simplicity. I didn't have to be a rocket scientist to understand God's Word. Thank you again for walking in Jesus' footsteps and teaching as He taught.

Dena

In the Eyes of a Child

As I sat on the floor in our family room watching TV, I listened quietly as the Rev. Billy Graham preached to thousands of people, telling them about the love of God. I did not know the impact that moment would have on me for the rest of my life. I recall Rev. Graham saying to the people, "You must be born again." In the eyes of a child, I did not understand what was meant by being "born again," but something about it sounded real good to me. The idea of being "born again" stayed with me until adulthood. I am now a born-again saint of God Almighty. Washed in the Blood and filled with the Holy Ghost. In the eyes of a child, the Rev.

Billy Graham's words were very simple to understand; so simple, in fact, that even a child could understand them. Thank you, Rev. Graham.

Victoria

A JOURNEY TO FIND JESUS

I thought I was seeking something real, something besides myself. I guess I was seeking God, even though I didn't phrase it that way.

In September 1971, Rev. Billy Graham was preaching a crusade from Oakland, California. I don't know when the crusade was taped; I just know that it was on TV that week in Alabama. I was so, so confused and angry about a lot of things. I really was on a journey of faith. I had been meeting with two Baptist pastors to discuss spiritual things, and yet I was angry about some of their answers, and the Bible made no sense to me.

On Thursday night, September 9, 1971, my mother and dad wanted to watch the crusade. I mentioned that I could not stand to hear any more preaching by my two Baptist friends, nor even Billy Graham. But that night from Oakland, Billy asked, "Where would you go tonight if you died? Heaven or hell?" I could not get that question out of my mind. I listened for the first time as Billy explained the Gospel and what it means to follow Jesus Christ.

I did not sleep much that night. Billy's voice was ringing through my brain in that clear way he has of speaking. *Where would you go?,* the questioned haunted me. I knew I needed to make a decision but I was scared and confused.

The next day, September 10, 1971, a Friday, I went in to work and was going to my work station when I saw one of my Baptist pastor friends. I spoke to him about the previous night and what I was dealing with. He said for me to have lunch with him, just the two of us. So, I had lunch with him, and somewhere around 11:10 a.m., I asked Jesus Christ to come into my life and to forgive me of all of my sins. I cannot express the physical reaction in my body, but it felt like the weight of the world passed from my shoulders, and I felt good, wonderful, joyful.

Years have passed, and I have continued worshipping God in Christ. I have attended many churches through revivals and special speakers. I began teaching a Sunday school class, and then I was appointed to several jobs in the church. Finally, I was appointed lay leader of my church. This was in 1978, and God began speaking to me about going into ministry.

I was a high school dropout, working at a plant in Birmingham. The United Methodist Church required ministers to attend college and get a two- or four-year degree. No one in my family had ever attended a school of higher education. However, the ministry was burning in my heart, and it was all I could think about. Should I give up my job and go to school? It was a hard time for me to decide what to do. By this time, I was speaking on Sunday nights, and I worked with my pastor (who was pastoring a circuit of three churches, including mine), who taught me (and allowed me) to lead worship services, praying and leading in worship. As a result, I had more experience than many seminary candidates for ministry.

I never forgot how and when I started my journey of faith. I shared with others what I had experienced and how important it was to make a decision to receive Christ as

Savior and Lord of one's life. I have served more than twelve different appointments in these years, and have had a wonderful opportuity to share the good news of Jesus Christ. It has been a hard and long journey, but I was not alone, for I knew that I was following the Great Shepherd of the sheep and that He would lead me through the long and hard valleys. I have made mistakes and have failed Him in many ways, but He has never failed me, for He gave me strength and provided for my every need.

I still remember Billy Graham's voice ringing clearly about receiving Christ and allowing Him to become the Master and Lord of our lives. I think I can say that without Billy's message that September night, I would not be where I am as a Christian and as a pastor. Thank you, Brother Billy, for your message and your willingness to preach the message of salvation and faith in Jesus Christ.

APPRECIATION

This is not a story, but a sincere note of appreciation. My wife, Linda, and I have been in full-time ministry among the ranks of independent Baptists for more than thirty-nine years. We wanted to offer a word of thanks to Billy Graham for clear preaching of the simple Gospel of Jesus Christ, who offers salvation by grace through faith without any works of righteousness on our part, freely offered to all who come unto God by Him.

Another thing we appreciate and admire about Billy Graham is that, in these years of ministry, there has never been a scandal attached to his name. This brings much honor and glory to our heavenly Father and helps the cause of Christianity greatly. To God be the glory, great things He hath done!

Ben and Linda

UNFORGETTABLE DAY IN ROMANIA

It was about twenty-seven years ago when Mr. Graham visited Romania. For a communist country at that time, such a visit was out of the ordinary. I lived in Bucharest, and God gave me the privilege to be part of one of his crusades. I remember being in one of the biggest Pentecostal churches in Bucharest when Mr. Graham spoke. Just seconds before he walked in (along with pastors and priests from all denominations), the combined choir and orchestra started to sing, and many, many lights came on in the church. At that moment, when Dr. Graham got on the podium, I felt like the rapture was occuring. I will never forget that day, that unique moment in my life. His sermon was simple, not complicated words, but very powerful. I feel honored and blessed by God that I was part of that wonderful moment in our country's history.

I HAVE TO WRITE TO YOU

I haven't met you, but I feel as if I *have* to write to you to thank you, Reverend Graham. God has given me a heart for the lost, and you share this calling with me. Your simple message of salvation. . .which is God's simple message of salvation, has helped God accomplish so much for His Kingdom. You have touched so many lives and have inspired me. You remind people that salvation is for all. God's love is never ending. I have been saved since I was eight. I am now thirty-one. It was such a pleasure to see you in Nashville in 2000. Praise God for you, Reverend Graham!

"God Hates Sin"

Billy, there is just something about the way you say what you say. There is something special about the look on your face. There is something very special about the manner in which you approach biblical principles.

I know how you always want the praise, glory, and honor to be given to God. You are always so humble and don't seem to like it much when people try to give you praise. Well, I'm sorry, but you are just going to have to be a little tolerant with me.

I am sixty-one years old, the youngest of eight children. My father passed away when I was two years old, leaving my very shy mother to take care of all of us. With God's help, she did a fantastic job.

I remember us watching Billy Graham on TV. I always had such a warm feeling in our home, like everything was going to be okay. One time, you were delivering a message and you paused for a moment and simply said, "God hates sin." That hit me so hard. I had always known that, but those three words convicted me. I thought I was a pretty good guy most of the time. I guess I was. When you said, "God hates sin," I thought of many things I had done that I am ashamed of. I asked God to forgive me and to come into my heart in a special way, and he did. I now start every day with Bible readings and prayer. My prayer is always that God would help me be the person He would have me be. Thank you, Billy Graham, and all of your team for everything.

John

CHILDLIKE FAITH

I have always been a churchgoer. I probably attended church before I was even born. My mother made sure of that. She somehow managed to get my siblings and me (four of us in all) to church every Sunday morning and evening and Wednesday night. Revival week was no exception. We went unless we were sick. I didn't mind, though; church was like home to me.

When I was about twelve years old, our little church in Mississippi decided to gather a group to go and see Brother Billy Graham in Jackson. I was on the list to go. (Like I had a choice!) I didn't dread it, but I wasn't exactly jumping up and down at the idea either. I had seen Brother Graham on occasion on one of the three channels we received on the one TV we owned. (Boy have things changed.) I admired him and decided this might not be such a bad experience.

I was somewhat surprised by the number of people attending the crusade. This little country girl was not used to such, but what tugged at my heart most was hearing the old familiar hymns sung by such a tremendous group of people. I was overcome with emotion. Then Brother Graham spoke. I will never forget the simplicity of his message; I had never felt the Spirit move so strongly. When the choir sang "Amazing Grace," I sobbed. I had heard it sung hundreds of times, but never like this.

I am now forty-two years old, not gray-haired and granny-like just yet, but certainly not a spring chicken either. I will never forget the sound of "Amazing Grace," the simplicity of the message, and the moving of the Spirit that night. I will always admire Billy Graham and his life of integrity. There is no doubt in my mind that one day he will hear these words from the One he knows so well: "Well done, my good and faithful servant, well done!"

A SIMPLE TRUTH

When I was seventeen, I was invited by a group of Christian friends to the Billy Graham crusade held at the Pepsi Arena in Albany, New York, on July 12, 1990. I had always believed in God but had no personal relationship with Him. I believed He was a distant Creator and wasn't interested in my daily life. I believed God was for Sundays and that was it. Then I heard Billy Graham preach the simple truth of God's amazing love and that He would have died just for me because He loved me that much. I also heard him talk about being eighteen inches from heaven, having God in your head and not your heart, and I thought, *That's me!* So I made my way down to the floor of the arena (from the nosebleed seats), met with a counselor named Heather, and prayed to accept Jesus as my Lord and Savior. In June 2005, I was a prayer counselor at the Billy Graham crusade in Queens and had the privilege of introducing others to the Savior I had fallen in love with. I have also chosen to do that with my life. Thank you, Billy, for your faithfulness and consistency in your walk. That is so desperately needed in today's world. Thank you for sharing the simple truth of God's great love. But most of all, thank you for introducing me to the love of my life, my Lord and Savior Jesus Christ.

I REMEMBER

I can remember when I was a little girl and we would sit around the radio and listen to Billy Graham preach. When we bought our first TV, we watched whenever a Billy

Graham crusade was broadcast. I was finally able to attend my first crusade, in Charlotte. I can't remember the date. Our choir members helped with the choir. I wished I could sing well enough to do that. When my husband was off work, we went together, and I went with the youth for youth night. It had been raining really hard that day. We all had trash bags along with our raincoats. I was so excited that my children would get to see and hear Billy Graham. Johnny Cash was also there that night. I remember Billy Graham saying that it was not going to rain for a while, and it didn't! It was so cloudy and looked like it would pour any minute, but it didn't. I worked as a counselor that night. I remember all the people pouring onto the field. It was so awesome! I'll never forget what a simple message he gave about God's love and Jesus loving us and dying for us. It amazes me how he can give such a simple message but with such love and humility that thousands would be saved. I hope we will see someone like him again. I *pray* we will see someone like him again, because we desperately need another Billy Graham now.

THANKS, BROTHER GRAHAM

I never got to go see him in person. I used to watch him on TV as a child and then as an adult. If he was on, I was watching. Brother Graham, you have helped me many times with the Word of God. When you spoke, a child could understand. Thank you for all the times that you were away from your family. God has blessed you and your family.

Pauline

INTEGRITY

Having been raised in the turbulent sixties, I saw firsthand many, many young people who rejected God and destroyed their lives. I also unfortunately saw many ministries fail and be reduced to shame. In the midst of it all, I would always watch Billy Graham every chance I got. His simple Gospel message and humility truly spoke to me. His message was always simple—"Jesus saves"—and yet at the same time profound. Seeing his invitation calls would many times reduce me to tears as the hundreds would come forward to receive Christ as their Savior. It was clear the precious Holy Spirit was working in a mighty way through Billy Graham and his entire godly team. I personally thank God for sending this world a Billy Graham. Thank you, Billy Graham.

THE HUNGER STILL BURNS IN MY HEART

In December 1968, while watching Dr. Graham on television, the simple Gospel message burned in my heart. I knelt down in our recreation room and recited the sinner's prayer. The presence of God flooded the room, and for the first time in my life, I felt the forgiveness of God. To this day, the hunger to know Him in greater measure still burns in my heart. The years have been exciting ones, seeing and experiencing the Word of Life, being baptized in the Holy Spirit, and interceding for those God shows me in dreams and visions. To this day, I still hand out Dr. Graham's booklet *Steps to Peace with God*, thus sharing the Gospel wherever I am sent. I owe Dr. Graham a million thanks for introducing me to such an awesome God as found in Christ Jesus. I praise God for the evangelistic outreach his organization has had worldwide. May God's richest blessings continue to be given to the

Graham family as they follow Him, just as Dr. Graham has all these years.

THE CLEAR, SIMPLE GOSPEL

As a little girl, I would listen to every crusade, and after each message I would ask Jesus to save me. I went to church every Sunday but never heard the clear Gospel like you preached. I would beg God to "know" Him. At thirteen, I finally accepted Jesus as my Savior publicly; however, I had already accepted Him personally at a Billy Graham crusade.

As a little girl, I tried to preach a message like you did, and after a few years I realized that the clear, simple Gospel is the best message to speak. Thank you for staying so clear all these years. I always say that when I get to heaven I want to look back at all of the spiritual children and grandchildren I was able to lead to the Lord. But Dr. Graham, it will be accounted to you, because you cared enough to preach the simple Gospel to a little girl hungry for the Lord. Thank you. . .to my spiritual dad.

Thank You, Billy Graham. . .
for Planting Seeds of Faith

BILLY PLANTED A SEED

One day, as I was painting my front porch, an older man drove up. (I live about a mile from the highway.) He said he wasn't sure why he was there. I replied, "Maybe God led you here." After his response, I asked if I could get my Bible to share a few things with him. He invited me to sit in his truck. As I shared the Gospel, he began to cry. You see, his wife had passed away some time before, and she had always wanted him to go to church. The previous night, as he had scanned the TV, he ran across your show, and it planted the seed needed to bring him to my house. He invited Christ in that day, and that was many years ago. Thank you, Billy.

MEMORIES

My mom passed away this past week. We had a memorial service just yesterday. She had been ill for a while, but she was always optimistic and concerned about her children and grandchildren and great-grandchildren's futures. Her life was difficult as a child, and her first marriage to my father was tough due to the drinking of both her parents and my father. Yet she never spoke ill of others and gave everyone the benefit of the doubt.

She always had a simple faith in God and his plan for our lives. She would never miss a Billy Graham crusade when I was a child. I was always drawn to them, and in time the seeds that were planted in those days took root and I gave my life to Christ. If it had not been for the TV crusades, I would not be able to say good-bye to my mom, who has been my rock for so many years. She brought hope when so much pain was in my life.

Because of her faith in God, and the seeds Mr. Graham continues to plant in our lives, I have learned that God is there for all people, no matter what their status in life. I thank you for the opportunity to share in this time of sadness and joy. And my best wishes for the Graham family as their father may also soon be called home.

I Finally Opened the Door of My Heart

I was probably ten when I attended an outdoor revival featuring Billy Graham. I remember it like it was yesterday. I wanted to go down at the end and accept Christ, but the church group I was with wanted to leave and beat the traffic. Many years of pain later, I finally opened the door of my heart to Jesus again. I believe that the Lord has always been watching over me and waiting for me to return. I believe that the Lord will use the pain from my past to help others. I believe that Billy Graham planted a seed in my life that could never be washed away. Thank you for giving yourself to draw others near to our Lord, Billy.

The Long Journey Back

I was raised in the Methodist church from when I was a preschooler, but I never really had any idea of what it truly meant to give my life to Christ. When I was twelve years old, my mother took me to a Billy Graham crusade. It was the first time I felt the tug of God on my heart.

From that point on, it seemed that my family and I were

under severe spiritual attack from "the adversary of our souls." When I turned thirteen, Dad became distant and rejected all my affections. Mother became so ill that it affected her personality. She was constantly losing her temper, yelling and screaming at Dad and me. She would throw dishes at my dad or just pull them out of the cupboard and smash them. She'd whip and beat me with whatever was within reach. Mother's condition was incorrectly diagnosed as mental illness. It adversely affected our family.

One month after my fourteenth birthday, my dad died while having an asthma attack. A year later, my mom had a hysterectomy, at which time the true cause of her illness was found—endometriosis (a massively infected cyst attached to her uterus). It took her two years to regain her health, and her emotional recovery was never complete. The damage done from the illness and the electroshock treatments they had given her based on the misdiagnoses had taken their toll.

By age sixteen, I could no longer tolerate conditions at home. I felt betrayed and abandoned by the God I had grown up with. From age thirteen, I had been told by my mom that I was enough to make a preacher cuss and that I was destined for a life of imprisonment. I had calluses on the backs of my legs and buttocks from all the beatings with belts, hangers, and tree switches. Nothing I did was ever good enough. I was under constant physical and emotional abuse.

Feeling unloved and unwanted, I attempted suicide. When that failed, I ran away from home and went looking for the "free love" I had seen on TV and heard people sing about in the music of the time. But instead of "peace and love," I discovered "sex, drugs, and rock-n-roll." By the time

I turned eighteen, I was well down the road of alcoholism, recreational drug abuse, and relationship addiction. On June 30, 1971, at the young and immature age of eighteen, I married. It was the year I should've graduated from high school. Instead, I was pumping gas in a small town in the Rocky Mountains.

Within the first year of marriage, I fathered my only "legitimate" child. But the marriage broke up shortly after the birth of my son, due to my infidelity, alcoholism, and drug abuse. I ended up living on and off the streets (Denver's notorious East Colfax Avenue) for a number of years. I played at jobs and women, but booze and drugs were my true love. Occasionally, I would sober up for a month or two because some "Christian" girl I lusted after was trying to convert me. But after a brief respite, I'd always go back to my old friends, "Bud Weiser" and "Mary Jane" (booze and marijuana).

When I exhausted all known means of support, I entered a two-week "alcohol awareness" program. It was near the end of that program that I met my current wife, Susan, at a nightclub. That was the only time I was sober and she was drunk. For the next twenty years, she was "a good little codependent" and tolerated my alcoholic lifestyle. If you have any questions about what hell is like, just ask her. Lord knows I put her through all kinds of it. But then, she stuck around for it, so in her own way, she was just as sick as I was.

On July 10, 1999, I began my journey down the road to recovery. I called a man I had met in an Alcoholics Anonymous meeting and asked him if he would be my "sponsor." When I asked him what the next step was, he told me, "Ninety meetings in ninety days and start going to church."

On August 12 of that same year, I quit smoking

cigarettes. On December 29, I quit smoking marijuana, as well. So, for all intents and purposes, I celebrate being clean and sober each New Year's Day—starting from January 1, 2000. Since that time, my wife and I have been actively pursuing a greater understanding of God's grace and His plan of salvation through Jesus Christ. I have come a long way, but I still have a long way to go. It's been said that "God works in mysterious ways." I hold that it's only a mystery if you don't know God! For, without God, one can never know true peace and joy. Therefore, I strongly encourage you to set aside any prejudices you may currently have about God and take the time to read God's Word—starting with the Gospel of John in the New Testament. Prayerfully ask Him to open the eyes of your heart to His love and kindness. The only thing you'll regret is that you waited so long. Thank you, Billy, for planting a seed in a young boy's heart.

Karl

A SEED OF FAITH

When I was eight years old, Pastor Graham planted the first real seed of faith in me. I accepted Christ from a TV crusade in the 1960s. I can remember that day well, because my mother and father had a verbal fight about his desire to change the channel on the TV. Yet my mother saw that I was completely glued to the TV. I know this was the day Jesus came into my heart. No church. We never went to church. It was twelve years later, after many unwise decisions, that I realized that God had a hand in everything I was doing.

Over the years, I have never forgotten the faithfulness of Brother Billy Graham. I love him deeply, and I know that God is allowing him to stay long enough to see a special miracle, one that will change the events of the world. Although just a man, Brother Graham is a friend of God's. Thank you, my dear brother, for your faithfulness and your unyielding compassion. Thank you for your years of prayers and commitment to the Body of Christ. I will cry and miss you when you leave this earth. But I will remember all of your words of God's faithfulness to his Body and wait for our Lord's return.

Just one sister in Christ who truly is grateful for your faithfulness

JESUS IS THE ONLY ANSWER

I first was saved as a young teen. I had been raised in a home where my mom was abused, and sometimes us kids as well. (My dad is a very changed man today.) I went to a crusade when I was thirteen or fourteen that was so awesome. I stayed with the life for a time but later got wrapped up in drugs, etc. Well, no seed sown can stay dead. Finally, in my early twenties, the seed sprouted. I am now forty-nine and married to my true love, a wonderful Christian man, for twenty-nine years. I am so thankful to Jesus for allowing wonderful men like Billy Graham to be born. He is one of a kind; none other like him. And one more thing I need to mention: my husband and I have five children, and they are all following Jesus. So that one seed planted grew into twelve more seeds out there planting more seeds (including our grandchildren). Thank you, Billy, for being such a wonderful servant.

SEEDS SOWN

I was a boy of fourteen or so when the Billy Graham crusade came to Columbus, Ohio. I went with the local church youth group because there were girls there. I heard Rev. Graham's words, and I felt the tug on my heart. I went forward, but I must admit it was because everyone else in the group had already gone onto the ballfield.

Eight years later, and many miles down the road—after moving to California in the 1960s and serving in the army during the Vietnam era—I made a heart and mind connection to give myself to Christ because He was who the Bible said He was.

As a pastor now for more than thirty-three years, I trace my spiritual fruit to the seeds sown by Billy Graham. They may have taken awhile to grow, but they were planted simply by this great servant.

Doug

MY WANDERING LIFESTYLE

I was a sixteen-year-old, pregnant, drug-abusing teenager when I walked into the Billy Graham tent on the beach in Southern California. I listened to Billy Graham and heard something that was a far cry from what I had learned in my Lutheran upbringing and in a home of child abuse and neglect. I went forward at the altar call and gave my life to Christ. A former prostitute with mascara running down her tear-streaked cheeks counseled me at that time. I left wondering what had just happened to me.

In two weeks, without any follow-up, I quietly turned off that new, vibrant part of me. But there was a new determination in me to "make it." The seeds of the Billy Graham crusade had been planted deep within me. I went on to have my baby, relinquished him for adoption, and began to live and work on my own, completing high school at night while living in a roach-infested, tiny apartment.

Soon my wandering lifestyle found me on a commune farm in the Shenandoah Valley of Virginia. Once again, God tugged on my heart as I grew weary with cohabitants who just wanted to take LSD and walk all over the mountain proclaiming that they were God. God blessed me with a job and a new place to live, but the devil had his plans, too. The humidity of Virginia caused me to become extremely ill, so I once again headed to California. This time, I took God with me. I found a similar church and began attending. The pastor was a shouting, judging, unkind man, rude to his wife and children in public, and demeaning to the hippies I convinced to come to church with me. I fled once again.

The following years were tumultuous, to say the least. In and out of colleges, biker gangs, relationships. There was always that still, small voice in my deepest parts, but I tried to bury it in rebellious living. I was successful almost to the point of death; deep despair and heartache drove me to the very edge of suicide. Was Satan going to win?

Once again, my merciful heavenly Father orchestrated a situation in which a room opened up in a house of Christian women just as I needed to move out of my previous location. I heard of this room from a coworker in the work/study program at the local junior college where I was again a student. I moved in and the callus around my heart grew stronger as the love of these new friends tried to penetrate. I isolated myself, tried to be rebellious. I think God was saying, "Your mouth says no-no, but your heart is saying yes-yes." And it was true, because the ever-present, never-ending love of God finally captured me, once and for all, and dragged me kicking and screaming out of the hand of

Satan and into the Light of Jesus.

It has not been an easy thirty years, especially the first five or ten, but with healing and mercy and patience, as only God can have, my life is awesome. I have three great children, plus the adopted child from my teenage years, with whom I was reunited by his choice when he was twenty-two. I am a missionary to Rwanda and soon to Thailand.

So. . .it's all good as only God can make it, because He is all good all the time. His plans and purpose are sure. He never wastes a hurt. His love is never ending, and His mercies never fail. His patience and faithfulness are my safety net. And it all began in a tent on a beach forty years ago when I listened to a man named Billy Graham.

FIRST SEEDS

In 1960, I attended a crusade with three other high school friends. At the altar call, I really wanted to go forward, but I was too shy. I felt my friends wouldn't wait for me, and we were forty-five miles from home that night. Back in the car, my date turned to me and said, "Did you want to go forward?"

"Yes," I replied.

"Me too," he said.

But we didn't.

My life was stormy until 1992, when I accepted Jesus into my heart. How different life might have been if I had answered the call when I was sixteen. I tried life the world's way, then my way, and finally. . .His way. I will never look back. The peace I have now is amazing. I still remember the pull I felt back then and wish I could have been bolder. God has sent me to Chad, Africa, three times, and maybe I will go again on a medical team. Who knows what God has in store for me?

SAVED IN SWEDEN

Take yourself back to your preteen years. Now see yourself as an American preteen living with your family in beautiful Stockholm, Sweden. You're trying to learn the language and adjust to being far from home. And occasionally you get to experience a slice of the good old USA. I encountered two remarkable Billys while in Stockholm: my first concert (with Billy Joel) and my first crusade (with Billy Graham). Both were All-American joyous occasions. But only one of them changed my life. . .Rev. Graham's crusade.

The opportunity to worship in English was welcome. Suddenly I was in a place full of love, listening to Rev. Graham describe the simplicity of coming forward to begin your personal journey with God. I remember a stadium filled with people, the music, and then the call. We were sitting pretty far back, and I'd never seen anything like it. But the tug of the Spirit at my heart couldn't be ignored. To this day, I can see myself getting out of those chairs, walking up front. . .and being surrounded in a circle of prayer and love.

My Christian journey took many twists and turns through young adulthood. But it was the personal relationship with God, a foundation laid down that day at a stadium in Stockholm, that planted a critical experience in my heart. Ironically, it was a seed that later bloomed in Billy Graham's backyard, in upstate South Carolina. Decades later, and just miles away from Billy's home in the mountains of North Carolina, the girl who had walked forward in Stockholm was making a home as a local news anchor in Spartanburg.

Through a Bible study for new moms, I was able to reconnect with that heartfelt desire to have a personal relationship with God.

We all know it's a small world, and making it even smaller was this: I wound up growing the seed that Rev. Graham helped to plant across the ocean, at First Baptist Church, the very church where Rev. Graham himself turned in his later years of life—the two of us sharing the same pastor and a loving God.

You Were the One Who Planted the Seed in My Heart

I wasn't even a Christian, but I occasionally watched your crusades on TV. I did not grow up in a Christian home. We went to church, but I never thought that much about God. Through school and halfway through my military service, my life was fine. Then my world fell apart. I felt like no one cared. I said if God didn't care, neither did I. I did things I never imagined I would do, ate like a pig to cover the guilt, and had a nervous breakdown. Still, I never sought help.

Some time later, I was assigned to another base. God put me right across the hall from two Christian girls about my age. I had been there about three or four months when I accepted Jesus as my Savior. Looking back over the years (thirty-five to be exact), I know that you were the one who planted the seed in my heart so that one day it would take root and grow into a "tree" for what the Lord had planned for me. Since I have been walking with Him, I have had highs and lows, but He has never left me nor forsaken me. He is always true to His promises. Mr. Graham, I have watched your crusades every chance I got. God has used you to touch my life in so many ways; I couldn't begin to tell you. The Bible says one plants and another waters, but God gives the increase. The Lord put a call on your life, and you were obedient. Thanks for being there to plant the seed. God bless you.

THE WALL IN MY HEART

I heard Billy Graham preach in Berlin, in 1990. One year after the Berlin Wall had come down, his words about grace changed my life. The wall in my heart came down, and I met Jesus for the first time. Back then, I was a very young man with many burdens, having grown up in East Germany without a father. Today, I am a happy father, husband, film and TV writer, director, preacher, and consultant to young people. The glory goes to God. Thank you, Billy Graham, for sowing the first seed in my heart, and thank you to all of those who have supported this ministry over the years.

A LIFE-CHANGING DAY. . .THANK GOD!

I'm a fifty-five year-old mother of six children. I thank God for Billy Graham and for what his ministry did in my life. I had a lot of trials in my life as a child. I talked to God a lot about the things I went through, and I attended church regularly. By twelve years of age, I had tried to commit suicide, but God didn't let me die. One day, I was watching TV and the Billy Graham program was on. I started watching it, really listening to the message. I understood what he was saying; it was so real to me that day. At the end, when he asked people to come to the front if they wanted Christ in their life, I began to cry. I cried hard, and God ministered to my young heart. I prayed and asked Christ into my life.

I went on serving God in church, singing in the choir, teaching Sunday school, etc. But then when I turned eighteen, I just didn't go to church anymore and lived my life. I went through more hard times—a very brutal first marriage, a difficult second one, sick children, and sick myself most of my life, another attempted suicide. My husband and I were going through some financial trials, and neither of us went to church anymore. God was calling us and we ignored Him, so He turned up the pressure. We finally had enough, and one day that week someone put a flier in our fence about heaven or hell. We called the number on the flier, and a pastor came to visit us and told us about Jesus and invited us to his church. We went as a family, and my husband and I rededicated our lives back to the Lord. We then went into ministry, and my husband became a minister.

You see, a seed was planted in my life all those years ago through the Billy Graham ministry. Was it the big crusade, the great preaching, the singing? It was the power of God and the anointing on a very obedient humble man of God. I want to thank his wife and his children for sharing him with the world. We needed the message he was born to preach.

There once was a man named Billy Graham
He preached about God all over the land
And now that he is old and gray
The seeds he planted will never fade away
They continue to spread all over the earth
Many a life experienced new birth
The goal you see is to get them heaven-bound
Not to that place under the ground
Billy Graham's ministry did this for me
Now my spirit is finally free

All praise goes to God our Father for using a humble servant, Billy Graham.

YOU PLANTED THE SEEDS

Dear Brother Graham: Greetings in the name of our Lord and Savior Jesus Christ. I was first introduced to your ministry many years ago as a young boy. My dad would always invite me to watch your crusades with him on TV. I was always impressed by the mighty healings that the Lord would do through you. Dad wasn't much of a churchgoer in those days, yet he had an uncanny type of faith. You see, Dad was a heavy smoker and just couldn't seem to find a church that would allow him to smoke in the pew.

I will never forget that one day when a neighbor stopped by and mocked you, saying to Dad, "You really don't believe all that hocus-pocus, do you?" Dad replied, "Yes, I do. I believe that Jesus has apostles today, just like He did when He walked the earth, and Billy Graham is one!"

Those messages planted a seed of faith, which bore fruit many years later. You see, in 1980, I was diagnosed with multiple sclerosis (MS). But in 1984, I gave my heart to the Lord and was totally healed through the prayers of a local ministry. That move of the Lord led Dad and other family members to give their hearts to the Lord, too. Dad went home to be with the Lord on July 11, 2007. Today, both my wife, Patti, and I are deacons in our local church. Again, thank you!

AT THE TOP OF THE STAIRS

When I was a teenager, around the year 1971, my parents were watching a Billy Graham crusade on TV. As I walked through the room to go upstairs to my bedroom, my father said, "Patti, you really should watch this. "My mother chimed in, "Yes, Patti, get down here and watch this." We were a Catholic family. My father loved to watch Billy Graham. My mother really wasn't that interested but watched because my dad did.

I said, "No, I'm going to bed." I had never heard him preach before and didn't want to watch him simply because my parents said I "needed" to. As I reached the top stair, I paused when I heard Brother Graham say something like this (not a direct quote): "If Jesus Christ isn't your main thought during the day, then He is not your God." I was shocked. I knew I didn't think of Jesus Christ every day, but I thought I believed well enough.

I don't know if my parents remembered anything Billy Graham said. But I've remembered those words all my life. I became a born-again Christian a few years later, when I was twenty, through friends who had gotten saved. But I know the very first seed planted in me was planted by Brother Graham that night as I barely listened at the top of the stairs. Thank you so much for your ministry!

BILLY SOWED THE SEED

As a Ugandan University student in London in 1984, I had the fortune to hear Billy Graham preach the Gospel one evening at a little chapel in Victoria, just around the corner from Buckingham Palace.

Billy Graham spoke in a low voice that day, because he

had either just had an operation or was not well. As I got up to answer the altar call at the end of the message, I was somehow dissuaded by someone I'd gone with, and sat back down again. Nonetheless, the seed had been sown in me.

It was to be another fourteen years of twists and turns in my life before I finally answered that call, back in Uganda in 1998. On the day I finally answered the call, I remembered the evening I'd heard the Gospel from Billy Graham. He had sown the seed, and someone else had watered it. Praise God!

NOT TOO DIRTY TO BE CLEAN

I was brought up in the church. My mother was a very prayerful woman, who was a powerful influence and witness in the lives of her five children, who all have now become ministers and pastors of the Gospel. Although I was brought up in the church, I somehow never felt accepted, nor could I ever seem to follow all the rules and regulations that would make me a "saint" according to my church's teaching. So, after giving birth to a child at age sixteen and later marrying the father, I went on to have three more children in this abusive marriage. I later began to use drugs and drink and sell my body to support my children while attempting to get through college after my divorce.

It was during this time that some women from my mother's church came to witness to me about giving my life to the Lord, but I simply expressed to them that I was not ready. The teaching at that time was that you "get ready," stop sinning, and then come to the Lord. I had no power to clean myself up. A few days later, I was sitting in front of the television and there was Billy Graham preaching in one of his crusades. He was saying that you can "just come" to the Lord and that being a sinner qualifies you for an opportunity to be forgiven, if you would repent and ask Jesus to save you. I listened and doubted that it could be that simple. I prayed, and felt the tears roll down my face as the Lord embraced me with his love. I still remember the warmth that came into my heart. But I dared not tell others, who had told me I was "too dirty to be clean," that I had been forgiven and accepted by Jesus. In listening to the teachings of my upbringing, I began to doubt that I had been saved and began to return to the ways of the world, but a seed had been planted, and about a year later, I gave my life totally to the Lord and allowed Him to clean up my life from drinking and the life I was living.

About five years later, I accepted a call into ministry, and cofounded a church in Hawaii. And because Billy Graham was one of my mentors in ministry, I thought I would conduct my altar call as he had. I began reading a book called *The Effective Invitation* and saw how people would come to the altar for salvation and prayer. Since then, I have been through many trials and now have relocated to Arkansas. My husband and I pastor a church here, and I always open the service with a reading from the devotional *Hope for Each Day: Words of Wisdom and Faith*, by Dr. Graham. I continue to hold Dr. Graham as my mentor. He and Ruth will truly have a soul-winner's crown worth its weight in glory.

THE CALL TO EVANGELISM

Dear Billy, thank you first of all for being faithful to the call of God on your life. As you preached to the crowds at a crusade, I too got saved in my living room in front of my TV set. I don't remember my age then, but I was a very young girl. The compelling Word of God you spoke into my life planted the seed of new life. I didn't realize then the course that my life would follow. All I knew was I received a hunger for God. My spirit yearns to fulfill my destiny in God. I trust and know God is not done with me yet. When you shared Jesus, I believe you planted words that God had ordained for me. I pray I will be as faithful as you have been until Jesus returns.

PRECIOUS SEEDS OF BLESSING

The Rev. Billy Graham has been a household name in my home for as long as I can recall. I grew up on a farm in South Georgia, and we worked hard. It didn't matter what we were doing, if Rev. Graham was going to be on television, my family was in the living room watching the one old black-and-white TV set. We only got three channels, but praise God, Billy Graham was on one of them! No one talked or moved around during the message.

My father was a strict disciplinarian, a WWII veteran, and was not even saved for part of the years we watched the Billy Graham crusades. I know that Rev. Graham planted and watered many spiritual seeds in our home, and in my life. My father's salvation when he was in his forties is one of the precious seeds of blessing. . . . I was not saved directly as a result of a TV crusade, but the seeds were definitely there. I finally was able to attend a crusade in the mid- to late 1990s in Atlanta.

THE FRUIT IS OBVIOUS

When I was a little girl growing up in Arkansas, in a family of six children, my mother used to watch the Billy Graham crusades. She was the first in her family of seven children to come to Christ. I remember her family making fun of her, and my dad would often abuse her. I never once heard my mother answer back with an unkind word. She faithfully took all six of us kids to church and lived a quiet strength devoted to Christ.

Because of her faithfulness, I wanted to learn the Word of God for myself, and even as a young child, I would try to read the Bible. Even as a young child, I could sense the presence of God whenever the Billy Graham crusades were on. It was obvious God was drawing me and had a great plan for my life.

I thank God for my mother, and I thank God that I had the experience of hearing the Gospel through Billy Graham as a young child. It would be the seeds that God would later water on in my life. Even now, I watch the reruns on TBN on Saturday nights. . .and the presence of God is just as strong now as it was then. It gives me a wonderful, comforting feeling.

I went on to have three sons, and my youngest joined the Marine Corps. In February 2004, I was driving my son's Jeep back from Cherry Point, North Carolina, to Tulsa after he had just left for his first tour of duty to Iraq. Having been on the road for several hours, I needed to stretch my legs and get some gas, so I took the next turn to the right. I noticed it was a beautiful little town, and as I stepped out of the car, I felt a presence.

After getting gas, I thought I would stop in one of the shops, and I noticed there were quite a few Billy Graham books—and one by Ruth that I had been looking for. When I commented to the clerk that I was so glad to find that book, she said, "Well, Billy and Ruth live right up the road." Then I understood what the presence was. . .you could literally feel

God's presence so strong there, in Black Mountain, North Carolina.

I realized, too, that the presence I felt was the power of prayer—the many prayers that had gone off that mountain, prayed not only by the Grahams but many faithful people of God. I realize that is probably as close as I will ever get to being around Billy or the Graham family, but, oh my, what a pleasant surprise it was that day. How beautiful is that little town snuggled by those mountains. Oh my, what a sweet presence of Jesus I could feel.

Thank you, Billy Graham. The fruit is obvious. . .oh so obvious!

Thank You, Billy Graham. . .
for Helping Me Find Jesus

BLOCKED IN MY CLOSET

When I was two years old, my parents divorced. Back then (1962), the father *never* got custody, but my dad did. But, being in the service, he could not take care of three children all under the age of five, so he put us in a Catholic orphanage in Texas, near the border with Mexico. Six months later (after begging the nuns not to allow us to be adopted), he came to get us with a *new* wife.

I grew up knowing hardly anything about God. My parents took me to catechism before I was seven, but with my father being in the service for twenty years, all that moving around made it hard to make friends.

By the time I was ten, my father retired from the navy and bought a 240-acre farm in northern Wisconsin. By the time I was thirteen, I was the product of a double divorce, with my stepmother gaining custody. I spent the next few years experiencing everything the world had to offer, using alcohol and men to try to fulfill my needs. I was very sad and lonely, and my life was going nowhere as I went to ladies' nights, nickel night, dance contests, and anything that was offered at any bar to try to forget my loneliness.

One day, I was at my one-bedroom apartment and decided to clean out my one huge closet. I pulled everything out and pushed it into the middle of the room, hoping to rearrange and fix everything from there. Instead, I found I had blocked myself into the closet.

I had the TV on in the other room, pretty loud so I could hear it in the closet. Then to my surprise I began hearing someone talk about God and Jesus, I didn't even know the difference between God and Jesus. Well, I did not want to hear anything from some "Jesus freak," but I was blocked into my closet and couldn't get out. I didn't want to make a bigger mess trying to get out, so I started arranging things much faster so I could march over to the TV as soon as possible to turn the channel.

Finally! I cleared enough room to make it over to the TV, but when I put my hand on the knob to turn it, I *couldn't* . . . . My hand stopped, and I stood there listening to what the man was saying. He was at the point where you call the number on the bottom of the screen. I said to myself, *I will call, but if I get put on hold or a busy signal, I will just hang up.*

I dialed the number, and when a man answered, I began to tell him how I tried to be a good person and that my mother had sent me a Bible and that I had it right next to my bed. (I didn't tell him that I had never even opened the Bible.) He very matter-of-factly said, "Then why did you call?" My response did not check in with my head; it came right out of my spirit. I said, "I want to accept Jesus Christ as my Lord and Savior." Instantly, from head to toe, I felt a tingling sensation. I was changed instantly, never to be the same again! And to this day, twenty-four years later, I am still living for, loving, and serving God with all my heart, soul, and might.

Maria

MY SALVATION

I grew up hearing and watching Billy Graham on TV. My mother was a faithful follower of Rev. Graham's. But when he was on TV, I never really heard the message. It never went to my heart. Rev. Graham was coming to Hartford in May 1985. My mother didn't have anyone to take her. None of my siblings wanted to go. Mom begged me to take her to see the crusade. I never can forgot going into the Civic Center and seeing all those people. Having stopped going to church quite a few years before, I didn't think people still had belief in God. We got some seats and started to listen to the program. It was okay, but not great to me. Then came Rev. Graham on stage. His message, though I don't remember it, spoke to something inside of me, something deep down. I wanted to know more about this "salvation" thing. What is this "trust and obey" thing? I needed God more in my life. And I wanted God then and there. When the invitation came at the end of the program, my mother and I went forward. I praise God now for the special bond my mother and I experienced that night, getting saved the same day and place. Mom is in heaven now, and I know someday I will be with her because of hearing and understanding Rev. Graham that afternoon. I have been saved for twenty-seven years. I am still growing as a Christian. I got to see Rev. Graham at Flushing Meadows a few years back. I praise God that I got to hear him in person once again. Rev. Graham will always have a special place in my heart, because of that special bond I had with my mother. Thank you for spreading the Word.

HE POINTED ME IN THE
DIRECTION OF THE SAVIOR

During my senior year in high school, my two best friends died in separate car accidents six months apart. Another close friend had died the previous year. I was miserable, lonely, and guilt ridden. I thought if I'd been there for them, they would've been okay. I was suicidal and on a downward spiral. I was drinking a lot, doing drugs, and hanging out with new friends who really didn't care about me. My parents were rarely home because of their own choices they were making. I felt completely alone.

My Christian brother, Bill, witnessed to me for a couple of years, but I didn't listen to him. He was living a dual life, partying at the same parties I was and bringing home different girls all the time. I used to laugh at him for being drunk and unholy on Saturday night and holier than thou on Sunday morning.

One night, I was home alone late. I was drunk. I turned on the stereo, and of course Bill had left it on a Christian station. I didn't have the energy to get up and change it. The Southern voice on the radio was a soothing one. The man sounded compassionate and intelligent. He was saying all of the same things I had read in the little tracts Bill always left lying around the house.

Suddenly, all of the things my brother had said that I'd been rejecting seemed within reach. This man didn't sound like my brother, two-faced and self-righteous. He sounded like he cared about *me*. He pointed me in the direction of the Savior. He told me to make a decision, and I did. I decided to turn my life over to Christ that night. I only wish I'd had the nerve to call the phone number and get more information. It took me years to learn how to go to church. Believe it or not, I didn't know a person could just walk in, sit down, and enjoy a sermon. I am very thankful to Billy Graham. I had wanted to die so I could join my friends. Now I know that when I die, I'll be surrounded by friends and family.

NEW CREATION IN CHRIST

As a child, I was brought up in a Christian home, but I did not make a decision to accept Jesus as my personal Savior until I was twenty-four. I was married and living in California, where my husband was in the Air Force. I was miserable with anxiety and not knowing what was happening in the world and with me and my two young children. I blamed my husband for my unhappiness. One day, a lady asked me if I knew Jesus. I couldn't answer her. That night, on TV, I heard Billy and his message about the Christ who died for me. It pierced my heart. It has now been forty years. I praise the Lord that I was gloriously saved and am a new creature in Christ.

Rachel

TROPHY OF GRACE

Dr. Graham, I am just one of your thousands of "trophies of grace." I grew up listening to you, but one night in 1972, in a drunken stupor watching you on TV, during your altar call, I knelt by my couch and asked the Lord back into my heart and life. I then returned to my childhood church in Detroit and made a promise to the Lord that I would now do whatever he wanted me to do in life. About six months later, the Holy Spirit rekindled the "call" that I had as a child to be a full-time evangelist. . .and I said "yes!" to that call. For the past thirty-five years now, I have traveled all over the United States and Canada preaching the Gospel of Jesus Christ. I simply cannot begin to tell you how God has worked in my life, family, and ministry since the night I surrendered my life back to Him after watching your crusade, and hearing God speak to me through you that evening. And all the lives that have been changed through my ministry all these many years now, I pray that God will accredit your account accordingly.

Dr. Graham, after traveling for thirty-five consecutive years now, I have just a little idea of the tremendous sacrifices that you and your precious wife and family made as you embraced God's will for your life, and I just wanted to take a moment to say a heartfelt "thank you!" Not only to you, sir, but to your entire family as well. I've always wanted to meet you, and I look forward to that time in heaven when I will. I realize that the line will be long, and I'll have to wait my turn, but I'll have an eternity with God and His people to do so.

WHY MICHAEL W. SMITH?

I am a forty-six-year old mother of a twelve-year-old son, whom I have raised by myself. I call him my angel because I became a born-again Christian when I became pregnant with him. I rarely dated, unless the men were Christian, and even then it was few and far between. I wanted to be the best mom I could be raising my biracial son by myself.

I have had a hard, hard life. I endured rapes, drug abuse, and near deaths, only to learn later in my life that God was the very One on High who sent his angels to me each and every time so that I might someday impact others with the truth of Jesus Christ.

One day, when my son was about ten years old, I was watching Billy Graham on TV and I saw Michael W. Smith for the first time. I thought, *Why Michael W. Smith? Why did Billy Graham choose him to play out of all choices?* You see, I had been to prison several years earlier, and when I got out, the first CD I listened to was Michael W. Smith—and it changed my heart with his music. I continued to listen and buy more CDs.

Two years later, I got married to a man I believed was a Christian. But three months after our wedding, I was in a horrible car accident, and my new husband left me when I needed him the most. It was then that I delved back into drugs, leaving my son with his grandparents as I mourned my life, asking God, "Why?"

For the very first time in my entire life, I sought God with all my mind, heart, and soul. Even though I had been going down the wrong path, I knew I was grieving the Holy Spirit. At night, the depths of my depression left me alone in my dark house. No husband, injured drastically from my car crash, my son away from my arms, my back problems, and the pain was unbearable. It was then that I tuned in to a Christian station and heard Michael W. Smith singing "Healing Rain." Even though I continued in my sin, something much stronger than the grip of Satan and his drugs came over me. It was God, answering all my questions through music on this one station that had only Christian music. As I continued to sin, I also continued to pray, cry, and groan with the Spirit who produced an amazing connection with Jesus Christ. I began to recall everything I had ever gone through—every person I had ever hurt, everything I had ultimately forgotten about my life, I recalled. At each instant of recollection, I prayed for that person, and I continued to search relentlessly in the Bible, and miracle after miracle happened *each* and *every* time I prayed. I had never had a glimpse of heaven until this most tragic time. No one will ever understand the miracles that took place. But God did. Groaning with the Holy Spirit and praying with tears flooding my room led to what I believe only angels could see.

After these times, this whole vision, dream, or what have you, left me. Only a memory remains. But this memory has been etched into my heart, starting with the question on TV with Billy Graham's crusade, and the question of *Why Michael W. Smith?* I will never forget that question that stuck in my head, yet God had prepared me for a miracle. In my darkest hours, I believe I was dying and fighting death at the same time. A peace that passed all understanding came to pass in my life. I knew that God is a God of peace, a God of comfort, a God of miracles, and a God of Mercy, and it was all for me. Jesus died for you and me. He knew every hair on my head, every thought, prayer, question, desire, hurt, pain, and despair. I thank Billy Graham and his ministry. My prayer is to someday mean something to someone. God knows my heart. I now am single again (separated from my husband, who never came back), on a road to seek God with all my heart, mind, and soul again, so that I may fulfill a blessed existence and purpose. Thank you for letting me share. I pray I can touch others, because I was given that gift by others.

I WAS A CRITIC

Around 1971, I was into drugs and was very lost as a teenager. The only preacher I had ever heard of was Billy Graham. At the time, I did not like what he stood for and was a critic—really without a good reason, never having heard him or seen him.

One night, I came home early after doing drugs, and my heart was searching for truth in this rat race of a world. I turned on the TV and heard a man speaking words of truth about man's sinful condition, the world problems, and God being the answer. For the first time, I heard words of truth, and the Holy Spirit began speaking to me. I'm not sure when I actually believed and accepted Jesus as my Savior, but listening to Billy Graham that night changed my life, and I have been grateful to Billy for his stand for Christ and his ministry that allowed God to speak into my darkness and bring light. Thank you, Billy Graham, for your integrity and stand for Jesus.

ALONE. . .VERY ALONE

I sat in my apartment, alone. . .very alone. I had been in the army for three years, with a great number of health problems—including being told that I had to have major back surgery. I sat in my apartment, watching TV, and the only person I felt comfort from was Billy. I dropped onto my knees and found Jesus. Jesus and I have walked many roads since then, and I've even been blessed to see Billy in person. (What a blessing that was!) I just wanted to say, from the bottom of this child of God's heart. . .thank you, Billy, for listening to the call Jesus obviously placed on your heart and life. May God provide you all the comfort in your heart that you have indeed been a faithful servant.

Thank You, Billy Graham. . .
for Bringing Me Back to Jesus

I Needed to Return to My Faith

Dear Billy, in the late 1980s I was living in Jacksonville, Florida, and I had developed a pretty bad drinking problem. Watching Rev. Graham one night on TV made me think about the Christian home I'd been raised in and how I needed to return to my faith. Through a series of events that can only be explained by God's intervention, I quit drinking and cleaned up my act. I have been sober for seventeen years now, praise God! Thank you, Billy. You changed my life.

Saved from Hell on Earth

Sometime in my twenties, I heard Billy's message and felt I accepted Christ. I worked with my church youth group and planned to go to missionary school. But Satan took over and I listened to him and went down a long road of living in hell for many years.

There was an intermittence of years when I tried living a moral life and prayed. Then, unfortunately, I spent years committing adultery, doing drugs, and drinking, all the roads that lead to hell. In my neighborhood, there were some Christian families that took pity on my son, Mark (praise the Lord for that). It was through their prayers and their work with my son that he went to church and accepted Christ.

I continued on my road to self-destruction until I hit the bottom and was on the way to losing my husband, son, and home. I decided to give God another chance, or commit suicide. I called my neighbor, Kay, who had been witnessing to me, and asked to go to church with her. I told her my situation, so she was praying that I would not change my mind about going to church. I had no intentions of doing so. I had to give God one more chance.

When the pastor completed his sermon and asked for those who wanted to give their lives to Christ, I knew I had to go forward. I was weeping so hard that I could not talk to my friend, so she went with me. We went and talked to the pastor, and I just kept nodding my head to all that was said. I also was baptized that day. To this day, I still remember the cleansing I felt and the weight that was lifted off of me when I came up from the water. I knew then I was free from the past. That was June 7, 1981. I truly believe that, through all the things I did during my days of hell on earth, as I call it, God never let me go. I thank Billy for that day long ago sharing your love for Christ to all of us on TV, and your dedication to our Lord.

"I'll See You in Heaven"

I have been a lifelong supporter of yours. I grew up in a Christian home, but when I became a teenager, I drifted away from the church and the Bible. I was totally immersed in the world. After two children and two marriages, I could no longer ignore the vacant spot in my heart. I started attending church and reading the Bible, but I seemed hesitant to totally commit myself to Christ. I felt I should publicly commit myself to Him. I promised the Lord that if Billy Graham came to my area again, I would go and give myself to the Lord. I was thinking this wouldn't happen, because you rarely made crusade appearances anymore. I was utterly shocked to read in the paper soon after that you were going to be at Qualcomm Stadium in San Diego. The Lord did His part of the bargain, and I kept mine. On Mother's Day 2003, my son Gary and I attended that San Diego crusade, and I came forth for my Lord, Jesus Christ. A year later, I was baptized. Billy, I will never forget you, or what you said as you walked off that stage that night. You said "I'll see you in heaven." I am looking forward to that, Mr. Graham. I love you.

Dr. Graham's Influence on My Life

I accepted Jesus Christ in 1977, at a very low point in my life. I was only eighteen or nineteen years old, and I was living with a bunch of guys I knew from my neighborhood in Huntington Beach, California. I knew that unless things changed, my life was going nowhere.

I met a man who told me about Jesus, and I professed my faith in Christ shortly thereafter. However, for years I lived with one foot in the world and one foot on Jesus, just not wanting to commit myself entirely. I began to listen to Billy Graham on TV and went to his crusade in Anaheim in 1986. It was then I began to realize that my faith—or lack thereof—wasn't doing it, and I was miserable. I began to listen to Billy Graham any time he was interviewed on TV, and I really began to admire him and his faith in Jesus Christ. I liked the fact that he never had a bad thing to say about anyone, no matter who they were, and that he preached the Gospel. I knew through this that I was loved.

I eventually began to go back to church and rededicated my life to the Lord. I liked the fact that Dr. Graham was friends with Pope John Paul II and believed him to be a man of God, unlike other Christian leaders who are much more critical of anyone whose beliefs may slightly differ.

My faith in Jesus Christ has grown, and I credit much of that to Dr. Billy Graham and his ability to speak the truth no matter what the cost. I have always liked the fact that Dr. Graham speaks the truth in love. If I would not have listened to Dr. Graham and his preaching of the Bible, I would have been hell-bound the rest of my life. I love our Lord and Savior Jesus Christ, and I will always admire Billy Graham. I wish I could give him a big hug, and I look forward to seeing him in heaven with all the other saints.

My mother, who is an agnostic and is not that friendly toward Christianity, even likes Dr. Graham, saying that he is a good man. Even those of the world recognize there is something different about Billy. Billy Graham truly thinks of others before himself and has remained humble. Thank you, Billy.

SET FREE

First, I'd like to thank you for your love of the Lord Jesus. Because of you, I have come back home for good. When I was younger, my grandmother and I would watch your show and we would get our Bible out. She would help me understand what you had talked about.

As I got older and higher up in school, I got in with a bad crowd, just to fit in somewhere in this world. Then, right before I graduated, I started to drink, and I became an addict for seven years. I lived to drink. It took over my life. During that time, my grandmother sat me down and told me that she loved me no matter what I did.

Not long after that, my grandmother was told she had cancer and she would have to have treatment right away. I was at my apartment one evening, thinking about my life, when you came on. You talked about backsliding. You said that God still loved me. So that night, I gave God all of me. When I told my grandmother, she was so happy for me that I gave my life to Christ and gave up alcohol.

My grandmother's cancer returned, and this time the doctor told us there was nothing more they could do. But before she went home to the Lord, she was able to see me sober and living for the Lord. Because of your ministry, I have been set free from alcohol for three years. So I just want to say a big thank you.

JUST BLESSED

I grew up in a church that did not teach the Bible. I was fervent, often attending services daily, even as a teen, but I did not know Christ. During my first year of college, I got into an argument with a student on campus about how to get to God. I told him I could get to God anytime I wanted. He told me that we can only get to God through Jesus Christ and quoted John 14:6: "I am the way, the truth, and the life. No one comes to the Father except through Me."

I turned away from him and left. But that verse would not leave my mind. All that night, I heard it in my mind. I heard it in the morning and at lunchtime. It went to class with me, and dinner. No one sat with me at dinner. Just a voice in my spirit, saying that verse again and again . . .

That night, by myself, I got down on my knees and asked Jesus to forgive me for all my sins and to come into my heart to be my Lord and Savior. Nobody had ever taught me to pray like this; there just seemed to be a leading in my spirit.

I was saved, but I didn't know it. I just knew that the presence of God seemed so close to me—right behind me, at my side. It seemed that if I turned around quickly enough I would see Him. One time I even tried! But I didn't know how to grow. For the next few years, I tried to pick up my Bible and read. I would start in Genesis, but usually all my efforts would die somewhere around Numbers. Or, I would play "Bible roulette," asking God for a verse and opening my Bible randomly. I was a baby!

I married, graduated from college, and moved to New Mexico. We heard that Billy Graham was coming to town. I was still going to a church in the denomination I had grown up in, but I felt I needed to go, so I went. At the end, when Rev. Graham gave the invitation, I knew I needed to stand and recommit my life to Jesus Christ. Here is where help came! Not only were counselors available to talk with me, but they also invited me to sign up for a Bible study.

How I loved those Bible studies! I filled them out and sent them back. Sometimes it took awhile before I sent back a study. I was now a busy mother with two children. But the counselors who received my booklets were always gracious. They sent back kind words and encouragement. I realize now that they were praying for me. I went through the whole series, and the last book included a copy of the Four Spiritual Laws. I thought, *I can't just learn this and set it aside.*

That night, at a party at my home, one of my husband's students asked how she could be saved, and I didn't know what to say to her. I was so chagrined. I took the booklet and gave it to her, but I felt so bad that I couldn't present the Gospel to her as I should have. I decided then that this would never happen again. If someone wanted to know how to be saved, I would be able to tell them. I got another copy of the Four Spiritual Laws and studied it. And I began sharing it.

Years later, Campus Crusade for Christ's "I Found It" campaign came to Albuquerque. I signed up, and God used me to present the Gospel to others. What a gift to bring someone to Christ! There can be no better blessing! I also kept reading my Bible. I went on to become a Sunday school teacher and to help others grow in Christ. I am still teaching God's Word today.

I am grateful. I have been so blessed by Billy Graham and his amazing organization, and I just want to say thank you.

Thank You, Billy Graham...
for *How You Touched My Family*

~~~~~

AT MY WITS' END . . .

I was in Augusta, Georgia, in 1996, with my three-year-old daughter, and I was at my wits end. I called in to the 800 number and asked the Lord into my life. Since then, Billy Graham has been an inspiration to me. I was in Nashville when he preached there, and I was again led to renew my vows with my Savior. My then seven-year-old daughter also gave her life to Jesus. We have been blessed all these years. It has been a struggle, but my faith remains that God has good things in store for us. I praise God for all Billy Graham and his family have done for everyone out there. He is my hero.

JASON'S CONVERSION

I took my three children to a crusade in Little Rock, Arkansas, when my son, Jason, was nine or ten years old. He was never an outspoken kid, he didn't tell you what was on his mind. When the altar call was made, I was very surprised when Jason went forward to be saved. I cried and cried with happiness that he was reached by Rev. Graham's message of salvation to give his life to Jesus.

MOTHER AND DAUGHTER BORN
AGAIN THROUGH TV CRUSADE

I want to let Billy Graham know the effect he had on my life and my family through his television crusades. I apologize for not writing him sooner and telling him the effect his ministry had on my life.

I was raised as a Lutheran and was in Sunday school by the age of three. I always enjoyed the stories about Jesus, and I believed He died on the cross for me and my forgiveness and eternal life. In seventh and eighth grade, I went to confirmation classes and was confirmed in the Lutheran Church. I always enjoyed talking about Jesus. Many nights in my room, I would talk to Him and cry because of my life being full of sin. My parents went to church on Sunday mornings, but that was it. No Bible reading at home, no prayer, except bedtime with my sisters. My family drank alcohol and went to bars and dances, so as a teenager I would drink on weekends with friends and went to dances.

I married right out of high school to a Lutheran farm boy. We attended a large Lutheran church. Praying only took place if there was a major problem or emergency in the family. I would get the Bible out to read but put it away if I heard my husband coming. I felt embarrassed, like he wouldn't approve of me. We were married five years and then came the birth of our son, and eighteen months later a daughter.

I always was irritated when Billy Graham was on TV. It took off my favorite programs. I can't remember the exact date, but one day in 1973 or 1974, I clicked on TV and Billy Graham was preaching. Instead of getting irritated, this time I chose to listen. I had never heard of asking Jesus into my heart and life—to be born again. Billy said you may have been a Sunday school teacher or gone to church all your life, but have you ever had a personal relationship with Jesus— asking Him into your heart and life?

The next day, I thought more about it and decided to get on my knees and said, "Lord I already believe you died for me, but I didn't know I should ask you into my heart and life. Please come in, and I give you my life." I didn't see lights or have a feeling-type experience, but from that day on I noticed a change in what I valued and how I looked at life and my decisions and choices. Jesus was changing me. I read the Bible daily and received literature from the Billy Graham organization to help me grow spiritually.

When my daughter was fifteen, I talked to her about giving her heart fully to Jesus. She said, "I believe, but I'll do that after I'm grown. Otherwise, I might not have fun now as a teenager." A couple days later, in the evening, I was watching Billy Graham on TV and she was in the living room with me and was watching. I received a phone call and left the room. Some time passed, and when I returned to the living room, I found that my daughter had just prayed the closing prayer with Billy Graham to received Jesus into her heart and life as he closed his crusade meeting.

So you see, the Billy Graham ministry impacted both me and my daughter, and it carried over to my son. At age twenty-one, he fully gave his heart and life to Jesus and is now a mighty man of God. My son and daughter are both married and today are still following the Lord with their spouses and children. Thank you, Billy Graham, for your obedience to the call and for touching me and my family with the truth of the Gospel. I pray you will get to read this letter personally.

Betty Jean

MY WIFE, NORMA

I had been asking God to give me a helpmate who loved Him first. When I met Norma, she was not a Christian, but I was in love with her, and I asked God to open her heart, because she would not listen to me. Norma is from Mexico, and at the time she spoke very little English. One of the people she knew was a Bible-believing Christian, and he had invited her to the Billy Graham crusade in San Antonio. Unfortunately, for the first two nights, Norma had to work. Finally, on the third night, she called me and told me she was going to the crusade. I lived in Houston at the time. The first thing I did was go home and get on my knees before the Lord. After two hours of prayer, He let me know that it was a done deal.

Here's Norma's account of the crusade: "I went to the crusade, the atmosphere was one of love, the singers sang their songs, and then that old man got up and began to preach in English, and I could not understand one word he was saying. I was so tired that I fell sound asleep. In the middle of the message, I awoke, and was clearly hearing the old man speak directly to me in Spanish."

Long story short, that night, Norma was convicted by the Lord and accepted Christ as her Savior. Later that year, we were married.

Today, we have three children. For years, the doctors had told me I was sterile and would never father a child. Yet, by God's grace, I have fathered three children. Today, we are involved in ministry. We want to take this opportunity to thank "that old man." Brother Billy, we love you and pray for you always. Thank you for being a willing servant. You have no idea how many people that crusade in San Antonio has touched through Norma.

HE TOLD ME I NEEDED A CHURCH FAMILY
I can remember listening to Billy Graham when I was a small

child. My parents watched him on the TV. I grew up in a very abusive home. Dad was a mean alcoholic. My mom died when I was thirteen of a brain aneurysm. I was pretty much on my own, with twin brothers who were months younger. It was tough. I met and married my own alcoholic husband, and we have two sons. We have been married for almost thirty-four years.

I was saved at the age of eight or nine. I had gone to Sunday school and church (though I was afraid of the screaming preacher). I learned from a Sunday school teacher that Jesus loved me and that He would take care of me. I was sitting by myself in a swing outside one night, about nine or ten o'clock, listening to my parents fighting, and I prayed to Jesus that one of them—and it didn't matter which one—would go to jail for fighting and hurting us all like that. About twenty minutes later, Dad was taken to jail. (He got out the next morning.) I knew in my heart that Jesus was listening to me that night, and I have known from that night that He would always protect me.

When my dad was old and in bad health, his doctor asked me if I attended church. I said, "No, but I am saved." He told me I needed a church family and that the day would come when my dad would die from his drinking and I would need that church family. I did not want to go to church. I had too many problems with all the drinkers in my family, I had two teenage sons, and I had a job. I did not think church was necessary. I even wrote to the Billy Graham Association to see if this was really necessary. They wrote back and told me that I did need to go to church and have a church family.

When Dad died, I was not in a church, and his body was

donated to science. There was no closure to his death, and it was very hard on me for a long time.

My youngest son left home at eighteen, and I prayed for his safe return. I told God that I would do anything He wanted me to do if He would return my son to me. God did bring my son back home, and I asked God what did He want me to do? The Holy Spirit let me know that God wanted me to go to church. I asked Him, "Which church?" He led me to go to the small church where my oldest son had been saved years before. It was close to my home, and I had an old friend who attended there. I have been in church for ten years now, and I have enjoyed every minute of it. I met a Jewish man at church one night, and he told me he was led to the Lord by Billy Graham in El Paso, Texas, a long time ago. My husband has been sober for seven or eight years now. My youngest son, who had turned to drugs, entered a faith-based treatment center that did not charge a penny, and he has been clean and sober for two years. He so loves the Lord that he is a youth leader in his church, and he is there every time the doors are open. Yes, God is good, and He loves us all. Thank you, Billy, for introducing me to the Lord.

MY DADDY WAS BROUGHT TO TEARS

I prayed and asked Almighty God to speak to you, Billy Graham, through His Spirit in me tonight. I am a fifty-six-year-old woman who was raised in a wonderful Christian Lutheran family, very close to my grandparents as my father was an only child. My grandfather was a prominent business owner in the automotive industry, yet always taught Sunday school. My father was a well-educated design engineer in the automotive industry—Michigan's primary industry—yet always a teen small-group leader and an evangelist. You,

Mr. Graham, were more highly esteemed and respected by these two men than I can express to you.

I remember the excitement in our home as we gathered to watch the Billy Graham crusade, and as we sat in anticipation, yet with the utmost respect for your passion for God and God's beloved people. I watched two grown men brought to tears as you asked all the lost children of God to come forward and make Jesus the Lord of their lives. As a child, I watched my precious daddy and grampa drawn to your calling, inspired by your conviction to glorify their beloved heavenly Father. I saw their humility as they prayed with you for those making their way up the aisles, at the sound of "Just as I am, without one plea, but that Thy blood was shed for me. . ." Thank you for inspiring the two earthly men in my life, whom I loved more than anything; now I realize that I was loving Jesus in them.

My son was nine years old in 1998, when we attended your crusade in Tampa. We walked forward, and my son asked Jesus into his young heart. My son now has a strong faith, strong leadership traits, and is not afraid to be a Christ follower; he's on his way in obedience in this generation today! God has a real plan for my son's life, and your diligent obedience to God started the process in 1998. Thank you, Billy.

Thank You, Billy Graham. . .
for *Helping Me Deal with Adversity*

A Whole New Me

I did a lot of things in my younger life that I'm not proud of. These things affected who I was and who I became. When you don't know God can help you through your life, you make a lot of bad decisions and do a lot of dumb stuff.

Both my parents loved me in their quiet way. I went to church all my childhood and teen years, but I did not understand that I could have a relationship with God. I was a quiet child, but I did not feel good about myself. I had a low self-esteem for some reason. Finally, when a boy showed me some attention, I thought this was what I needed. When I dated, I ignored God's promptings to wait for the man God had planned for me. I wanted to make all my own decisions. I did not want anyone controlling me.

I was sad most of my adult life over my marriage problems, mainly because my husband belittled me by name-calling and later cursing at me. To make matters worse, he thought he was right in every situation. I blamed my husband and God for all my unhappy circumstances. I wasn't such a bad person, so why did I deserve this meanness? So I looked at everything as an attack against me. I became even more negative. Because my husband said a lot of mean things to me, I started to say mean things back to him, and my heart became hardened just like his.

I didn't know what to do to fix my marriage. I wanted out after twenty-five years. I had tried everything I knew to fix my problems. But my husband did not see any problem; he didn't even know I was unhappy! It was just me who had the problem. I was very depressed. It seems that I had to first hit the bottom for things to change. All this led to severe depression that lasted for the next ten years of my marriage.

In November and December of 2004, I began searching for something else, but not knowing what I needed. I tried a hypnotist to "cure" all my problems. That was a flop. But, thankfully, I was searching for help. I went home and got my childhood Bible. Then one night in January 2005, while my husband was in the other room watching TV, I turned on my kitchen TV, which got only three channels. I happened to stop on a Billy Graham crusade. I was curious and watched it. I cried out for God to help me, because I had tried to fix everything that was wrong in my marriage and I could not do it anymore. I needed Him. I finally gave up.

God was just waiting for me to call upon His name. He waited until I was done trying everything, and I finally gave up and asked Him for His help. He was ready and waiting to help me. I felt like He reached down from heaven and gave me His hand and pulled me out of the pit I had put myself in. I asked Him to forgive all my sins. I even confessed every sin I could remember since I was a little girl (I was now fifty-eight).That day, my whole life changed. First of all, I got a sliver of hope. God took my hardened heart and gave me a new heart and a new attitude, and peace flowed over me. I finally knew that God really loved me, and I believed it in my heart, and I had a desire to please God. He forgave me of so much that night that I was so exceedingly thankful for what He did for me. I now wake each day and end each day and go through the entire day praying to Him and focused on

Him. He did a total transformation of my life. I am a whole new me.

I still have the same circumstances; however, I feel God's presence helping me to cope and to respond now in a way pleasing to Him. It has been an uphill climb, and I am not there yet, but I try not to go around the same mountain so that I learn to press on toward God's goal for my life. God is an awesome God.

I am so humbled when I say that I give God the glory, and I thank Him for his faithful servant, the Rev. Billy Graham. Thank you, Billy, for being faithful to God's direction in your life. I was forever changed.

Dawn

A YEAR OF NEW BEGINNINGS

In June 1972, I was twenty-nine years old. My life was a mess. I had reached the bottom of the barrel. One night, my husband and I had been out drinking and had gotten in a fight. We were at his parents' house. I stormed out the door at midnight and just started walking. No one ran out to bring me back in, so I kept walking. I remember looking up at the stars, and in my half-stupor state, I said, "God, help me." Those three words saved my life, because with what happened next, no one would have ever seen me or heard from me again.

I had this idea that I was going home, which was a hundred miles away. I was walking on a highway, and three teenagers picked me up. They drove me about four miles down the road and dropped me off. Then another car stopped, and a man picked me up and took me to a George Webb restaurant. So now I'm sitting in this resturant, telling the waitress that I am going to hitchhike back to Milwaukee. As I'm sharing this, another man sat down next to me and apologized for listening in. He offered to drive me home. (I believe he was an angel.) Well, by 4:30 in the morning, I was walking into my house.

At this point, I was feeling really bad about myself, and I decided that my husband and children would be better off without me. So I decided to leave them. I asked a friend to take me to the bus station, and I bought a ticket to Las Vegas, where an uncle of mine lived. At this point, no one—except God—knew where I was.

When the bus stopped in Salt Lake City, there was a layover, so I decided to do a little sightseeing. I came to the Mormon Square, and I saw a hippie guy passing out pieces of paper. I thought he looked really weird, so I kept on walking. After another block or so, I saw a woman doing the same thing, only she looked more normal. By now I was curious, so I stopped and asked her what she was doing. She said she represented the Billy Graham Evangelistic Association, and she was there simply to share with people about Jesus. They weren't discrediting the Mormons but just sharing about the Lord.

I said, "Well, I'm a Catholic, and I know everything there is to know about Jesus." (Yeah, sure.) I think we stood there for more than two hours talking. She gave me a Billy Graham New Testament and some of his books. She never pressured me. I still remember her name—it was Nancy. She wrote something on the front page of the Bible she gave me.

I went back home and got right with my family. (At this point, I was still not saved.) One night, when my husband was gone and the children were in bed, I got out that Bible and decided to start with page one. In the front part of the Bible, Billy Graham had inserted "How to Become a Christian." He had written out the four spiritual laws, and I read them, and then I came to the sinner's prayer. I read it and thought, *What does that mean?* (I'm slow at understanding.) So I read it again, and all of a sudden the light came on, and I said, "Oh, that's what that means!" So, then I read it a third time, but this time was different, because I read it from my heart and not just from my head. Jesus was waiting for a heart surrender.

Let me tell you, when I prayed that prayer a third time, my living room came alive with the presense of the Lord. He was so real—what was happening to me was so real. I could feel the burden of sin being lifted off of me, and my whole being was changed in an instant.

I will always have that sweet girl Nancy, from the Billy Graham Evangelistic Association, to thank for taking the time to talk to me. My salvation was sealed on June 25, 1972. This is the first time I've ever written out my testimony, and the first time I've given credit to the Billy Graham ministry. It was through his ministry that I first heard about being born again.

Thank you for letting me share my story.

Sandra

"DON'T FORGET TO GO TO CHURCH THIS SUNDAY"

One night in May 1984, I was in a desperate mental condition. I went into my bedroom in anguish and wept before God on my knees. I had looked for God in many different places and through different religions, but in my quest to find Him, I had always come up empty. All I could do at the time was cry out from the depths of my heart and plead for forgiveness for all my wrongdoing. I told God that I didn't want to continue to live a life of sin and that I wanted to please Him and be like Jesus. I had been depressed and under heavy mental oppression, as I was suffering from paranoia and social anxiety disorder, and lived a very distressed and unhappy life at barely twenty-four years of age. Since my life had been disastrous up until that point, I went in desperation once more to seek God. As I pleaded, I suddenly felt the presence of someone in my room. I opened my eyes to look but saw no one. I instead felt a dumbfounding peace that engulfed me to the point where my anxiety subsided and I was able to think with clarity and go about my business. Glory be to God.

A couple of days later, in the middle of the week, I saw Billy Graham on television and felt an enormous compassion coming from him that melted me away and caught all of my attention. I don't remember his message, but his words moved me to the point where I began to urgently desire what he was conveying. He made the altar call, and I saw people in a huge stadium running to the altar from everywhere to take what he'd been offering. I started to panic, because I wanted to run to the front, too, but couldn't from my living room, and my heart sank in my chest with disappointment; but thank God for immediately moving Billy to say that if you were at home and couldn't come up to the front, you could just do it at home by putting your hand on the TV as a point of contact. I was gratefully relieved as I did. He led me to the Lord at that moment and at the closing of his ministering, said: "And don't forget to go to church this Sunday." Those words stayed with me, and I sought out a friend and neighbor who had become a Christian before me and who lived on my same floor, and asked her if I could go to church with her that Sunday. She happily obliged.

I've been saved for twenty-three years now, by the grace and mercy of God, and during my most difficult times in my walk, when I felt unsure about continuing, and when I was tempted to walk away from Jesus, I would come across Billy Graham again on TV, and God would speak through him regarding my very situation and encourage me. Praise be to God. I love Billy with a special love and gratitude that I can only feel toward him, because it was him that God used so that I might receive the forgiveness of my sins and salvation through Jesus Christ.

Thank you for your love for the Lord, your commitment, and dedication, Billy. My life has never been the same since I saw that first telecast in 1984, and you've been a source of encouragement for me many times after that. You became selfless when you came to Christ and accepted His calling on your life, that I might one day receive newness of life, and I can't thank you enough for sacrificing for me like that. I love you dearly and look forward to one day meeting with you in heaven.

Mayra

I KEEP PRAYING AND READING SCRIPTURE

Dear Mr. Graham: I heard you speak in Detroit, Michigan, when I was a teenager. I gave my heart to Jesus at your crusade but fell along the way. I believe I'm on the right track now. I attempted suicide in 2005 and believe that God gave me a miracle, because my life was spared with no residual effects. I give thanks to God every day for that! I keep praying and reading scripture every day in hopes that I will be forgiven, and I ask God to help me one day at a time. Your presence in my life as a teenager and at the present time (I'm now sixty-one) is what keeps me going each day. I thank you so very much for all that you have given me and this world. May God bless you and your family.

I Could Feel God's Love
through My Daughter's Birth

During the free-spirited summer of 1969, at the young age of fourteen and while still a virgin, I found myself in a musky, dark apartment being violently raped by an older teenager. In retrospect, I believe I may have been very near to death through that experience, as I was "floating" above my own innocent, bloody, and defeated body. I remember feeling so sorry for "her." I could see every single bad thing that was being done to me. It was both disgusting and horrifying to me, but I did survive. I awoke to find myself changed, permanently tainted (I thought), and on a direct path of careless self-destruction. My idea of love and affection was drastically skewed, and I lived the rest of my teenage years in a post-traumatic mental state. I hated myself, and I even hated my own name. As if I were not even alive, and now unable (without God) to make good life choices, I repeatedly mutilated my own body by allowing nearly every male I dated to abuse me sexually. Having no relationship with God, this was not a very hard thing for a girl to do, even though I despised every single thing about sex. Despised it. Sadly, because of these events, my heart and soul grew void and dark, beyond description. Deep depression and crying spells came.

At age nineteen, and in another abusive relationship, I became pregnant with my precious daughter. The day she was born, I somehow knew there was a God who loved me. My daughter's birth was a miracle to me. I could feel God's love through her! I could see it! I had a sudden, anxious hunger to be cleansed. I wanted to make everything in my life all right but didn't know how to do it. I do not remember the specifics, but some wonderful Christian gave me Billy Graham's book *Peace With God*, and I read it as quickly as I could. Not many days passed before I gave my heart and soul to Jesus Christ. Now at fifty-eight years old, I can say the journey has been long and not always easy, but I was cleansed and reconciled to the One who created me. I praise His sweet and Holy name for saving my life and soul.

Teresa Grace (I gave myself this middle name.)

MANY THANKS

I became born again in 1981. Since that time, I was fortunate enough to meet some young Christians who guided me in my journey. I have always watched Billy Graham on TV, when he was at many different crusades. I was honored to serve at one of Franklin Graham's crusades in the 1990s at a small arena in Niagara Falls, Ontario.

It was a very difficult time in my life during that crusade. I was director of evangelism at a local church when I found out that my husband (now ex) was stealing money from our church and had borrowed money from some very close friends in the church, saying it was for me. Many so-called believers rejected me and turned their backs on me. It was a nightmare.

My husband was a very bad, compulsive gambler and had started a Gamblers Anonymous group at our church. But he could not break the habit and was charged with theft and was awaiting a jail sentence. During the time of the crusade, I was devastated and broken.

I volunteered at the office that was doing the work in preparation for the crusade. I served there and applied for a counselor's position for the crusade. Never have I been closer to the Lord, and I wrote on my application that God was my breath (for indeed He is).

When I received an answer concerning my application for counselor, I was overwhelmed that I had been chosen to be a supervisor at the crusade. I felt very unworthy, particularly because of the embarrassment and humiliation I was suffering because of my husband.

When I went to the crusade, I was so shocked to be sitting with a group of pastors. The people who had rejected me saw that I was in that group, and that broke me how great God's love is. I felt a bit like Christ, who was rejected and beaten.

I am so thankful to the Lord and the Billy Graham Evangelistic ministry. The crusade experience saved me and helped me heal my broken spirit. I was honored to pray with a young girl, share the steps to peace with God, and ultimately share in the joy of a new convert.

God is so good, and I thank you, Billy, and the rest of your team for a lifetime of ministry and how God has so richly blessed those who love Him.

ONE BOY LOOKING FOR THE CREATOR

God bless you, Billy Graham and family, for giving up each other's time for the anointed calling in your lives. I lived my young life always on the road, staying (living) with many people. My mother was in hiding from her past. I was fortunate to have God come to me as my protector from things chasing my mother and me. God showed himself to me in a dream when I was a child—as a gigantic rainbow with a blinding glow. My mother was agnostic; therefore, we did not go to church or even watch it on television. However, I knew that rainbow from my dream was more than a dream, because the next day (after the dream), I started feeling a much higher presence than myself. A short time later, while watching TV, I heard Billy Graham speaking of God the Father and Jesus Christ. Time went by (unsure how much), and I crawled to the cross and into the arms of our Lord and Savior Jesus Christ. Thank you, Billy, for giving the Holy Gospel the way it's meant.

Chad

THE NIGHT GOD CAME INTO MY HEART

My name is Meg. My husband and I live in Kentucky, where he is an equine veterinarian. We have two wonderful children and have a very blessed life here. The Lord has been very good to us all of our lives. Growing up, I was raised in a Christian home and taken to church every Sunday and Wednesday. Of course, our home was not perfect, but we knew we were loved and that our parents cared for us very much.

I was the youngest of four children, and I was very soft-hearted. I watched the Billy Graham crusades on television quite regularly with my mother, whenever they would come on. One particular night, while watching a certain sermon, I became convicted by the Holy Spirit and started crying while listening to the message of Dr. Graham. He was preaching about our sins and how we were in need of a Savior. I knew that without Jesus, I would die in my sin and go to hell forever. I knew that I did not want to go there, so I prayed the sinner's prayer and asked Jesus into my heart. After the broadcast was over, I talked with my mother more in length about the decision I had made, and I knew I was born again! I wrote to Dr. Graham and received the literature he sent to help me with my walk with Christ. Of course, I have never regretted that decision to follow Christ.

God has always been more than faithful and has seen me through some very tough times. He has blessed me with a Christian husband, and both of our children have accepted Christ into their hearts. Jesus is absolutely my very best and dearest friend. He has never left me, and I know He never will. To God be the glory!

Thank you, Dr. Billy Graham, for being obedient to the call to follow Christ and proclaim the message to the lost and dying. Because of your faithfulness, I came to know Jesus Christ as my Lord and Savior. I will forever be grateful to you.

Thank You, Billy Graham. . .
for *Saving My Life*

SAVED AT NIAGARA FALLS

In 1960, someone handed me a book with testimonies of some of the people who had been saved at a Billy Graham crusade. I was sitting in my car trying to get the courage to jump over Niagara Falls and end my life. As I read the testimonies, I thought that maybe Jesus could change my life, too. And I could always come back next week and jump.

I had a tract in my hand, and I prayed the prayer on the back and asked Jesus to forgive all my sins. God changed my life that day. For all these years, I have followed the Lord, reared eleven children, and have been in full-time ministry for many years. I have seen thousands of people saved through SOS Ministries USA, which my husband and I founded in 2001. Thank you, Billy Graham, for your faithfulness and being instrumental in my life. Also, my son-in-law was saved watching you on TV. His family (five children) are now faithfully serving the Lord.

DELIVERED

My seventeen-year-old sister and I were living on the edge in San Diego. We were doing drugs, going from man to man, doing everything under the sun except serving God. We were raised in church, but we were as far away from that as we could get.

My sister was dating a guy who was using LSD. Before long, she was doing it, too. I was strictly into pills: uppers and downers. We would stay stoned from Friday to Monday morning, pulling it together only long enough to go to school and work.

One night, a nervous Johnny dropped my sister off and peeled off in his Camaro like the devil was chasing him. It turned out my sister was overdosing. She started screaming at the top of her lungs, clawing at her face and arms. "Get the spiders off," she cried. "There's a dead man! Make him get away! He's come to get me! The skeletons! Skeletons are trying to eat me!" She cried like a baby. I held her through the night until she started to come down. It was horrible.

I didn't have the presence of mind to take her to the hospital. I prayed for the first time in a long time. "Lord please help us." Thank God, she didn't die. However, that was just the beginning. She returned to that hellish place in her mind many, many times thereafter. Mostly without warning. Sometimes in public. She had to drop out of college.

It was fear that stopped me in my tracks that night. Your crusade was on TV. My mom sang in the choir at your Baton Rouge crusade. I remembered your literature coming to the house during my teenage years.

"It's youth night," the announcer said. You came on and immediately pulled out all the stops. It seemed you knew everything we'd been doing. By the end of your sermon, I was crying like a baby. I prayed the prayer. You said to get in a good church, so I started asking around. I hadn't been in church in eleven years. One of our partying girlfriends told us about a church she had grown up with nearby. I went there the next day, even though it wasn't Sunday. When I walked in the door of the Baptist church, some people were sitting around a table in a meeting room off the foyer. It turned out to be the board of trustees meeting.

"Can we help you?" asked a kind, older man. "My sister, she's on drugs," I said. "We need help." I told them the story. They prayed and asked me to bring my sister. We went the next Sunday. That was the beginning of my walk with the Lord.

Today, I am rooted and grounded and established in the Lord. I'm a member of a church in Houston. I love the Lord with all my heart, soul, and mind. He is the center around which everything flows. Life has not been a bed of roses. There's a devil loose. However, I know without a shadow of a doubt that if you hadn't been there that fateful night, neither my sister nor I would be alive today. Your message opened the door to a new world, to a new life. I am a new creature in Christ Jesus.

Tish

THE WORDS THAT SAVED MY LIFE

As a young girl, I was among the runaway/throwaway children living on a Ft. Lauderdale beach. I was either hiding or trying to sleep under bridges. I was bounced around in Christian runaway shelters and foster care homes from ages twelve to eighteen. I was hated by my mother for looking like her mother-in-law. I was seen only as a financial burden. I was thrown away and unloved.

I was considering suicide one day when I found a book by Pastor Graham. The book said that someone loved me and gave His life up freely on the cross! God loved me! Well, that fifteen-year-old child knelt by the water, cried, prayed, and asked God to be her Father.

I rose and saw the sky, and decided to stay alive! If it were not for Jesus and the book Mr. Graham wrote that gave me hope, that girl I was long ago would have died. From my two sons and grandson, who would not have been born if not for your words, we say, "Thank you, Billy Graham!"

THE GREAT INTERRUPTION

I was born in Chicago in 1952 to parents who had recently arrived from Puerto Rico. My parents were simple and poor people, my mother went to school barefoot and got only as far as the second grade, and my father was able to complete high school in the army, where he served during World War II.

My father became an alcoholic throughout most of our growing years, and as we six kids grew up without any direction or discipline, we all went our own reckless ways. At the age of fifteen, I left home, with my mother's permission, to get married. She thought nothing of it. I got caught up in a relationship with a young man who did not know anything about taking care of someone, let alone the two children who came later. I was beaten and left to take care of myself. Eventually, I left and went back home.

After finding employment, I went out on my own and lived as a single parent. Six years later, I legally married another young man who also knew nothing about being a husband and left me for another woman. As time went on, my life consisted of the party life—getting high, depressed, and of course the typical sinful lifestyle. One night, while high on marijuana, I changed the channel on the TV and began listening to the Rev. Billy Graham. As he spoke, all I heard were words that assured me that God was actually speaking to me directly. I called the number as instructed and gave my life to Christ. The next day, I recalled what I had done, but I did not understand to what extent it would take me.

During that time, I began to notice that I was not thinking the same, and my brother contacted me to tell me that he had his church praying for me. I got excited, and when he visited me, he planted me in a church he had attended. I was thirty years old. Today, I'm fifty-five and still loving and serving the Lord. I have served in the church as nursery director, Sunday school teacher, director of women's ministry, and so many wonderful acts of service. My life has not been without trials, but God has grown me up, and I know my purpose for living. I have shared the Gospel with many people, and just recently with a woman on her deathbed. I am wholeheartly grateful to Rev. Billy Graham. I love him and esteem him. He is my Moses. May the Lord continue to bless and keep him.

Gloria

BILLY SAVED MY LIFE

In mid-1975, I was five months pregnant, back living with my mother, and looking to get a divorce started. I was in an awful relationship, and I had just about had enough of being beaten every other day. I still had bruises all over me from the last beating as I sat in Mom's living room and saw Billy Graham on TV. *Yeah, yeah,* I thought, and was about to switch it off, when Billy Graham seemed to look straight at me. He seemed to be talking directly to me when he asked this question: "Have you given your heart to the Lord?" I watched the complete broadcast, and that night I sat in my bed with my Bible and prayed for the first time in seven years. I now had hope. Thank you, Billy, for saving my life!

SAVED FROM THE BRINK

Mr. Graham, I thank God that your crusade came to my hometown of Niagara Falls, New York. At the time, I was working part time, going through a divorce, and drinking every day. I had four children and knew I wasn't doing right by them, but I just couldn't stop. As I was waiting for the bus one day, I noticed on the side an advertisement for one of your crusades at the convention center. That night, I was drinking again and decided to walk down the street to the center to see the crusade. It was being led by Leighton Ford.

I remember sitting in my seat when he called for people to come up and receive Jesus. I do not remember taking that walk—I only know that I ended up in the front, crying uncontrollably. I accepted Jesus that night, and one of the workers talked to me for quite a while and gave me some literature to read. I walked in the rain that night after the crusade and felt truly cleansed. That was the beginning of my walk with Jesus.

I've learned since then it doesn't happen all at once; and I didn't change overnight, but I know without a doubt that God is with me in my walk and I continue to grow in my faith. I thank you for all the books you have written and the crusades you have put on, for they have been a great source of inspiration to me and have helped me in my journey. I know they will continue to do so.

Thank You, Billy Graham. . .
for Everything

My Salvation Experience

I have long wanted to write to thank you for your faithfulness to the Lord. I was saved after listening to one of your crusades, televised on September 9, 1976. God had been dealing with me about my spiritual condition since I was a young teen. I just didn't feel good enough to go to heaven. For many years, I went through periods when I struggled with my sinfulness, and as I got older, it got more intense and more frequent. I got married and started visiting a Bible-teaching church with my wife. When I heard the Gospel, I knew it held the answer to what I needed. After a week of revival at that church, and listening to the evangelist preach and give the invitation, I knew I needed to accept Christ; but I just couldn't give up, I had so many questions that I felt I needed answered. The night after the revival ended, I was at home thinking about what the preacher had said, and I was in so much turmoil. It was then that I turned on the TV to provide some distraction, so that I could get this salvation stuff off of my mind. The TV came on and there was Billy preaching the Gospel. I got up to change the channel, but when I got to the TV, I just couldn't do it. I sat down on the floor in front of the TV and listened to Billy preach. The Holy Spirit had him say the things I needed to hear to give up the struggle, and when the invitation was given and "Just As I Am" was being sung, I gave my heart to Christ there in my living room. I am so thankful for the faithfulness of Rev. Graham and his team. Since then, my wife and three kids have been saved. I have taught Sunday school and been a deacon in the church and a witnessing Christian. I felt it was time to send a personal thank you.

Barry

MOM AND THE BOTTLE

My mother, who passed on to her reward in heaven last year, accompanied me to the Carrier Dome in Syracuse in 1989 to see Dr. Graham. Mom had been battling the bottle for more than twenty years at that point (since the loss of my grandfather in 1969), and she was struggling again after the loss of my dad, her husband of nearly forty years, in 1987. She knew that unless she found a direction for her life, she would eventually lose this battle. Dr. Graham's words reached down inside her like no one's ever had before! She took his message to heart—to give her life to Christ—and the healing began that very day! She began to attend church regularly and to *look forward to it* for the first time since I was a little boy. After several months, the change in her was remarkable! Her life *was* Christ's! She'd found her way to God at last, and Dr. Graham was the signpost. So completely did she change that she never went near the bottle again and never even *wanted* to. I believe now, and will believe to my dying day, that Dr. Graham saved her very soul! Thank you, Billy, from the bottom of my heart!

"I WILL"

I was leaving work one day and heard on the radio that a Billy Graham crusade was going on. Something prodded me to go, and I thought there was no way I would be able to get tickets or parking. But I thought I would drive by. Right in front of the stadium was a parking spot waiting for me. So I parked and headed up to the stadium. When I saw security, I thought, *This will be the end of this.* Instead, they waved me in to the stadium. I thought, *Well, I'll be in the nosebleed section and barely hear him.* Well, some man waved me down the aisle to a door and down some stairs to a seat that was directly across from Billy Graham. I was stunned. I listened to him talk. He called for those who would give their lives to Jesus. I felt someone picking me up, and I walked right up to the front of the stage and looked at Billy and said, "I will." He saved my life that day, and I will never forget Billy Graham.

CHRISTIAN FARMER

As a young farm lad, I loved to listen to Billy Graham's *Hour of Decision* on the radio. I remember sitting in my farm ute out in the paddocks, listening intently and not wanting to miss a word, and to hear the entire programme before going back to the homestead for dinner.

When I heard about the Melbourne crusade in 1969, I quickly made plans to attend. I traveled the 350 kilometres with a friend from our tiny bush church. When Billy extended the invitation to accept Christ, I went forward, along with many others. I was not left standing for long; soon a volunteer counselor approached me and guided me through helpful literature about giving your life to Christ. It was an unforgettable experience. The counselor kept in touch with me after my return to the farm, and over several weeks I was guided on my new walk with Christ.

It is now thirty-eight years since I made that decision; I remember that crusade as if it were last week. I have since married, and we have four adult children. I take part in many

Christian activities, such as roles in our little church, camps, and seminars. Due to our geographic isolation, we cannot attend city gatherings, but we are blessed by printed and Internet material from many sources, including Billy Graham literature, which helps our understanding of the Bible and our growth in Jesus. I am always grateful for his unique style and total commitment to God.

THANK YOU FOR GIVING TO THE LORD

Like the song "Thank You for Giving to the Lord," Billy, you have given yourself to the Lord, dedicated your whole life for His work. Mine is a life that has changed, and I just wanted to say thank you, Billy. Thank God for you and your ministry.

Shirley

THANK YOU FOR BLESSING
US WITH YOUR MINISTRY

Ever since I was old enough to watch TV, my family and I would run to the black-and-white television and watch Billy Graham. It was a time of celebration for our family. Through much chaos happening around us, we were always blessed in rural Mississippi by watching you on TV. Thank you, Billy, for blessing us with your ministry.

FROM A FREIGHT DOCK

As a young woman, age nineteen or twenty, I worked at McClellan Air Force Base, in Sacramento, California, as a clerk typist, before going on to college. One day, an order was handed down that anyone who wanted to could leave work and go hear Billy Graham speak. (I'd like to see that happen in government today.) There he stood on a freight dock as the people assembled. The power of God came with the words that Billy spoke to us that day. I'll never forget it, though it was nearly sixty years ago, that great godly man standing on a freight dock, delivering the same message he's always delivered: God loves you, and He'll change your life if you invite Jesus into your heart. Thank you, Billy, for faithful service to our Master, regardless of the circumstances.

JESUS AS MY LORD

I first came to Christ when I was fifteen, through reading the Bible and listening to Christian programs on television. I was at a point of suicide in my teenage years, but I accepted Christ one night in 1973 while watching a Billy Graham crusade. I knelt and asked Jesus to be my personal Savior and then wrote to the address given on the television.

I was sent the Gospel of John and read it. I memorized the cards given to me as well, filled out the questions and sent them in, and received my certificate from the Association. I still have that certificate to this day.

Soon after becoming a Christian, I was excited about the idea of becoming a missionary in Africa—specifically Uganda (where Idi Amin was in control at the time). As I started going to church, I did not get proper discipleship and did not understand making Christ the Lord of my life. My mother died when I was nineteen, and we moved to a new town in southern Illinois, where I knew no one. I had lost so much, and I was really struggling. I went into the business world and became a very hard worker (which was my way of dealing with the pain inside all of the losses).

At the age of twenty-nine, I came out of a two-year

relationship with an alcoholic (whom I almost married) and thought it was the end of the world again—though I never forgot Jesus and what He did for me. I continued to remember that.

In July 1987, Billy Graham did a crusade in Denver, and I went with my little sister from Big Sisters of Colorado—and both of us, with tears streaming down our eyes, went forward. This time, the Lord made it clear that He was more than just my Savior but also my Lord, and He wanted to be everything to me in my life. I then, at the age of thirty-two, left my job (where I was making a good salary) and went to school at Colorado Christian University. I began to prepare for missions. I am now a missionary in Uganda, working with orphans and AIDS patients. Thank you for sharing, Billy Graham, and loving people enough to do so. May the Lord bless you now and in heaven (and I know He will).

HAPPY MEMORIES

My father, my friend, and I packed a lunch and headed out to Flushing Meadows to hear Billy Graham. We had no idea what the day would bring, but we knew it was something my father, Harry, who was ninety-five at the time, would love to witness. He had been a Christian most of his life and had helped many people along his journey. He listened to Billy speak whenever he could.

When we got to the park, it was packed and very hot. We were afraid Dad would get overheated, but God guided us to one of the only shaded areas in the park. Because of Dad's age, the guards let us stay there and listen to the speakers. It was an amazing day, and although Dad was losing his eyesight, he was still able to hear everything that was said. He was so happy to be there and witness all the love that was there. He thanked us so many times for bringing him there to hear Billy speak.

My father went to be with the Lord this year, but I'm so glad we had this opportunity. We just wanted to let you know that one of the happiest days of his life was spent with you. Thank you for doing God's will and spreading the message; heaven knows how much we need it.

HE SPOKE AS ONE WHO HAD AUTHORITY

Throughout my life, it has been the voice that gets me. No matter where I have found myself, if that voice is on the television or radio, I am compelled to stop and listen. The message is so simple and so clear that it draws me back to all that matters—my relationship with Christ and where I will spend eternity. I am compelled to listen, because like the Savior he directs me to, Billy Graham speaks "as one who has authority."

I have worked in the field of child protection all my adult life. I have seen and served children who are beaten, burned, bound, bludgeoned, raped, and murdered. This work, combined with the ordinary sadness we all face, has on many occasions left me with a hole in my heart and an unbearable ache in my soul.

And yet, in my darkest hours, as if God had it planned, I have mysteriously found that voice while sitting in my hotel room flipping around the television channels or radio dials. Every time I hear the voice, I feel a greater presence.

I've seen Billy Graham only once, at a crusade in Sioux Falls. He began his sermon by saying he had good news and bad news. The good news was that he had spoken with the weather service and the storm clouds behind him were at least an hour away. The bad news, he said, was that he had called the weather service an hour ago.

He spoke for only a few minutes that day as the storm descended on us. I don't remember how many people stayed in the rain. I only remember that I did. I had to. The voice compelled me.

Victor

WELL DONE, MY GOOD AND FAITHFUL SERVANT

Jesus came to earth to make everlasting life available to us all. He sacrificed his life on the cross, teaching us about God's love. Billy Graham has spent his entire life repeating this same story to the world, in order that all who hear and believe will be saved through Jesus Christ our Lord. Thank you, Billy Graham and the Graham family and evangelistic team, for your lives of service to God. We all must strive to be good and faithful servants. May the story continue be told, and to God be the glory.

JUST AS WE WERE

My husband and son attended one of Dr. Billy's crusades at a university stadium in Houston. I don't remember the year or the exact location, but I will never forget the experience. Our hearts were so tugged to go forward. We had been believers since childhood, but Dr. Graham's message compelled us to go down and rededicate our lives that evening. I am so grateful for his dedication to our Lord. He is such an inspiration, and he has passed that to his son. Thank you, Billy Graham.

BEAUTIFUL STORY

I wish I was able to write what I feel in my heart about how you have helped me hold on to my faith in God our Lord Jesus Christ. I know if I could, it would be one of the most beautiful stories in the world. Through your television crusades, I have learned, felt shame, begged for forgiveness, become closer to God, and was made aware of what is really important—my life with God. I hope when we are in heaven I will be able to tell you, "Thanks, Billy Graham."

Christine

MY DAY OF SALVATION

Brother Billy, just a short note to thank you for the one and only time (I believe) that you came to the University of Florida for a one-day crusade. Although I had been raised in the Methodist Church, it was the first time I was challenged by the Holy Spirit to receive Jesus as my Savior. God bless you, and thanks from the bottom of my heart.

Steve

THE GOODNESS OF OUR GOD

Dear Dr. Billy Graham, I just wanted to say thank you. Thank you for allowing God to use you over the airwaves for these many years. I remember, as a child, my grandmother listening to you on the radio. What a blessing. Then, a number of years ago, I had the privilege of seeing you at the Nassau Coliseum in Uniondale, New York. I'll never forget that night. One day, when we all get to the other side, we'll sit and reflect about the goodness of our God.

Carol

THROUGH YOUR WORKERS

During your Houston crusade (1963?), after the message, my twin sister Barbara and I simultaneously got up from our seats to answer your call to those who wished to come forward to "be saved." When we reached the arena floor, we were met by one of your workers (prayer team). He looked only at my sister and asked her, "How do you know you are saved?" She answered, "Because God told me so." I remember looking at her, astonished, and thinking, *I didn't hear anything.* I remember that I had the desire, but for some reason I didn't internalize it. I have always believed that you were certainly served by people in your ministry who were really in tune with God.

Thankfully, ten years later, watching a program on TBN in our apartment one afternoon, I realized I had never prayed to receive Jesus as my Lord and Savior. That day, I knelt and asked Him into my life, remembering the words my sister had said. In my heart, I heard His words as well!

When my husband came home that evening, I told him about my experience, and he thought I had gone nuts. He would not listen to me at all, even when I showed him scriptures. He said, "Oh, that's just a Baptist Bible anyway (which completely hurt me, as I wanted him to receive the assurance and joy that I was experiencing).

After several tries, I realized I couldn't save him. God showed me that it was He who would save him; all I had to do was to pray and trust Him. I was able to give my husband over to the Lord, and exactly two days later, he prayed and asked God into his heart, after seeing the change in my life. That Sunday, God blessed us as we were both baptized the same day.

Due to your crusade worker's sensitivity to God's Spirit ten years earlier, in knowing just what to ask or say—and to whom, I was prepared later (and also my husband) to personally receive Him. Another ten or eleven years later, our son also received Him. Thank you, Billy.

WALKING THE AISLE

My family plays Gospel music. My sisters wrote a song called "The Road To Calvary" as a result of the many times our dad would sit and watch your crusades. He is blind now, but he recalls the times when he could still see and he would watch as thousands came forward to accept Christ while the choir sang "Just As I Am."

Sitting in his recliner one night, he was watching your crusade, and just like many times before, the choir began to sing and Dad said that, in his mind, he watched as people got up from their seats to step forward to make a bold confession of their need for Christ. He said that, even though he was sitting in his chair at home, in his heart and spirit he got up and made his way to that old-fashioned altar. Now his kids do the same thing frequently.

We've served the Lord for many years, and we still make a trip with others, walking the aisle. Jesus walks the aisles of our hearts, and when he beckons for us to come and receive of His grace and mercy, we simply cannot refuse. Your ministry is precious, as is the Christ you serve. One day, we will look upon His wonderful face as He says, "Well done, thou good and faithful servant."

ONCE WAS ENOUGH!

I am an African American female who grew up in a small town in Mississippi. I watched Dr. Graham on our black-and-white TV set. It was hard growing up in the South during the 1960s, but when I saw Dr. Graham on television, I knew in my heart that there *is* a God and that things could be so much better, if I trusted Him.

At the end of each sermon, Dr. Graham gave an invitation to accept Christ. No matter how many times I watched him on television, I accepted Christ over and over and over again, each time he gave the invitation. Until one day, listening to him preach, I came to realize that when I accepted what my Lord and Savior had done for me on the cross, and asked for His forgiveness, and believed in my heart that He is the Son of God, I was saved. *Once was enough!*

I HAD HELL SCARED RIGHT OUT OF ME

I've been a churchgoer all my life. I like to say I was born on a "Baptist blanket." More than that, I have loved Jesus as far back as I can remember. Why, I was even baptized at the age of five. I was so mad at Peter for denying Jesus that I wanted to be baptized.

Then, in December 1969, I was listening to Mr. Graham on the televsion. He was preaching about hell. The Holy Ghost had been dealing with me for about six months that I wasn't truly a Christian—that my belief and security were resting in those baptismal waters. And then, that is exactly what Billy Graham said—that our faith and security had to be in the person of Jesus Christ. Then he talked about how awful hell would be—that we would be all alone in darkness, forever separated from the God who loves us. Well, that scared hell right out of me! When Mr. Graham called for the invitation, I knelt beside my television and received Jesus Christ as my Savior. I was baptized a second time—this time for the right reason—as a show of what Christ has done for me. Thank you, Billy Graham! I am a life that was changed. I'll see you in heaven.

THANKS, BILLY!

Dear Billy, I've read your columns in our newspaper every day for the last twenty years. Your columns have been instrumental in developing my relationship with Jesus Christ. Thank you for all you have done over the years, for me and for countless millions around the world, pointing us to the Lord Jesus Christ and His truth. God bless you and your family. Keep it going!

GOD IS LOVE

I was raised to believe in God and Jesus, so I had the basics. But we were not encouraged to read the Bible. God was always someone I was afraid of. I learned about Jesus, but I didn't think of him as my Brother, or how prayer can change lives, until the first time many years ago when I tuned in to Billy Graham on television. Through his preaching, Billy Graham unlocked the door for me to have a personal relationship with Jesus. I began to see that I didn't have to *earn* salvation, that it was a gift. All the good works were good to do, but they were not how I was going to get to heaven. Billy Graham opened my eyes and my heart to the truth that God loves me and that salvation is a gift for the asking. I consider Billy Graham as my first step on my walk with the Lord. I began to read the Bible, to really pray and spend time with the Lord each day. I went to a crusade that he gave in Philadelphia some time ago, and I remember looking at the thousands of people who were listening to Billy Graham that day and feeling the strong presence of the Lord there as well. Billy Graham has been a strong influence in my life, and words could never convey how much he has helped me and opened my eyes to the love of my Savior Jesus.

A BLESSED TIME TO REMEMBER

Our United Methodist youth group in a little town in Iowa (population 400) raised money all spring long so that we could rent a bus with a group from Ames to go to the Explo '72 crusade in Dallas, Texas. We did many things, including a spaghetti dinner, and also sold our strong arms (doing work for people) to raise money. It was my first time to be so far away from home without my parents. We had a great time during the days we were there. I accepted Jesus as my Lord and Savior during this crusade. The stadium was so full and crowded the night that I accepted Jesus that we did not walk to the front as you normally would have people do. Instead, we stood up where we were on the stadium field and prayed the prayer as you guided us. I was seventeen years old.

Today, I am fifty-three years old, and I still remember that time with great love and thankfulness. Our group came back to Iowa with the fire of the Holy Spirit in us, and we spoke in many churches about our time at the crusade. We took another group the very next year to St. Paul, Minnesota, to Key '73. Our church was blessed because of those crusades. While at the St. Paul crusade, I volunteered to sing in the choir. I enjoyed that very much. When I hear the familiar songs of the crusades, even now, my heart is warmed and I sing along with them.

My life has brought me many trials and hardships, but my faith has always carried me through. I'm so thankful for Billy Graham's crusades, for helping me build a strong relationship with my Lord Jesus. I can truthfully say I have felt God's love and guidance my whole life since then. Praise the Lord!

YOUTH CRUSADE ON TELEVISION, CIRCA 1962

My younger brother and sister were asleep, and my mother had gone out for the evening. I was fifteen years old and was sitting on the couch watching TV. My parents were divorced. I wasn't doing well in school, and I liked to run around with the other teens who were drinking and smoking. I was depressed all the time, and I had been molested by my mother's ex-boyfriend. I went to the Catholic church when I was younger but had stopped going. I talked to God once in a while but didn't know if He really heard me or not.

As I turned the channels, I came across something that looked interesting. On the screen was a man in a stadium somewhere, talking to the youth. He said things that really touched my heart. I remember because I started crying. He held my interest, and when he had finished speaking, he said, "If you're watching this on TV, come and kneel in front of the television and give your life to Jesus." I knelt in front of the TV and prayed with Billy Graham, and I now know that Jesus did come into my heart and life.

I didn't call or write to Billy afterward. Not realizing exactly what I had done, I kept on with the way I was living. Many years later, I finally gained the understanding I needed and have been serving the Lord ever since. My mother used to tell me that I must have the best guardian angels watching over me, because I lived in spite of my behavior.

Now, forty-five years later, I am still alive and serving the Lord. Thank you, Billy Graham, for your love, faithfulness, and obedience to God. You pointed me in the right direction, and Jesus came into my heart at the most difficult time of my life. Even though I didn't change right away, God was with me, and I wouldn't have made it without Him. I've told many people about you over the years and told them how much I love and respect you. God bless you forever.

Lynn

BORN AGAIN

I want to share my story of how God used the faithful preaching of Billy Graham to introduce me to a relationship with Jesus Christ. I was born in Uniontown, Pennsylvania, on April 10, 1940, the youngest of five children. There was a ten-year difference between my nearest sibling and me. My mother always said I was a mistake. My father was an alcoholic, but I considered him a good man. He taught me how to cook, helped me with my homework, and was always there for me in my life. He wasn't a violent man, he just kept to himself until he died. He and my mother never got along.

When I was four, we moved to Washington, DC, where I attended Catholic school. My dad was a Catholic and my mother was a Protestant. We lived very near the DC Armory, which held many different attractions. So many people attended these shows that they would park their automobiles all along our street and walk to the armory. One particular day, I asked my mother, "Who are these people going to see at the armory today?" She replied, "Some preacher called

Billy Graham." I never forgot that name!

After I graduated from high school, I worked at Catholic University as a secretary. When I was twenty years old, I met my husband-to-be. He was a musician. We married, both twenty-one, and traveled a bit. When I became pregnant, we settled in New Jersey for about three years. During that time, I was watching TV one night when I heard a gentleman introduce a man called Billy Graham. I finally got to see this person I had always wondered about. I didn't know that I had to be "born again" in order to get to heaven. When I finished listening to him speak, I cried and gave my heart to the Lord. My husband was working at the time. I told him later about my experience, but it didn't seem to faze him. Nevertheless, years later, before he died, he gave his heart to the Lord as well.

Thank you, Mr. Graham, for never giving up on the world. Your teachings have changed my life forever, and millions of others. God bless you and your family.

Judy

THE COVE

The ministry of The Cove covered me for about five years. I was able to see it as a home, and it was the place where I could walk in the woods and just talk to God. The Spirit-filled rooms and seminars, the fireplaces and hot chocolate, all the good conversations with like-minded people—all blessed me immensely. The Cove was part of Billy Graham's vision, and through it I came closer to God. Thank you, Billy and Ruth Graham, for all that you have given me. Your ministry and your willingness to follow the Lord's leading changed me in ways you could never know until eternity.

A LIFE WORTH SAVING

I first was introduced to the Rev. Billy Graham at the age of seventeen, while channel surfing one night. At this time of my life, I was very depressed and I thought of suicide. I saw Rev. Graham and listened to his service and was deeply moved to tears. I had gone to church all my life, but I hadn't given my life to God until that night. I called in, someone prayed with me, and I surrendered my life to God.

I later received reading and lesson materials to enhance my commitment, which I enjoyed very much. That day, I took my life a step further and joined a church, and in that church my love and closeness for the Lord grew. Seeing Rev. Graham's service that night was the foundation I needed to be rooted in the Lord. Despite all the trials and tribulations that may come my way, I now know that the Lord is with me and He loves me, and I have leaned on him ever since. It all started with that night of watching Rev. Graham's moving service. Thank you, Rev. Graham, for saving my life.

Theresa

ONE OF THE MILLIONS

Dear Billy: I would presume to call you by your first name, not for lack of the deepest regard and gratitude, but because you are, to me, a friend. I am a brother who is counting on walking and talking with you someday. Your life has blessed and shaped mine since I was a child growing up in rural Oklahoma. I am one of the millions of lives you have touched who will probably never get to tell you on this earth—*thank you!* My eyes filled with tears and yearning to have you know how deeply grateful I am for your unashamed love of Jesus.

John

JOINED A FRIEND

Billy had spoken and made the altar call, and my friend felt she was called to go forward. So as not to lose each other in the crowd, the rest of us went with her. When we got to the floor, I burst into tears. A helper came to me, and I ended up rededicating my life to Christ and have never looked back. My husband and I went on to Bible school and continue to follow after Christ to this day. Thank God my friend (whom I have now lost track of) was called to the altar of Christ, for my life was turned around, and I serve Christ to this day. Thank you, Billy Graham and your family, for the giving of your lives so others are saved.

A LONG OVERDUE THANK-YOU

Many times over the years, the Lord spoke to my heart to write to Billy Graham with thanks and gratitude for my life-changing experience. Finally, I replied to the Lord, "How will I do this?" I did not expect the answer to come from turning on the television.

A few days later, I was amazed to hear about the Thank You, Billy Graham website that allows people to not only send their thanks and gratitude but also to share their stories. No way was this a coincidence.

My life-changing experience began when I was a young teenager. Although I was a Christian, I had not yet experienced the power of the Holy Spirit. I was invited to attend a Billy Graham crusade with a friend. I had no idea what this was but thought it sounded like a good way to get out of the house. We rode on the church bus to the crusade, which was a very quiet ride. At the end of the service, I attended the altar call. I was anointed with a glorious experience, but I was not sure what was happening. We returned home on the bus, singing and praising the Lord—a very different experience from the bus ride going to the crusade. This was the night that changed my life forever.

For the next thirty years, my life continued with marriage, children, self-employed business, college, and other events. During the years, my family and I journeyed through many of life's challenges. No matter how difficult the situation was, we always overcame by the power of the Holy Spirit through Jesus Christ.

Thank you, Billy Graham, for being part of my supernatural experience with the Holy Spirit. I cannot express enough what a life-changing experience this was. Daily, I seek to serve and love the Lord. Each day, I continue to seek the Holy Spirit with a love that keeps growing more and more each day. What an awesome God we serve. Most important, the power of God impressed upon my heart to send this thank-you. Thank you, Billy Graham! I will continue to pray for you and your ministry.

MY POEM FOR YOU

I have listened to your crusades for years via televison. I write spiritual poems and children's stories. Several years ago, I wrote a poem titled "Just As I Am," which I dedicated to you. I never sent it to you because I could never figure out the correct address—and I still don't know. I trust that you will finally have a chance to read it here and be encouraged. Thanks again for your wonderful commitment to serving the Lord all of these years. God bless you.

Eva

Here is my poem:

"Just As I Am"

Just as I am, Just as I am
The song the choir softly sings.
Come to Jesus, Come to Jesus
All of your burdens bring.
I got up from my seat
Walked down the aisle
And at the altar I lay.
Repeat these words after me
I heard the preacher say.
I believe Jesus is the son of God
That he died on the cross for me.
If I confess with my mouth
And believe in my heart
He'll forgive me and set me free
The worldly pleasures I once craved
No longer pull me down
Since I gave my heart to Jesus Christ
I now know that I am heaven bound
If you too will repent of your sins
And ask Jesus to come into your heart
He'll forgive you of all of your sins
Then your life will have a brand new start
Then you must try to start each day
By reading God's Word, the Bible
Most of all you should take time to pray
Find a church where you can worship
Then you must be faithful to attend

Be sure to share your born-again experience
With others, perhaps a neighbor or a friend
Then ask them to pray the sinner's prayer
Just think that when they pray with you
You will be fullfilling the Great Commission
Just as the Lord Jesus commanded us to do
There will be another sinner saved by grace
Then one day Jesus will say to you well done
Thou good and faithful servant
When we see Him face to face.

I SHARE A BIRTHDAY WITH BILLY GRAHAM

Both of my parents and I share the same birthday, November 7. In fact, my dad was born in 1918, so he always mentioned the fact that he had the same birth date as Billy Graham. He even told it to telemarketers in his later years. This little connection makes Brother Billy even more special to me. His preaching captivated me as I watched him on TV in my early teenage years, and on June 24, 1965, I had another "birthday" and "made sure" of my relationship with Christ while sitting in front of the TV set. Even though I grew up attending church, there was something about the way Billy Graham presented the Gospel that caught my attention and got me to examine my life and relationship with God more closely. I will always be grateful for his wonderful influence on my life. And yes, because he is such a faithful and esteemed servant of the Lord's, I feel very privileged to be able to say that my birthday is the same day as Billy Graham's.

THANK YOU, LORD JESUS

In the spring of 1957, I was a mixed-up, self-destructive college dropout with a severe stuttering problem (and a far graver sin problem) when Dr. Billy Graham and his team came to New York City, my hometown. A BGEA-trained counselor reached me with God's Word just in time; my life was saved and my soul instantly reborn when Matthew 7:7—"Ask, and it shall be given you" [KJV]—hit me right between the eyes, and I responded, "Lord Jesus, please come into my heart." (He did!)

Dr. Graham's messages at Madison Square Garden led me to go forward and surrender fully to Jesus' lordship. His preaching on "abiding in Christ, the Vine" (from John 15) culminated in a life-transforming filling by the Holy Spirit. During the crusade, I experienced untold blessings and took my first steps in Christian service and witness.

Subsequently, and very surprisingly, Christ called me to preach the Gospel and has since trained and used me in evangelistic ministry, graciously healing my speech impediment in the process. Many special people (especially my wife and parents) have helped to mold my life. . .some in profound ways. But no one has had an effect so deep, so revolutionary these past fifty years as Dr. Graham, starting with my second birth to the present.

The Billy Graham Classics currently shown on TBN continue the discipling work begun five decades ago. The new birth is a miraculous, indescribable gift. For such mercy and grace, and for everyone whom God uses as a conduit of His astonishing favor, I can never praise and thank the Lord enough, in this life or the next. Truly, salvation "was the LORD's doing; [and] it is marvelous in [my born-again] eyes"

(Psalm 118:23). Thank you, Dr. Graham, for fulfilling God's call so faithfully.

ETERNAL LIFE AND BEYOND

During my sophomore year of college, I started trying to figure out what it really means to be a Christian. My parents had always told me we were Christians, but we never attended church. Even though I was attending a church, my grandparents urged me to go to the Billy Graham crusade. It was the first time in my life that I ever heard the concept that Jesus had actually died for *me*. When Billy gave the call, I could not believe how many people went up. I thought, *I now believe this, but I'll just tell someone at the church.* Graciously, the Holy Spirit made me get up and go forward. What I don't think most people who have been saved by the crusade realize is how much the crusade works with local churches. Within the next week, I was going to a new church and am now a member of the Navigators. I thank Billy not only for showing me what eternal life means but also for giving me the tools to live as a born-again Christian from that day on.

THANK YOU FOR YOUR FAITHFULNESS

Dear Billy, I was eleven years old the night my aunt and uncle took me to see you at Madison Square Garden. I was visiting them in Kings Park on Long Island. I'm from Florida. We were up so high that I couldn't tell for sure it was you until you spoke. I always loved your accent. No one knew at that time what God was going to do in your life, and all the millions of lives you would touch.

I didn't get saved until 1969. I often listened to you on radio and watched your crusades on TV. Your message of salvation always touched my heart. Even before I got saved. I never had to worry about false doctrine, showmanship, or being led the wrong way, because you lifted up Jesus and you never got off track.

Your faithfulness to your own team meant so much, too. All your guest singers were good, but no one could compare to George Beverly Shea singing "How Great Thou Art." Cliff Barrows was like a rock—so strong, and his presence was one of meekness and love.

No one will ever hear or sing "Just As I Am" without thinking of you and praising God that He does take us just as we are. Thank you for obeying God. I love and respect you more than words can say. All your children are a blessing also.

INSPIRATION

Thank you for always being an inspiration of what it means to live your life for the Lord. It always inspired me to see your photograph hanging in the halls of Northwestern College, and I've always appreciated the ministry you have. I pray for my sons to one day grow up to serve God as you have.

HEARTSTRINGS

In 1972, I went from Idaho to Dallas for Explo '72, and Billy spoke there. He asked for college students to volunteer and join him in Cleveland in July. Every time he said the word *Cleveland*, I felt like my heart was a harp and God's fingers were strumming the strings. I was a brand-new Christian and finally decided that God was calling me to go to Cleveland. I went and served in many ways and ended up staying in Ohio for two more years. While there, I met some students from a small Bible college in Indiana. Once again,

I felt God leading me—this time to go to Indiana. I went to school there and met my wife from Minnesota, where I now live. God used Billy to give my life direction, and I will never forget the adventures I experienced because of the calling to go to Cleveland in 1972.

DRUNKEN SAILOR CHANGED

In 1954, I went aboard my ship and went wild—drinking, chasing women, and all other things a young sailor away from home for the first time would do. A shipmate took me to a Youth for Christ meeting where they showed a film by Billy Graham. I accepted Christ as my Savior on December 5, 1955. I would love to say that ended all my problems, but after the honeymoon was over I found I was in a battle zone. I was wounded by some people in the church and went back into the world. I must say that God is faithful to His children, and even when I was in the world, He was wooing me back to Himself. I read most of Billy's books, and they helped bring me back to Christ. Thank you, Billy, for sharing your love for Christ; it changed my life.

A COUNSELOR BROUGHT TO TEARS

I have been a follower of Billy Graham's for more than thirty years, and I had the opportunity to serve at one of the crusades in St. Paul, Minnesota. I remember the night, as a young Christian myself, when I served as a counselor for the first time. When Billy gave the altar call, I was brought to tears even as I went forward to receive other people who were coming forward. A couple of other counselors saw me coming up front with tears flowing down my cheeks and said, "Could we pray for you to receive Jesus Christ?" I said, "I have already received Him, and I am also a counselor, but I am so touched by the Holy Spirit of God here that I cannot stop weeping." Finally, I was able to pull myself together and help some who had come forward.

In 1981, I got a job at the Billy Graham Evangelistic Association, on the computer side of the ministry. This was a great honor for me, and I was able to meet Mr. Billy Graham a couple of times. I even have a picture of myself and my five children all around Mr. Graham. Thank you, Billy, for your service to God and the world we live in.

COMING HOME

Growing up in a US Air Force family, I was always moving and therefore had no church home. The air base held a Sunday service but not distinct in denomination. I was always hungry for God but didn't understand anything about Him. My mother told me stories about how she was stationed in Germany while expecting me and the incredible loneliness she felt. She turned on the radio and heard the voice of Billy Graham. It was a poignant moment for her as she sat in a foreign country awaiting my father's return from flying. It comforted her in such a way that she never forgot it. That was in 1956.

Fast-forward now to 1967. We were stationed in Goldsboro, North Carolina, and because my father was a fighter pilot, he was out of the country. When my mother and siblings were out of the house one evening, I turned on the TV and noticed that Billy Graham was on. . .so I listened. I was fascinated that he could speak to my heart. I had never felt God's presence so strongly and was surprised that there could be such a peace in my heart. I wanted more, and when Billy prayed at the end of the telecast, I prayed with him. I asked Jesus to forgive my sins and to come into my heart.

From that day on, my life changed and has never been the same. Though I came from a family that was constantly uprooted and can never really call anyplace home, Billy Graham gave me roots. And I can always think back to one moment in time, one place, when I was a teenager and felt at home.

For a family who served their country, and for the many times when my father was away on missions, Billy Graham filled a need in my life. He was away from his family, too. His mission was of a different kind—an eternal mission that changed my destiny. Now I am fifty years old, and my four children and my husband know the Lord. Who knows how far-reaching our lives will go, but I know it will be great. I want to say thank you to Billy Graham and his family for their faithfulness. I am so grateful, words are not enough to convey what is in my heart. Thank you for helping me come home.

Melinda

GOD LOVES YOU!

For more than fifty years, I have heard this man of God preach the Word; such power behind those words, "God loves you, and he can change your life." I can hear those words in my mind over and over, just as he spoke them. What comfort they bring.

MY LIFE CHANGED DIRECTION

On Friday, 9 November 2007, the ABC on their program *Can We Help?* replied to a viewer's question about the record crowd at the Melbourne Cricket Ground. After showing various scenes of football matches, cricket matches, and the Olympic Games, they came up with the absolute record crowd of 140,000 people (more than we had previously been told) at the Billy Graham crusade in March 1959. That number will never be reached again, because on that occasion people were allowed to sit on the hallowed turf.

As a twenty-five-year-old, I was in that congregation, and as a result my life changed direction. I was a Christian at the time but was trying to live in two worlds. I didn't go forward at that Sunday afternoon service. However, after hearing Billy Graham's sermon repeated on radio, I realised I needed to surrender my ambitions to be an actress, and even any desire to get married, and I rededicated my life to God. Less than a month later, I was on a train to Alice Springs to work at a children's hostel. Two weeks later, I was engaged to an Englishman I met on the Ghan [railroad] on the way. Five months later, we were married at the John Flynn Church in Alice Springs.

When my husband's parents migrated to Australia, we all settled in Adelaide and later welcomed two children into the family. I will always be grateful for God's faithfulness, and Billy Graham as His messenger, for getting me sorted out at that particular time. We worship a great God.

A Godly Servant

Billy Graham has been an inspiration to me for my entire Christian life, more than fifty-five years. Whenever a crusade was anywhere near to us in Texas, we would be there. When I was old enough to sing in the choir, I did three times—once in Lubbock, and twice in Houston. Billy Graham's message was so plain and easy for anyone to understand, and you knew he was a true servant of God. He did not do anything to bring the glory to himself, but he met with everyone just as a humble representative or ambassador of our Lord and Savior Jesus Christ. Thank you, Billy Graham, for what you said, how you said it, and how you lived it. You and your ministry changed my life.

The Fruit of Faithfulness

I asked Jesus into my heart while watching Billy with my mom. Well, the truth is, I really didn't want to watch Billy Graham; I wanted to watch *Green Acres*. So, I pretended not to listen, but the Holy Spirit spoke to my heart, my mom answered my questions, and that night I knelt by my bed and prayed a simple salvation prayer. I was nine years old.

Many years later, when I was in high school, our youth group went to the Minnesota State Fair, where Billy was holding a crusade in the Grandstand. I was thrilled to see Billy in person!

Fast-forward to the mid-1990s, when he came to the Metrodome in Minneapolis. I was married with three children. All three had a personal relationship with Jesus but had not seen a Billy Graham crusade. My sister managed dcTalk (they were part of the music for the crusade), so my family had a box that overlooked the whole field. I wanted my children to have a visual image of people going forward to meet Jesus. And what an image it was! The sea of people pouring onto the main floor is still etched in my mind! Billy Graham has been used by God to reach generations of people. He has been faithful to obey God. Thank you for your faithfulness, Billy. Your obedience changed my life.

A FREE AND UNEXPECTED GIFT

When I was at a very low point in my life, I walked into a church I had not been to before. In the rack on the pew, along with the hymnal, was a little card that offered a correspondence Bible study course. I took that card, mailed it to the address listed, and in the return mail I received a little booklet. It contained the Gospel of John, with several questions at the end of the book. I read the book, answered the questions, and mailed it back. A few days later, in the mail, came another booklet containing another book of the Bible and more questions. This process continued until I had completed the entire course.

At the end of the process, I received my grades for the course and a copy of a Bible concordance as a free, and very unexpected, gift. There was never a request for money, not even to cover the cost of the materials. All of these materials, and the person who read and graded my answers, were provided by the Billy Graham Evangelistic Association.

This was a turning point in my life. God had been watching me and drawing me, but He used Billy Graham and his ministry to actually teach me how much I was loved! I wish to thank Dr. Graham personally for his dedication, perseverance, and most especially, for his godly walk. I will forever be grateful to God for allowing me the privilege of living during the lifetime of one of God's most faithful servants. I pray that God will bless you with unspeakable peace and joy. To God be the glory!

A Tribute

I have many memories from my childhood of sitting in front of the TV and listening to many of your crusades. Being very young (seven or eight), sometimes it was difficult to be attentive, but I can remember crawling up in my mother's arms and watching her face as she listened to you. There was such a smile on her face and a calmness about her as you spoke.

I was eleven years old when I knew I wanted to give my life to Christ. My mother talked to me about what a commitment it was to truly give your life to Jesus, and that to help me understand that decision, she wanted to get the booklet you had published on what it means to become a Christian.

I remember sitting at our kitchen table and finally completing it and talking with her about it. I was so excited. I knew there was something different about me. My story is no mountaintop experience that many have, but I was saved because of your commitment to spread the word of Jesus Christ.

When I was fourteen, I lost my mother to cancer. She suffered terribly but never once blamed God. Instead, when able, she would go to church and praise Him. I am told the last word she said was "God," and I believe she was truly in His presence. So, thank you, Billy, for helping me receive Jesus Christ so I can one day again see her wonderful smile and spend eternity with God.

Those Were Truly Great Days

Thank you, Billy! I remember as a young child going to your crusade here in Melbourne, Australia, with my parents. We also used to listen to your broadcast on the radio. We were so blessed. My mother had your photo in a frame on our mantlepiece. You could sense God's presence over the radio as you preached. Those were truly great days! Your ministry changed my life. Thank you, Billy.

AN OPEN LETTER OF THANKS

Dear Dr. Graham, my spiritual destiny was set in motion when my Christian parents took me on vacation to attend your crusade in 1957 in New York City at Madison Square Garden, when I was eleven years old.

I have no memory of what you said in your sermon that night; however, the Holy Spirit seized your words and with them wrapped my soul with the strength of eternity. I could not resist the beckoning of the invitational, "Just As I Am," and made a mad dash to join those who felt the same tug of the Holy Spirit, an enormous crowd of people (which overwhelmed me not only in number but also in height). When I arrived in the decision room, a very nice woman led me to the Lord.

Not long after that, you held a crusade in Louisville. My parents and grandparents had a party to welcome you and your staff. I remember meeting you. I recall looking up at this very nice, very tall man with incredible eyes. Standing there speechless, I thought I had just met and shaken hands with Jesus.

Only years later did I totally commit my life to the Lord. Through many hardships, trials, and health issues, I have learned to depend entirely on Him for everything. In doing so, He has shown me that every Jordan barrier converts into an open portal, every pit offers golden nuggets, and every hill of difficulty transforms into a mount of deliverance. The Lord has proved to me over and over this promise, which has become my very favorite verse: "Did I not tell you and promise you that if you would believe and rely on Me, you would see the glory of God?" (John 11:40 AMP).

I celebrated my spiritual birthday this summer; I was fifty years old. That is why this letter is so special to me. I cannot imagine my life without the Lord. I shudder to think what might have happened to me had I not been in NYC fifty years ago to respond to your invitation to accept the Lord. I thank that special woman, whoever she was, for leading me in prayer to receive Jesus as my Savior. However, I truly want to thank you, Billy, from the depths of my life, for your obedience to follow the Lord in the calling and purpose for your life. I am eternally grateful. Catch you on the other side!

Lynn

BORN AGAIN. . .THANK YOU

At Explo '72 in Dallas, I remember Billy Graham and Bill Bright sharing the Gospel with the people there. Most of all, I remember taking a stand and confirming my faith. I was a religious person and had attended church all my life, but after the meeting and prayer I knew without a doubt that Jesus Christ had come into my heart to be my Lord and Savior. I praise God for Billy Graham, because of the souls that he has won to Christ and because he stepped across denominational lines, took a stand for what he believed in, to bring unity to the Body of Christ and defined what the word *Evangelical* means. I believe Billy is a model for every minister sharing the Gospel, because he has not only talked the talked but led his ministry with integrity and purity of heart. God bless you, Billy Graham.

MEN GOD USED IN MY LIFE

Thank you, Billy, for your faithfulnes to God and His Word. I am walking with God because of how you did your part in His plan to reach me. When I was twelve, Billy pointed me to Christ, and at age twenty-four, men from the Navigators helped me learn to walk with Christ. I wanted you to know that godly men live on in the hearts of the ones inspired by them.

AN ELDER BROTHER . . .

I have watched Billy on TV ever since I came to Jesus back in 1975 at the age of ten. I have attended a few of his crusades in the New York metropolitan area. I have always enjoyed hearing him preach. Even more than that, I have admired watching him grow older with the Lord's grace. He has been through many things as his body has aged, yet he keeps his youthful love and humility for the Lord. That is something I want to emmulate in my own life as I continue to follow Jesus.

Kyle

NEW FAITH IN CHRIST

My wife and I are thankful for the ministry of Billy Graham, because we both came to trust Christ as our Savior in our senior year of high school. I trusted Christ at the 1969 Billy Graham crusade in Anaheim Stadium. A friend invited me to go and sing in the choir for the crusade. On the last day of the crusade, I finally gave in and went forward. That was an amazing experience for me. I have never felt happier in my life. I invited my wife to come to the crusade, too. (Of course, she was not my wife then.) She said no. But we had a long talk about spiritual things on a date in April 1970. I got to share my journey to faith with her. She was very interested. So I invited her to our youth group meeting. The night she came, we saw the Billy Graham movie *His Land.* She trusted Christ shortly after the movie. We got married a few years later and have been married for almost thirty-five years. We have been very involved in ministry in several churches and have led short-term missions trips to Russia. So, here's another way God has used the Billy Graham ministry. Thank you so much for being obedient to God's call.

STAFF DEVOTIONS

My respect for Billy Graham has always been high, but that respect grew tremendously after my interaction with the staff of BGEA. My only exposure to Billy Graham was through books and the occasional crusade on television, until I moved to Charlotte, North Carolina, to plant a church. Several BGEA staff attended our small congregation, and I was invited to speak to the entire BGEA staff for their morning devotions. As you can imagine, I was overwhelmed, honored, and intimidated at the same time. What could I possibly say to a staff that was serving the Lord with Billy Graham? I was greeted with warmth and treated like family when arriving at the BGEA offices. After nervously addressing the staff and delivering a short devotion on the love of God, I was encouraged and sincerely thanked by many of the BGEA team. They presented me with a limited edition Billy Graham book and made me feel like I genuinely belonged. I will never forget the Jesus-like acceptance and love I felt that day from the BGEA staff. I haven't met Dr. Graham personally, but I believe the measure of a man can be found in those around him. The people at BGEA are truly the shoulders on which Billy Graham stands, and my reason for respecting him more than ever.

Derek

MIRACLE

Dr. Billy Graham, thank you for coming to Pittsburgh in 1968. My eldest son, then ten years old, received Jesus Christ as his personal Savior. He had a severe reading disability, diagnosed then as dyslexia. We were told by the neurologist there wasn't anything that could be done for him. The next year, during Lenten season, the Episcopal church in Monroeville had a series of lessons entitled "God's Presence in Everyday Living." My husband and I attended. The first night was on salvation, and I knew I was saved. The second evening was on the baptism of the Holy Spirit. I prayed, "If this is real, make it known to me." A soft voice in me said, *"Say thank you."* I quietly said, "Thank you for Your gift of love." The third night, the topic was on healing. We were told that if we wanted to see demonstrations of healing by God to go to the Baptist church in Oakmont on Saturday evening. The whole family went, and a Rev. Chuck Trombley told of his son's healing of brain damage from a motorcycle accident. My son asked if he could let Rev. Trombley pray for him. We skeptically agreed. Our son was totally healed over a period of the next three years. The first thing I noted was that he had depth perception. Then his grades came up from Cs and Ds to Bs and Cs. He continued to improve and by ninth grade was received into the National Honor Society. Today, he is a graduate of Grove City College as a chemical engineer and now teaches advanced math in a Christian school in California. He answered the call of God to leave engineering and teach God's lambs. He is presently forty-nine years old, with no symptoms of disability. Thank you, Billy Graham, for laying the Gospel groundwork for the charismatic renewal in Pittsburgh.

SINCE WAY BACK WHEN . . .

During the 1970s, stacks of *Decision* magazines sat in the small drugstore in our home in Indonesia. Friends who could read English helped themselves to a copy or two. As a teenager, I read them voraciously. English just happened to be my favorite subject in school.

It was my mother's oldest brother who started it all. He'd attended the Southern Baptist seminary in our hometown. And he was all for you and your ministry. I guess his excitement rubbed off on us. From his contacts in America came extra copies of Sunday school materials. Judging from the parcels of *Decision,* he must've been in touch with BGEA. (One issue I recall had a fiery-red "World Aflame" as the front-page/main article.) Then someone asked him to help translate these materials into Bahasa Indonesia. He got hooked! For decades, he translated tracts and Christian magazine articles from Dutch and English. He had the tracts printed and distributed them to various corners of our home country.

Translations of articles used to be staple fare in church magazines, but sometime in the 1980s, my uncle ran into trouble. The BGEA representative in Bandung notified him concerning copyright infringements. (It was way too late to do anything about the problem.) In any case, Dr. Graham, I hope you'll find it amusing to learn about this incident. My uncle went home to be with the Lord in 2003, at the age of eighty.

SALVATION

I have watched Billy Graham on TV for most of my life. I thought I was saved when I was five, but as an adult I realized I had never really turned control of my life over to God. I was in an unhappy marriage, had a three-month-old baby, and was suffering from postpartum depression. The only relief I got was reading the Psalms. One day, I started reading an old Billy Graham book that was my mom's. In the middle of reading, the Holy Spirit touched my heart. God showed me a struggle going on between Him and my will. He spoke to me and said, *"Don't you think what I have for you is better than anything you could have for yourself?"* I got born again that very minute! Only God knows the number of people drawn to Him because of Billy's ministry!

I'M A PREACHER NOW

Some of my earliest memories growing up in the church were times I'd sneak upstairs to the sanctuary when no one else was around and pull up the pastor's chair to the pulpit so I could stand and pretend I was the Rev. Billy Graham. I'm a preacher now and don't need that chair to stand behind the pulpit.

RESTORED AT LAST

I was a gang leader at the age of nineteen. I wanted so desperately to find God, yet didn't know how to go about it properly. I fancied the girl who invited me to Billy's crusade and went with the intention of disrupting the meeting. However, I sat and listened to the message, and when the time came to go forward for the altar call, I found myself being lifted from my seat and going forward under some other force than my own. I received Christ into my life that night and felt His overwhelming love pour into me. I called it His first love. All I wanted was to do good for everyone, and even after leaving the park I went to the centre of the city and started praying for those whom I felt were lost like I was. His love set me free from seeing others' faults. It was a tremendous occasion for me. I am now sixty-eight years old and still in love with Him, more so than ever. "Whom the Son sets free is free indeed." I thank Dr. Billy Graham for his time and effort in preparing himself to come to New Zealand, and for the message he spoke that night. Some years later, I became a foreman at a job making fridges and freezers and had to go into the city for some parts. It was there that I met again my counselor who prayed for me and laid hands on me for the receiving of the Holy Ghost. I was so excited that he remembered my name. Praise God for people like you, Billy. May you be richly blessed in all you do. I know God has set aside a mansion for you, and when the time is ready, you will hear him say, "Well done, my faithful servant." Bless you and all your staff, in Jesus' name.

Lawry

A TESTIMONY

In May 1959 (the year Billy Graham came to town), I was only a young man, in my eighteenth year. At the time, I was living with my father in a home fractured by divorce. I was regularly seeing a girlfriend who was a Christian. (However, I was not aware of this.) I went with another (very sceptical) friend to the Billy Graham crusade at the Wayville Showgrounds in Adelaide, and God began speaking to me that night. After the meeting, on the way out,

I purchased a Bible, much to the disgust of my mocking friend. Despite that, with determination I began reading the scriptures at home.

The following Sunday (May 31), I rode my bike (twenty kilometres) to see my girl and to share dinner with her family. She asked me to go to church with her. During the service, she went forward for the Lord's Supper (she had missed the morning Communion service), and as I witnessed that act, God touched my life with a profound sense of a deep and desperate need. My heart burned as if on fire, and my soul was deeply disturbed. When we arrived home after the service, Bev took me into a quiet room and turned on the radio, tuning in to the *Hour of Decision* broadcast.

The Holy Spirit met me in that hour, and when Billy gave the invitation, I called the crusade counseling line in Adelaide and gave my life to Christ. Bev was very excited, and I was totally overwhelmed, not realising just how much my life would change after that night. I soon found myself baptised, in a church, teaching Sunday school, and was invited to be a member of a beach mission team, playing piano accordion as the team musician. I played wonderful choruses for children on the beaches and at night played to the adults in tent missions. Best of all, I played songs from the Billy Graham crusade songbook at those meetings.

The next step was full-time Bible college for three years—and what amazing adventures God had planned! Marriage, missions, more training, more study, pastoral ministry, many trials, countless defeats, victories, failures and mistakes, countless miracles, faithful provisions, amazing grace.

In 1959, I read and memorised the following quote from one of Billy's books: "Study the Bible, read it and then live by it; only then will you be able to show to a confused world the transforming power of an indwelling Christ." By God's mercy and grace, I have. What a precious and wonderful Savior Jesus is.

Thank you, Billy, with all my heart. How often I have wished through these years that I could meet and pray with you.

Alan

SAVED AND SEALED IN BUTLER, PENNSYLVANIA

I was raised in the Pittsburgh area as the only child of two loving parents who were faithful with church attendance and service in a mainstream Protestant denomination, yet I had no personal relationship with the Lord Jesus Christ. In Sunday school, I was taught from an early age to love God. As the middle school years approached, I was surrounded by Roman Catholic girlfriends, so my interest in their faith peaked, and I began to practice Catholicism, reading my Bible and going to Mass. My parents were horrified, yet wisely refrained from forbidding me. God had a marvelous plan ahead.

By age sixteen, I was determined to convert when I turned eighteen and would not have to have parental consent. In December 1969, I was grounded over Christmas break because I had seriously disobeyed my parents. I was sulking in my room one evening a few days after Christmas and turned on the battered black-and-white TV that only got one channel via rabbit ears. A Billy Graham crusade was in progress. I normally would not have watched such "Protestant heresy," yet something in Dr. Graham's voice and his earnest appeal, coupled with the simplicity of the Gospel message, snagged me. I watched the entire crusade, and at the close, alone in my room, I sank to my knees and I gave my life to

Christ, unreservedly, forever. I knew I would never convert to Catholicism. I knew I had found the Way, the Truth, and the Life. I followed up with Martha Cumberland, a crusade counselor in Butler, Pennsylvania, who came to my home and led me through the plan of salvation and then discipled me actively for two years. My parents came to faith in Christ shortly after I was saved.

Now residing in Raleigh, North Carolina, I will celebrate forty years with Jesus this December. I have made Him Lord as well as Savior, and I have no regrets. Because of many who prayed, and those who raised and taught Billy Graham, he was able to usher me into the presence of the living God so that I could have the most significant encounter of my life on one cold, northern night. I am confident that the Lord will finish what He has begun in me. Thank you, Dr. Graham, for being His instrument!

Susan

"IT'S TIME TO COME HOME"

I remember it like it was yesterday. I was living in St. Paul in 1990 and had just found out that my father had cancer. I was sitting at my kitchen table, thinking about what I could do. I was the younger of two girls, and my sister, a single parent, had a young child of her own. I knew she could not take time off from work, nor would she be able to give the support my mother would need to take care of my father and his illness. I knew they would need a lot of help, possibly twenty-four hours a day, and this was going to be the ordeal of a lifetime. Having been an oncology/hospice nurse, this was difficult, because I wanted to be with them and do the things nurses do.

As I was sitting in the quiet, I heard a Billy Graham crusade come on TV. I did not realize that I was unconsciously listening. (My mother had listened to Billy Graham crusades when I was growing up, but I had never spent time listening to them.) As the topic of the crusade was being introduced, I looked up at the television and I was stunned! The topic of the crusade, and I believe it was also printed on the TV screen, was "It Is Time to Come Home." At that very moment, I had peace and knew exactly what I had to do. God told me it was time to go home. A decision was never so easy to make in my life, as I knew that God was talking to me. Those few words changed my life.

I called my mother and father that night and told them, and two weeks later, I moved home. God was so good to me. He even had a job lined up for me when I got there. Due to that Billy Graham crusade, I found out how much I needed God. Since that day, I have understood that I depend on God every day of my life. I realized I can do nothing in my life without Him. I watch Billy Graham now every time I can. I tell this story often, especially if it might be to someone who needs to hear about God. I want to say thank you to him for just being there, as I know I'm not the only person who was changed for a lifetime by his hard work and his crusades.

Sandra

FOREVER CHANGED

I was raised in a nominal Christian home. My mother often watched Billy Graham crusades on TV. One evening, I was in the family room alone and happened to switch channels to a station that was carrying a Billy Graham crusade. I decided to listen. It was not so much what Billy preached, but the passion with which he preached. I struggled with agnosticism, but that night his passion for the Lord actually made me reconsider. I thought to myself, *This man really believes in what he is preaching.* When the invitation was given and the choir began to sing "Just As I Am," I made a decision. I went into my room, knelt down and prayed for forgiveness, asked God to reveal Himself to me, and made a commitment to Christ. The Holy Spirit spoke to me immediately and said that I must examine the evidence. I began to read the Bible daily, and my faith and understanding grew. The Lord led me to a wonderful church with a godly pastor, and I have served the Lord in many capacities throughout my life. I have taught Christian education, and I have been a leader in that ministry. I have worked in a group home.

Thank you, Billy Graham, for being faithful to God and for your impact on my life.

INSPIRATION

Times were hard when I was growing up. I lived with fear on a daily basis. I knew there was a God, and when things got really bad for me, I would hide and pray. In the 1950s, I saw Billy Graham on TV at a friend's house. I was not allowed to watch him at home. When Billy Graham spoke, I understood. It was like he was speaking only to me. He has been such an inspiration to me all of my life, and I am now sixty-six. As long as I can remember, I have wanted to tell him that. He helped a young child fight to survive and want to live. When I felt like I had no one, I knew that God loved me and would protect me. Billy Graham taught me that. I did survive. Thank you, Billy Graham.

HOPE FOR THE TROUBLED HEART

I was a sixteen-year-old mother and crazy in love with my son's father, but we were not married. He played minor league baseball and traveled a lot, and I was home going to school full-time and working at night. Life was very hard, and once my boyfriend moved back to Asheville, our hometown, we started living together. I had been brought up in a home where we went to church but not consistently; however, I always had "a conviction" and even played church when I was a little girl. So I knew it was wrong we were living together outside of marriage, but I loved him so much I couldn't let go. Well, I was working at a dental office and business was really slow, and I would sneak and read *Hope for the Troubled Heart.* During this time, I re-dedicated my life to my Lord and Savior. I went home and told my boyfriend and moved out of our bedroom until we were married thirty days later. I will always attribute my love and dedication to the Almighty using his faithful servant Billy Graham. Thank you, Billy.

MY BROTHER

My brother, Howard, was saved at one of your crusades in Memphis. He was a graduate of Annapolis and afterward taught at the Air Force Academy. He was planning to make a career in the service. He went to Vietnam because he did not want his son to have to fight in a war. Before he left, he told me that if he did not come back, to not worry about him. . .that he knew where he was going. At that time, it didn't mean much to me, but after he was killed in Vietnam, I have recalled those words a million times. Since then, I also have been saved, and because of your crusade and my brother's hearing the Gospel and going forward. . .praise God I will see him again. Words can never express my gratitude.

Among Unbelievers

Many years ago, I was a young divorced woman raising two small children with no help. We were living in my parents' basement at the time. My parents were unbelievers. We had a small TV in our apartment. One night, with all doors closed, I turned on Dr. Graham's crusade. I learned so many spiritual things that night. I was so afraid that one of my parents would come downstairs and open the door. They never did. Two years later, a friend at work asked me to attend a Baptist church. I had to keep that secret, too. Then, one night, I attended a church softball game. There was a sweet retired Baptist preacher there. He sat down beside me on the sidelines and led me to the Lord. He shared the Bible verse, "All have sinned and fall short of the glory of God" (Romans 3:23). We prayed together. I could feel the angels rejoicing that night, before I ever learned that the Bible says they rejoice whenever people get saved. Praise God for Billy Graham, who planted God's seed in my heart and has forever changed my life.

Cindy

My Grandfather

My grandfather was a great man. He and my grandmother provided the rudder with which I run my life now. Anything good in me comes from having lived with them.

My grandfather was born in 1889 in the mountains of northern Georgia. He left a large family to be educated in college and with a fresh diploma became a schoolteacher in a two-room schoolhouse in southern Georgia. He was a fierce disciplinarian, as a few of his former students have told me, but was also regarded as a great scholar who saw education as a way to a better future for his pupils. He later became a farmer and a local politician, and helped establish the crop quota system and other significant farmland programs as a federal employee with the Department of Agriculture. He died in 1970 when I was eighteen years old. As I was going through some of his business papers a few years ago, I was amazed to discover he had actually had more than two thousand dollars in the bank during the Depression of the 1930s.

One thing I remember most of him was his affection for Rev. Graham. He had the proud occasion to be a participant at one of the crusades, in either Atlanta or Washington, DC, in the 1950s or 1960s, and he would repeat to me how he stood and listened as Rev. Graham spoke and how impassioned the preaching was and his conviction of faith in Jesus Christ. This deeply affected my grandfather, and he told me the story several times. I'm not sure whether he just forgot he had already told me or if he wanted to imprint the dialogue in my brain; either way, it did make an impression on me.

I also had the chance to participate in a Graham crusade in Atlanta during the 1990s. My beautiful daughter, Sarah, was five years old and she and I went forward when called, and I received Jesus Christ as my personal Savior. I felt my grandfather's presence and knew how proud he would be of me. More important, my young daughter was a witness in a way that I also was a witness to my grandfather's faith.

SINCERE THANKS

Dr. Graham, I want to give you my sincere thanks for leading so many people to the Lord. I am one of them, even though I did not keep on the straight road for a long time. I am now fifty-eight years old and have truly given my life to Jesus

Christ. He is faithful to His promises, which I see in my life. I owe this in large part to you. May the Lord richly bless you.

GROWING IN MY FAITH IN JESUS

Dear Billy: I was already a believer and follower of Jesus Christ when you came to Toronto in 1995. I signed up to become a counselor at this evangelical event. I went to the training every Saturday, and it was after this that I decided to get up early each morning before going to work and spend time with the Lord in the reading of His Word and in prayer. That practice has changed my life. It is wonderful to start each day praising the Lord, thanking the Lord, confessing my sin to the Lord, and crying out to the Lord for those things that concern me. I go to work lighter, knowing that I cast my worries and concerns upon the Lord Jesus my great High Priest, who intercedes to our heavenly Father on my behalf. It is wonderful to be able to pray for my family, friends, and others, for the concerns of my church, the school where I work, and the things happening around me. This Christian journey is exciting, and I want to thank Billy for his influence on my growth as a Christian. Because of my involvment in his ministry, my relationship with Christ grew tremendously.

ENCOUNTER IN NIGERIA

While serving as national director of the Assemblies of God Women's Ministries from 1976 to 1985, I was privileged to minister in several countries overseas, as well as in the United States. In May 1985, I traveled all over Nigeria for various women's meetings, with Stella Ezigbo, the national Women's Ministries leader. One day, we stopped at Stella's home. At noon, I was seated in her living room with a Nigerian brother, and Stella brought us two avocados to share for lunch. In our conversation, I learned that this brother had come to Christ through reading one of Billy Graham's books. He pointed to a van outside, well identified as a Gospel literature distribution vehicle. Sharing the Gospel was now his full-time occupation, and he was enthusiastic about it. I regret not getting his name, but God knows, and will see this Nigerian brother as another of the countless souls influenced by Billy Graham, along with those who come to Christ through this brother's witness. Thank you, Billy, for your faithfulness.

Elva

WHAT A BLESSING!

Dear Rev. Graham, you have been a faithful servant of Jesus Christ. You have given your life to Him, but He gave His life for you. I grew up watching your crusades on televison, and I still watch them today. To God be the glory. I hope to have your strength in my later years. The world has been blessed to have you. Your light will shine forever and ever.

THANK YOU, BILLY

I went forward at the 1964 Columbus crusade at Jet Stadium, and my life was forever changed. It's been a long road with Jesus since then. He has cared for me, protected me, and helped me all along the way. Thanks to Billy and his team for staying on the straight road all these years. Their honesty and integrity throughout the years has glorifed our Father in heaven.

CANCER

When I was eighty years young, I had melanoma cancer. I had surgery and then radiation and chemotherapy. There were days when I was on radiation and chemo (I took radiation in the morning and chemo in the afternoon, five days a week for six months) and had a horrible life at times, but I never lost faith that God would heal me. Then my children stopped the treatment, because they felt it was killing me. We all prayed about this. I was supposed to take the chemo for six more months. I am now eighty-eight years young, and I am cancer free. I know God healed me. He still works miracles. I have watched every Billy Graham crusade that has been on TV. Dr. Graham, you were such an encouragment and a blessing when I was so sick. Thank you, Billy.

Grace

WORTH IT ALL

As a twenty-two-year-old young married, I went to the crusade at the Atlanta ballpark in November 1950. I responded to Billy's invitation to come forward, and did so, accepting Christ as my Savior. My wife had become a Christian the previous spring. We grew in the Lord during the next years, becoming active in church life. Twenty years later, we responded to the call to become missionaries and ended up with Wycliffe Bible Translators, first in Mexico and then in Peru, for a total of thirty-five years, before returning to the US and serving at the JAARS center for a couple of years before retiring. Billy, I praise the Lord for your faithfulness to His call in preaching the Gospel. I don't know just where I would be in this world if I had not responded at that opportunity.

Vernon

MY JIM'S SALVATION

I have been a Christian since I was seven years old. I was saved at a Southern Baptist revival in a tiny town in Oklahoma, where my entire family on both sides attended the Baptist church. Christ has always been a friend and a blessing to me. I moved with my family to Oklahoma City in 1949, when I was thirteen. Many years later, on a Wednesday evening, we were in our prayer meeting when our pastor said he had a guest and had asked him to speak that evening. It was Billy Graham. He wasn't so well known then, but I knew who he was and thought I knew the path he would follow. And I did.

I fell in love when I was sixteen with a boy who had been raised in the Catholic Church and educated by their schools. He was a wonderful, loving, caring boy, who just made my heart do flips. We married on April 3, 1956.

In 1957, we attended a crusade at the Oklahoma City Fairgrounds on a stormy Sunday evening. Billy walked up to the pulpit to a standing ovation, looked up at the sky, and simply said, "If it's all right with you, God, we had rather not get too wet tonight." This is the truth—the storm quickly moved on by, and no rain fell. To make the evening even more memorable, my young husband, Jim, was converted and baptized. My family and I had prayed many times that he would come to know Christ as we did. Our prayers were answered that stormy Sunday. I have chills now just writing about it.

What a soldier for God Billy Graham has been. I know the feeling of loss he has with the loss of his beloved Ruth. I lost my Jim seventeen years ago, but thanks to a message delivered by Billy Graham, I know I will see him again. God bless him and all of his family.

Faithful Servant

I deeply appreciate all Billy Graham has done to honor our Father in heaven. With his wisdom, I have learned to walk by faith in all aspects of my life. Each story or excerpt that Billy has written gives me encouragment to share my story as God shows me when and how. I have been saved by Billy Graham, for without his knowledge, and leaps of faith in our heavenly Father, I too would be struggling to find a deeper connection to God. With Billy's help, I have attained new growth, and my salvation is an outpouring to those around me. I will always remember Billy as the one who led me to God, and he will be someone I will see in heaven.

With Gratitude and Blessings!

Dear Dr. Billy Graham, it is with much gratitude and joy that my husband and I pass on blessings in the fullest measure to you. We have been ministered to greatly through the *Decision* magazine we receive once a month and the *Day By Day* devotional, personally written by you. The Lord has taken the words you have written to speak very tenderly to our hearts, affirming us over and over again that Jesus is closer than our very breath and we can trust Him. We love your challenge not to take anyone else's word for God and to find Him for ourselves so that we, too, can know Him by the warm tugs on our heartstrings. He is there, and absolutely nothing can separate us from His love. From reading your devotional over the past couple of years, I feel as if you are the "spiritual grandfather" we never had, and one we have come to adopt and love as our very own, with much gratitude.

Blessings, "Grandfather" Billy. "Your love has given [us] great joy and encouragement, because you, brother, have

refreshed the hearts of the Lord's people" (Philemon 1:7 NIV).
—*Judy* and *Ron* (your new adopted grandchildren)

GOD IS GREAT!

Between fifth and sixth grade, more than forty-four years ago, I listened to Billy Graham on television and sent away for Christian literature and started reading a red-letter-edition Bible. In so doing, I realized that I was a sinner and needed to accept Christ as my personal Savior. In fifth grade, I was lying, fighting, cheating, and getting C's and D's in school. After accepting Christ as Lord and Savior, during the sixth grade, I did not get into one fight; I stopped lying and cheating, and received A's and B's in all my classes. At the end of sixth grade, I received an award as the most improved student for the year.

During my college years, I attended Explo '72 in Dallas, started a Bible study, and distributed Bibles on campus. I received a master's in social work and was hired by the New York State Office of Mental Retardation and Developmental Disabilities to help move hundreds of people locked in institutions to family care homes in the community. As the district family care coordinator, I was able to encourage many Christians to participate in the ministry of hospitality. I recently retired at fifty-five years of age, and we just started a donation-funded street school, Eagle Wings Academy, this past fall. We consider ourselves full-time urban missionaries, having eight staff and twelve volunteers working with twenty children who want, but cannot afford, a Christian education. My hope is that the children will have a similar opportunity as the one that Billy Graham gave me forty-four years ago.
—*David*

MAN OF GOD

Thank you, Billy Graham. I am a fifty-nine-year-old widow, and I have a great faith. I am a Christian Catholic, and your words and your life have had a great impact on my life. For years, God gave you a wonderful gift of reaching to the whole world; to me, the Holy Spirit dwells in us all, and you brought Him to life in many of us. I only know that you will see the face of God one day, and I pray that your wife, Ruth, will be there to hold you once again in paradise. We thank God for sending to us a great man to fill us up with what is the only importance. . .faith, love, and charity. I love you. God bless you, and thank you for being a part of, and changing, my life.

HE IS WELL PLEASED

Dr. Graham, I want to write you a quick note to say thank you. I was saved at nineteen at a camp meeting in Ohio. Shortly thereafter, you came to Cooper Stadium in Columbus and held a meeting. I was raised in a church that basically taught salvation through works and not the precious blood of our Savior. I want to say thank you for your unwillingness to yield to the pressures of this world to ever be less than God intended you to be.

Your ministry and integrity have been the hallmarks of your life. You have always had the God-given gift to find something in this natural realm to compare with scriptural truth and share it in a way that even a child could understand. I pray that you have all you want and want for nothing, because you, along with your wife and children, have poured your lives out for Jesus as an offering—and, dare I say it, He is well pleased. Thank you from the very bottom of my heart for the countless lives you have changed for eternity. I don't know if I'll ever get to thank you in person. If the world had more fathers and grandfathers like you, it would be a much better place.

MY HISTORY ESSAY

During my senior year in high school, we were given an assignment called "A Study of Powerful Leadership," and I chose to study you. It was such a blessing to study a man of God for a school assignment! I was able to study your rise; the team around you; the many ways in which you stood at great moments of history and changed the world; the way you have influenced the future leadership of our world; and the sacrifices you made in your personal life that have benefited the entire world.

I can't help but think of all the previous centuries and the men and women who have defined them, and that, for centuries to come, when people look back on the twentieth and twenty-first centuries, they will see Billy and Ruth Graham. Thank you for your life, your ministry, and your dedication—doing this assignment has changed my life.

I WAS A REBEL

My experience with Billy has to do with his openness to embrace change and growth within the church, and in his own life, and admit it openly! I was a rebel. When I came back to the Lord, praying for God to show me His truth, He did! If Billy had not embraced change, I may not have survived "the growth process." I know that we have all different styles of Christian music openly available and embraced today because of Brother Billy leading the way. He never ever judged denominations or styles; he watched the fruit and tested it against the Word and never attacked people publicly! That is a testimony and example to the Body of Christ that I hope will live on. I heard Franklin Graham say on TBN that Billy questions whether or not we'll remember him and if he made a difference with his life! That touched my heart, and I had to post. The enemy (Satan) is still so threatened by Billy that he's tormenting him with lies and doubt! You are loved, respected, and appreciated by all of us in the Body of Christ.

I minister to young Christian adults today and encourage them to "hang on" by exhorting the Word to them. Sometimes I send them songs, or song lyrics, that I may not have had were it not for Billy's heart for people. The body needs to quit beating up its own and help one another to grow up! If the angels shout "*Holy*" every time God moves, and have done so forever, then how arrogant and ignorant of us to believe that we know all there is to know about God and His Word. I've found Him to be so amazing and exciting, and His Word, too, that the more you know, the more you want to know. And with all that, you realize you have only barely touched all that He is. If the world could see *that* knowlege on our faces, they would beg us for Him. I love you, Brother Billy. I look forward to seeing you when we get home.

MEMORIES

As a young girl when revivals and crusades were so big in the world. . .I just barely remember my family attending the crusade here in Chattanooga and sitting on a bench. . . . I was fortunately born in a Christian home and have followed Billy Graham's ministry all these years with love and respect. God has truly blessed us for knowing him and has blessed Billy with such a great ministry.

Early Memories

I accepted the Lord at the age of nine, when chalk artist Ding Teuling was speaking at the Rumney Bible Conference grounds in Rumney, New Hampshire. But one of my earliest memories is of hearing Ethel Waters sing "His Eye Is on the Sparrow" on a Billy Graham radio broadcast. Reading her autobiography later, by the same title, I realized what a great man Billy Graham is. His clear and real message is that God wants us just the way we are. The change would come after. Thank God for that message. The clarity of that has been the difference between people accepting Christ or waiting till later, maybe to eternal doom. Dr. Graham has made a real difference in many lives. God bless him and continue the work he started all those years ago, through his children, grandchildren, and those He led to the Lord.

Where Would America Be?

I live in Texas and have never had the privilege of attending one of your crusades, except by television. I just want to say a simple "thank you" from the bottom of my heart for your service to our Lord Jesus Christ. My oh my, where would America be without having the foundation laid by your ministry? I am praying for God to raise up another "Billy Graham," and He may very well have done that through your son Franklin! "The LORD bless you and keep you; the LORD make his face shine on you and be gracious to you; the LORD turn his face toward you and give you peace" (Numbers 6:24–26 NIV).

Thank You

Dear Billy Graham, thank you for all your years of evangelizing to the world by way of TV. I can remember, as a boy growing up in Greenville, Illinois, my mother and father would make us watch Billy Graham when he came on the TV. We had no other choice! When Billy Graham was on, we all had to sit down in front of the TV and watch him preach the Gospel. I am now in full-time ministry, so thank you for all of the years that God has granted you to preach the Gospel of Jesus Christ. I pray in Jesus' name that He will give you many more.

MY DAD HEARD THE GOSPEL

I grew up in a very traditional Roman Catholic family where we were taught about God by the priests, but Jesus was never discussed outside the church walls. My dad has passed away now, and for a while it weighed on my heart as to where he is spending eternity. Then I remembered the nights I would walk into the living room, where Dad was sitting alone watching TV, and I noticed he was watching a Billy Graham crusade. Not only watching, but was drinking in every word that Dr. Graham said. Being a teenager at the time, it didn't register what was happening until many years later. I remember asking my dad, "Why are you watching this?" He answered, "Billy Graham is a really good speaker." That memory coming back to me has reassured me that my dad heard the Gospel message loud and clear, and drank it into his heart. Though he would never talk about it. . .a family rule of sorts. . .I am certain that my dad is in heaven today because of the faithfulness of Dr. Graham sharing the Gospel message all those years. I thank our Lord for using Dr. Graham in this way, and I thank you, Billy.

Hope for Each Day

Recently, a friend gave me a copy of the little book of daily devotions, *Hope for Each Day*, which you published not too many years ago. It has reminded me many times of an incident in the past—from 1960, to be exact.

You had a crusade in Africa and visited Nigeria. I was a missionary in Ibadan, Nigeria, at the time. The missionaries on the Ibadan station got together weekly for a prayer meeting. You attended the meeting in one of our homes when you were there. That has been in my memory ever since. I praise God for all that has been accomplished in the world for God's Kingdom through your ministry, and pray the peace and joy of the Lord be with you.

My Billy Graham Story

While living in South Florida in the 1980s, my wife and I attended a Billy Graham crusade in Fort Lauderdale. I wanted to take this opportunity to thank you for being faithful to God's commandment by sharing invitations to accept Jesus Christ as our Savior and Lord. As the Word says, "Faith comes by hearing, and hearing by the word of God" (Romans 10:17). Your sharing and preaching the assurances of God for salvation through Jesus Christ were instrumental to my accepting Jesus Christ as my Lord and Savior. "And this is the testimony: that God has given us eternal life, and this life is in His Son. He who has the Son has life; he who does not have the Son of God does not have life" (1 John 5:11-12).

The youth preparation leading up to the crusade in Fort Lauderdale involved our taking the youth group from our church in Plantation to the events held before the crusade, and then on to the crusade. I went forward during your invitation, accepting Jesus Christ as my Savior and Lord. I can't say that at that moment my life completely changed, but it was the beginning of a journey in growing closer to Christ. Beyond that, my wife went forward at an invitation at our church, and our children accepted Jesus at Christian festivals.

The impact from an offer at one night's crusade, as it affects me, are not known; but God knows. It was a ripple effect, far greater than one person. As mentioned in Romans 10:9, "If you confess with your mouth the Lord Jesus and believe in your heart that God has raised Him from the dead, you will be saved." My assurance in Christ is secure because of your obedience to God's calling on your life. Your being the person who brought God's promises to me, and that being the starting point for my salvation, I must say, "Thank you, Billy Graham."

MY MOST MEMORABLE CRUSADE

The power and presence of God has flowed through the Rev. Billy Graham to the world—but especially to me. I have looked up to Rev. Graham all the days of my life. My family either attended or volunteered at every Billy Graham crusade in the New York area while I was growing up. I have volunteered and sung in the Billy Graham crusade choir many times.

My most memorable time was when we attended the 1971 Billy Graham crusade at Shea Stadium. The power and presence of God flowed through Rev. Graham so strongly that when he gave the invitation, everyone *ran* to the altar—young and old, saved and unsaved. Nothing could hold back the drawing power of God flowing through that beautiful, awesome, servant of God that day. My family brought a busload of people to the crusade, and all of them either gave their hearts to Jesus or rededicated their lives to the Lord.

Later that week, my family was invited to eat dinner with Rev. Graham and the crusade team. We were seated close to the head table at the restaurant. We looked up when he passed by our table and saw a bright light—there was a halo of light surrounding the Rev. Billy Graham! We cried to see such a sight. What a blessing the Rev. Billy Graham has been to the entire world—but especially to me. Thank you, Billy.

To the Graham Family

Mr. Graham, I have watched you on television for sixty years, and what a blessing you have been to me. My mother loved to watch you, and we both felt the love of Jesus through the television. You preached as if we were the only ones you were talking to; it was marvelous. I will continue to pray for you and your family. May God bless you richly with His love and grace.

The Boston College Crusade

Many years ago, you preached a crusade at Boston College. At that time, I was a young seminary student. You paid my way to attend your school of evangelism and allowed me to participate in the crusade each evening. It was a wonderful experience that I will never forget.

One evening at the crusade, I was seated by a family visiting the United States from Africa. We talked briefly while waiting for the crusade to begin, and I discovered they were unbelievers. I immediately began to pray that God would speak to them through your powerful message and they would come to know Christ as Savior. You can imagine my joy when the entire family went forward during the invitation to receive Christ. They later wrote their names in my Bible, which I continue to treasure today.

Mr. Graham, you have been to me, and countless others, a great example and mentor in the faith. My prayers are with you and your family in the home-going of Mrs. Graham. May the peace of God comfort your hearts during this time and in the days ahead. Thank you, Mr. Graham, for the tremendous impact and influence you have had on my life. And thank you most of all for your faithfulness across the years to Jesus.

'Cause Billy Graham Said So

I remember as a child growing up watching Billy on TV and wishing my regular show was on and not him. I started listening to Billy, really listening, when I was around twelve. My grandmother supported Billy's work, sometimes with money that could have gone to something else.

The joy that Billy brought into our lives was worth what was sent to him, and then some. I remember that Billy would send us a book every time we sent money to help do God's work. I looked forward to those books coming in, and I read them all. My grandmother could not talk about the Bible or God without saying, "And Billy Graham said. . ." That was the bottom line, 'cause Billy Graham said so.

No other teacher of God's Word has touched me as much as Billy Graham has. God gave him the voice and the words to reach right down to your soul, and it felt like you were going to bust if you didn't read more about God and share with others what Billy just led you to know about the Lord. It was, in a sense, magic, just the pure magic of seeing Billy and his wife's love for Christ. Billy and Ruth seemed so at peace, and it was the type of peace you want, so you start searching God's Word and praying for that peace and love that you felt when Billy was telling you about Christ.

THE DAY WE SAW YOU AT THE ROSE BOWL

Thank you for being a blessing to so many. My family and I will always treasure the day we saw you at the Rose Bowl in Pasadena, in 2004. We felt the presence of God in that large crowd. God be with you.

THANK YOU FOR BEING AN INSTRUMENT IN GOD'S HAND

Thank you, Dr. Graham, for allowing God to use you mightily over many years and touching our hearts and our conscience where God speaks to us directly. Thank you for being an instrument in God's hand to change my life.

I THOUGHT EVERYONE ATTENDED YOUR CRUSADES

Thank you, Billy and Ruth Graham, for being so devoted to God's call in your lives that you have influenced millions to have a wonderful life with Jesus as the center. You both are such wonderful role models of high Christian values and morals. Oh, that everyone would be such good role models!

In the 1950s, when I was a child in Louisville, my parents took us to your programs, and I didn't realize at the time how fortunate we were to be present there. Coming from a strong Christian family, I thought everyone attended. As the years have passed (I am now in my sixties and blessed with two beautiful children and six beautiful grandchildren), I realize how much your ministry has meant to me and so many multiplied millions all over this earth. It will be such a great honor and pleasure to meet you both in heaven! Thank you for being there as such inspirations!

SAVED AT ONE OF THE FIRST CRUSADES

I want to say thank you for the ministry of both Dr. Graham and Ruth. My dad was saved at the age of sixteen at one of the first crusades, in Boston. If it wasn't for the crusade, my father said that he probably never would have heard the Gospel. He went on to college and got involved in the Campus Crusade for Christ ministries and then of course raised his children to love the Lord. My dad was a dairy farmer and would have us watch the crusades on TV after barn chores were over. My husband got saved at the age of six, as a result of watching Billy Graham on TV with his mom. I have enjoyed watching Dr. Graham over the years and have had so many of the close people in my life saved as a result of his ministry.

WHAT A MIRACLE!

Since 1970, I have been thanking God for Billy Graham. While watching a telecast in August that year, I heard him ask the question: "If you should die tonight, do you know for sure that you would go to heaven?" He went on to say that he had absolute assurance that if he were to be killed in a plane crash on the way home, he'd go straight to heaven. Oh, how I wanted a "know so" salvation like that! So, for the next two months, I searched the Bible and Christian literature and listened to Christian radio, until one morning God made it clear to me through a radio preacher that I was a lost sinner . . .not a Christian at all as I had thought because of my baptism, confirmation, and church membership. So, in October 1970, I fell on my knees in my living room and in childlike faith confessed to God my sin and asked Jesus to come into my life as Savior and Lord. What a miracle! Immediately, I experienced a peace and joy that I had never known before! And I gained that assurance that Billy had confessed to having. I knew that I was saved and on my way to heaven! For the past thirty-six-plus years, God has been teaching me and growing me. My husband and all five of our children trusted Christ soon after that. And now nineteen of our twenty-one grandchildren have placed their faith in Christ as well. I have grown in my faith through the many books from your ministry. Thank you, Billy!

THE "FIRST COUPLE" OF AMERICA

Billy Graham was my hero when I first became a Christian and read one of his biographies as a young foreign university student in New Zealand in the mid-1970s. Ruth was the paradigm of the the virtuous wife, the godly woman of Proverbs 31, the Esther in the book of Esther; and, to me, Billy and Ruth will always be the First Couple of America. There never will be another Billy and Ruth, but God has more heroes of faith for the Gospel. God bless America once more and raise up more couples like Billy and Ruth.

HEALED FROM WITHIN

The last decade has been one of trials and of growth for me. Being a survivor of childhood abuse has taken me down many paths that are dark and full of bends and turns in the road. With the help of Jesus, I have walked with Him and listened to His voice as He healed me from within.

I grew up watching Billy Graham with my parents, and together we have gained insight through Billy's messages. The reason I am able to type this today is because of the amazing grace that I found from the Holy Spirit working through Billy. My parents have suffered a great deal, knowing that their only daughter was violated at a young age, and I am finding that we are now walking the winding road together.

I am not bitter, just grateful for the work that God is doing in my life. Thanks to Billy's willingness to share the Gospel boldly and fearlessly, I *know* where I am going when I die, and I have no more doubts. I remember being suicidal and had planned to end my life, and that night, there was a Billy Graham crusade on TV, and that night, I totally surrendered everything to God and walked away from those thoughts for good.

Thank you, Billy and Ruth, for your ministry around the world. I thank God for you as I type this with tears pouring down my face.

BLESSED, JOYFUL, AND FULFILLING YEARS

My husband and I would like to thank Billy Graham for his faithfulness to God over the years. It was almost thirty-two years ago when we listened to Billy Graham preach one of his crusades on TV and believed in Christ. We had been witnessed to by a family member for four years, but never made the commitment to Christ until that crusade in 1975. We have been serving the Lord ever since. They have been blessed, joyful, and fulfilling years, serving the One who is faithful and worthy of our praises and service. We are eternally grateful for our Lord Jesus Christ and to His faithful servant, Billy Graham.

SUCH FAITHFUL SERVANTS

I was honored to sing in the choir at a Billy Graham crusade about forty-five years ago. I was a young lady of twenty at the time, and the crusade was in Philadelphia. It was one of the highlights of my Christian life and something I will always remember—working behind the scenes, doing what I could for God's glory. God was so kind to let me be a mall part of the crusade at that time. And ever since then, Billy and Ruth Graham have been very special people in my life—a part of my daily prayers as I saw Billy go around the worldfor Christ. God bless you, Billy and Ruth, for being such faithful servants of our Almighty God!

AMAZING GRACE

Billy's crusades were a part of the confirming process for me as a new born-again believer. When I hear his voice and see how his calling is so great, it reminds me of how my heart was opened by such loving grace. "Amazing grace, how sweet the sound that saved a wretch like me. I once was lost, but now am found, was blind but now I see." Thank you to all the Grahams.

A TRUE APOSTLE OF THE LORD

Billy Graham was the one person who could always get my attention while I was flipping past all the channels on the TV. He has the power to grip you, keep your attention, and bring about the love and conviction of Jesus Christ better than any man. A true apostle of the Lord. I love you, Billy Graham!

You Walked Alongside
Me and Encouraged Me

I just want to say thank you with all my heart. I thank God for your submission. Even though you were not here in person to speak to, the Lord used you to walk alongside me and encourage me in the journey with Christ. I truly appreciated your wife and her wonderful ways. I loved her, and I loved her way. I greatly appreciate all your help and teaching. God bless you and your family.

I Didn't Always Appreciate
What You Taught

As a child growing up on a farm in Nebraska, I learned about Billy Graham from my grandfather. The latest copy of *Decision* magazine was always on the parlor table next to his Bible. I have to confess that I didn't always appreciate what you taught, but now as the mother of five and grandmother of two, I am so grateful for what I learned from your ministry. I thank you from the bottom of my heart. In addition, I am continually blessed by the Ruth Bell Graham scripture cards that are an integral part of my daily prayer life. May God give you peace during these difficult days, knowing that you will join her and our great God Almighty.

"Old Faithful"

As far back as I can remember, Rev. Graham has always been there. Whenever I'd turn on the television, there was "Old Faithful" reaching out to touch lives for Christ.

Back in the late 1970s or early '80s, I was suffering from panic and anxiety attacks and felt lost emotionally and spiritually. I'm Catholic and wasn't practicing my faith at the time, and when my life was turned upside down, I didn't know what to do.

Rev. Graham was on television, and I prayed the sinner's prayer and wrote to him for information about what to do now that I was saved. That opened the door for the Lord to step in, and today my relationship with Jesus is the most important part of my life. Without Him, I wouldn't have the gift of life, my wife, children, and sobriety. Life is a gift from Him to us, and what we do with it is our gift back to Him.

Praise God for using Billy and Ruth to touch the lives of so many people. (Now Franklin is doing such an awesome job.) I could never repay Rev. Graham for always serving and carrying Christ's message. . .no matter what crisis he may have been facing. I know when he returns home and stands before the Lord, Jesus will embrace him and say, "Well done, thou good and faithful servant. Enter now into the Kingdom I've prepared for you since the beginning of time."

His Message Always Stayed the Same

Where do I start? I cannot think of another man of God on this earth for whom I have more respect. I was raised in Charlotte, and when I was young, that's what drew me to Billy, because he was a hometown boy. I was blessed even as a young child hearing the Word; it was planting seeds. You see, I came from an alcoholic family, and while growing up I was lonely. I enjoyed hearing Billy. He made me realize that I can have a private, close relationship with Jesus Christ. As I got older, I read some of Ruth's books. She is the same as Billy, a godsend. Then, in the 1980s and '90s, so many "men and woman of God" fell from grace, so to speak, and the media alway showed the "bad" side, trying to take our eyes off of Jesus. There stood a man whom everyone could relate to—from world leaders to the common person. His message always stayed the same—Jesus loves you, and He took sin for you, and died and rose from the dead for you. Someday He is coming back for us all, world leaders and common people alike.

The Lord's teachings and words have truly lived in Billy. My whole life has been blessed by Mr. Graham, and he taught me to love our Lord and that He loves me.

THE STIRRING OF THE HOLY SPIRIT

In 1974, during one of Billy Graham's TV crusades, I accepted our Lord Jesus Christ as my personal Savior. I became a devout Catholic then drifted; a Jehovah's Witness then drifted; studied the Course in Miracles then drifted. I continued to seek the Lord, and in 2003, Jesus Christ was gracious to me and I was forever saved. I attribute my being saved (finally) to the beginnings of the stirring of the Holy Spirit in my heart in 1974. I pray every day that Billy Graham will be blessed, and I thank God for him and his ministry.

THANK YOU, FAITHFUL SERVANT

Dr. Graham, thank you so much for being a faithful servant of God to the world! Many lives have been changed as a result of your hard work, dedication, and sacrifice. May He truly bless you and your family with His grace, salvation, and mercy in this time of need.

I WILL NEVER FORGET THAT CRUSADE

I just wanted to say thank you so much for coming to Philadelphia in 1992. I had the privilege of being part of that crusade by being a counselor. It was my very first experience as a believer to witness an event that is bathed in prayer. Truly, I will never forget that crusade and the power of God. Thanks so much for giving your life to the Lord. He has used you to encourage so many others, like me. To God be the glory! Great things He has done—in you, to you, and through you. May the peace and comfort of God be yours at this time, and may you continue to find Him faithful.

WHAT AN IMPACT

In 1960, I met Dr. Graham at a pre-meeting with other pastors in Jacksonville, Florida. What an impact he had on me and others at the meetings. Forty-seven years later, with a wife and two grown children, I thank God for him and the impression he had on my life through the years. I'm sure he will receive many rewards in heaven, and one day we believers will meet again with him in the company of our Father.

I ADMIRE ALL YOU HAVE DONE

Rev. Graham, I want to thank you from the bottom of my heart for your using your life to serve and preach the Word. I admire all you have done in your lifetime, and I know that our Lord is so pleased with how you have used the time He has given you. I have always admired your life, and also the life of your precious wife and your children. You have all served Him well, and I just say thank you for all you do, and may God continue to bless and keep you in His care.

HIS EYE IS ON THE SPARROW

I was blessed to be part of the choir at Billy Graham's crusade at the Meadowlands in New Jersey in 1988. It was a true

Holy Ghost meeting, and I felt the Spirit moving throughout the whole night. Joni Eareckson Tada was there, and she
was very discouraged that night. She wept, and her husband,
Ken, had to wipe her tears and runny nose for her. CeCe
Winans then sang "His Eye Is On the Sparrow" to Joni (and
all of us), and it was an unforgettable experience. I learned
the glory of reality. We aren't always bright-eyed, but God's
eye is always on us.

Then Billy stood up. He was not well, even then, and
rather feeble, but he brought the presence of God into that
stadium with his words of hope and salvation through Jesus
Christ. I think I understood for the first time what it *really*
means to be saved. Thank you, Billy. You are amazing.

THE GREATEST EVANGELIST

I really do not know how to express the words to explain how
much Billy Graham has changed my life. It has been more
than thirty years since I first gave my life to Christ. Billy
Graham has played a major role in my walk with the Lord.
Out of nine children, I was the first in my family to give my
life to the Lord. I used to get up late at night and watch Billy
Graham on TV. When he got finished preaching and made
the altar call, I would cry and ask Jesus to come into my life.
His preaching moved me in a mighty way that still affects me
today.

I can truly say that Billy Graham is the greatest evangelist
that lived during my lifetime. Ever since I was a teenager, I
always wanted to meet him. I am now forty-nine years old. I
have never been to one of his meetings, but just listening to
him preach was like being there in the Spirit. I thank God for
this great man of God, and I know he has a special seat in the

Kingdom of heaven. I wish I could personally sit down and let him know how much he means to me. I want everyone to know that I love and thank God for him. He will always be a special part of my life. Thank you, Billy Graham, for changing my life so that I could know Jesus as my personal Savior.

I ASKED JESUS TO FORGIVE ME

When I was a teenager, I had friends in school, but I was still not happy with myself. When school was over for the day, most of the time I was in my bedroom with nobody to talk to or call. I knew somehow there was much more to life. By the time I graduated from high school in 1985, I had an idea to join the US Navy. After I got out, my mom and my stepfather thought it was a good idea for me to move out. My Christian walk at that time was very weak. I found a job as a day care teacher's aide. I was still searching in my heart for something better. I became involved with a "Christian" family I knew from the day care center. The family turned out to be part of a pretty serious cult, and I was left even more confused.

Thanks be to God, my brother saved me from this bad time in my life. He came and got me and took me back to my family in Virginia. The very next day, I was watching Billy Graham at home. The words he said on the TV really touched my heart. So right there, I gave my heart 100 percent to God. I asked Jesus to forgive me. I started all over again. I know now my first love is Jesus Christ, the King of kings! Thank you, Rev. Graham, from the bottom of my heart.

I HOPE ONE DAY TO THANK YOU IN PERSON

I've never gotten to meet you, though I did attend one of your crusades a few years ago. I do not have a great "story." I'm only writing here because I want to say thank you. I hope to one day be able to say it in person, when both of us have crossed over. May God continue to bless you.

PRECIOUS MEMORIES WITH MY MOTHER

My mother went to be with our Lord two years ago on July 8. She loved the Grahams. Every time Billy was going to be on TV, we would call each other and watch and reflect after the show was over. Billy Graham was, and still is, the most listened-to man I know of. He makes it very simple, just the way Jesus would want it. Jesus died for us, gave His blood for us, and wants us to have a better life here and (most important) life after death with Him. I know today that my mother is in heaven with Ruth, singing old hymns and praising our Lord. God bless you, Billy, and thank you for those precious memories with my mother.

YOU COULD FEEL THE ELECTRICITY

I first heard Billy Graham in the early 1970s. I was a new Christian and was a witness at the Billy Graham crusade at McCormick Place in Chicago. It was an intimidating experience. Thousands of people were energized by the message that Billy Graham gave. You could feel the electricity and the presence of God in that place. I have never forgotten the feeling or the passion I experienced that day so long ago. Thank you for your gift of sharing the Gospel.

YOU DON'T ALLOW THE
WORLD TO CHANGE YOU

Dear Dr. Billy Graham, though I have never had the opportunity to attend a Billy Graham crusade, work with the ministry, or even shake your hand, I have followed your telecast and broadcasts, read most of your books, and used your training manuals since I was very young. I am fifty-seven years old now, and I must say that the greatest impact on my life is the fact that I have never heard or seen you change the general basic thesis of your message: Accept Jesus Christ and be saved.

As an ordained evangelist, I have learned that you don't allow the world to change you, but you present the Gospel of Jesus Christ in a clear and concise way to change the world. I know that you (like everyone) have your faults and struggles to work through, but in your messages they were not evident.

I later began to hear and read about your precious wife, Ruth. As a pastor's wife, I was able to glean understanding and stamina from her words and books. Therefore, as hundreds of thousands of people you don't even know pray for you and are blessed by what you are chosen of God to do, I say thank you for sticking to the Gospel of Jesus Christ and for being so strong in the Lord and in the power of His might.

HIS SINCERE AND BASIC MESSAGE

I remember my mom, who was a Christian, and even my Dad, who was not, listening and watching Billy Graham programs on TV in the late 1970s and '80s, when I was a child. I didn't realize how much of an impact his ministry had on our family and the world until I became a born-again believer myself. Now, as an adult with small children of my own, I appreciate his sincere and basic foundational message of the Gospel of Jesus Christ. Rev. Graham never changed his message, and because of this, many souls will come to Christ. Thank you Rev. Graham. I know that one day we will meet in heaven.

I Observed My Grandmother

I am so grateful to my grandmother and Billy Graham's ministry. As a child, I observed my grandmother watching the Billy Graham crusades on television. I also saw her reading books authored by Billy Graham. Most important, though, is the fact that my grandmother and Billy Graham's ministries led me to the Lord.

Imitating Billy

"I wish I could be like or imitate Billy Graham." This is what I used to say when I was younger. Then I realized Billy was imitating Jesus Christ. Now I try to be like Billy—imitating Christ.

There Was No Time to Be Antsy

As a young girl from a very small rural town in Ohio, I remember my parents always watching Mr. Billy Graham whenever he appeared on television. Even then there was something compelling I didn't understand. Shortly after moving to Cincinnati to attend college, I gave my heart to Jesus in a small Baptist church. A year later, a friend asked me if I would be interested in working at the Billy Graham crusade that was coming to town. We attended all the meetings to work as ushers, but that first evening there was such an overwhelming crowd of people, especially for a country girl like me. There was no time to be antsy as the people were coming, and there never seemed to be an end to the lines of people. We greeted and smiled and helped, and everyone was so friendly and cheerful. Such a memorable event that left such an impression on my life.

Mary

I'VE NEVER FORGOTTEN MR. GRAHAM

I was there in 1957 in Madison Square Garden, sitting on the left of a row on the main floor, almost nine years old. My parents, Salvation Army Corps officers in New Jersey, brought a delegation to the crusade. I'd never been in such a crowd. When we sang, music filled the space. I don't remember the message, but I do recall Billy Graham's intensity in preaching, the tugging in my heart, and my response to the Lord. I've never forgotten Mr. Graham.

Over the years, we have received inspiration from *Decision* magazine and from television broadcasts of crusades from various cities. We have prayed for the team and felt proud to see such an upstanding minister of the Gospel not only welcomed by many countries but also appreciated by all of our US presidents. We were thrilled to attend the Billy Graham crusade in Tokyo in 1994, when we were stationed there with the Salvation Army. What an impact this man has had on my life.

I HAVE BEEN BLESSED

I just wanted to say thank you to Mr. Graham for his unwavering dedication to preaching the Word of God and for being a light to the world for our Savior Jesus Christ. I have been blessed to see Mr. Graham twice in my life, once as a small child and the other as an adult in my late thirties. Both times were impactful and inspiring. Mr. Graham, you are definitely a vessel in the hands of the Lord. He has used you to touch and change many people's lives, due to your diligence in speaking the Word of God to a world in such desparate need! Thank you, Billy.

TRANSFORMATION

As a little girl, I used to watch Billy Graham with my grandma. I wasn't always sure what she found so entertaining, but as I grew in my walk with the Lord, I understood the importance of evangelism. While living in Jacksonville, Florida, I had the opportunity to attend one of Billy Graham's crusades. I had invited a nonbeliever to go with me, and I witnessed firsthand the transformation of a life for Jesus. What a blessing. I have also read one of Ruth Bell's books and loved every minute of it. Bless you both for the many, many lives you have touched over the years (including mine).

A MAN SENT BY GOD

I attended a revival Billy Graham preached in Baton Rouge in the 1950s, and it help start my spiritual growth. When I lost my father a few years later, Dr. Graham became my spiritual father, giving me guidance to God's will. Dr. Graham gave biblical guidance to America, calling us to God's love and forgiveness. We would not be the nation we are today had God not sent Billy to preach His Word. Only a man sent by God could have said and done what he did. America depends on men like Dr. Graham. Thank you, Billy.

MY GRANDMOTHER WAS GLUED TO THE TV

I was a little girl when the Rev. Billy Graham began to broadcast his crusades on TV. My grandmother raised me and four other grandchildren. When Billy Graham came on TV, it was the first thing we had to watch, and nothing else. He would be on TV for three nights, and that is what we watched. My grandmother was glued to the TV, and so were we, just as kids. As an adult, I came to appreciate the tent revivals, because there aren't very many now. It seemed that tent revivals were more personal to the lost souls than the Internet, so to speak. Thank you, Rev. Billy Graham, and your lovely wife, Ruth, for your contributions to the many souls that were saved with the love of Jesus Christ. Be abundantly blessed, and thank you again. Let your children also know that we thank them for sharing their parents with the world. All so we could get to know about getting our hearts right with the Lord Jesus Christ.

I WATCH BILLY EVERY TIME HE IS ON

I can remember when I was a little girl, my dad and I would watch Billy preach on the TV. Dad would not go to church, but we would always watch Billy. Now, I watch Billy every time he is on. I put myself in the place of the people who come down at the end. Billy has been a tremendous influence in my life, and I love God and I love the Bible. I am currently taking classes to be a pastor and spread the Word of God. Thank you, Billy, and may God bless you.

IT ALL BECAME CLEAR

I grew up a "good Catholic girl" in an all-Catholic community, did all the things I was supposed to do, but was never satisfied. Sometime between 1971 and 1975, I attended a Billy Graham crusade in Baton Rouge, mainly because I had heard him on TV and something about what he was saying touched me. I had no clue what a born-again Christian was. I listened intently and was touched by what he preached. I didn't go up for the altar call, because I still didn't understand what was going on. And, shortly afterward, my life went back to the usual (heading in a very wrong direction).

In 1976, I was saved by the message of some former in-laws. I knew I was different but still didn't understand the gift of salvation. About three weeks after I was saved, I was reading one of Billy Graham's books (I don't even remember which one). Somewhere in this book, he was describing the great price Jesus paid for us. All of a sudden, it all became clear. I was at the foot of the cross, and I finally understood.

My life has never been the same. I know now that Billy Graham planted the seed at that crusade. Then his book was alive with revelation to my heart. I will probably never meet him on this earth, but I look forward to meeting him in heaven someday and thanking him personally for myself and for all the lost he brought into the Kingdom.

YOU WALK THE WALK

Dear Rev. Graham, I do not have a lot to say, but I wanted to let you know this: when I am confused about something about the world or my family, I know if I listen to one of your crusades or interviews, my questions are answered. I trust your belief, and I trust in God. You walk the walk and talk the talk. You are one of God's special angels, and I just trust your thoughts. Thank you for your trust in God and belief in the Word.

I WAS VERY SHY

Dear Graham Family, I grew up in Liberty County, Texas, as the eldest of four children. I was very shy, but I did accept the Lord Jesus Christ as my personal Savior at seven years of age. I served God faithfully, and we used to listen to you on our battery radio out in the country, as we did not have electricity!

I grew up, moved to Houston, got a job, got married, and had children. However, I was still shy. In the late 1960s or early 1970s, you came to Houston and held a crusade at the Rice University Stadium. I had learned sign language and was an interpreter in my church. Your staff put out a call for volunteers to come and interpret the services. I volunteered and was so blessed and privileged to share the Gospel to the deaf via sign language as you preached. My shyness was gone and God's anointing was upon both of us—and the deaf accepted Jesus as their personal Savior! Thanks for your godly life and your preaching of His Gospel.

MY EXPERIENCE WITH
A BILLY GRAHAM CRUSADE

Fort Worth, Texas, hosted its first Billy Graham crusade in 1951 in the Will Rogers Coliseum. This was during my second year of teaching school. I told my students that my husband and I would pick them up, take them to the crusade, and return them to their home if their parents would allow them to attend. We had a carful for each of the four Friday nights. God worked through these services and the local Baptist church. At the end of the crusade, all of the students in my classroom were Christians. Most of the new Christians had joined the local Baptist church and had been baptized.

I treasure this experience and was grateful for the positive influence it made in my class.

We moved from Ft. Worth and some years later went back for a visit. I was going to pick up my sister-in-law, Nita, at the insurance company where she worked. Nita mentioned to one of her coworkers that her sister-in-law, Selma, was coming to pick her up. The coworker asked if Selma had ever taught at Bludworth School. Getting a positive reply, she began to share that Selma had been her teacher for two years. She also shared that Selma and her husband had filled their car for the four Friday nights during the Billy Graham crusade. She explained that she was one of her students who had been saved during this crusade. It was such a surprise to see Marcella when I arrived, and to catch up on her life's experiences. She was now married, and her husband was a student at Southwestern Baptist Theological Seminary in Ft. Worth. It encouraged me to know that our efforts were continuing to bear fruit. Jesus really did make a difference in their lives during the Ft. Worth Billy Graham crusade.

Selma

HERE IS SOME OF MY LIFE'S FRUIT

Thank you for being God's servant. God's good work in me became evident when I sang my first church solo for Him at age six and then made the decision to give my life to Jesus at a local Billy Graham crusade at age twelve. Since the planting of those early seeds, here is some of my life's fruit: little farm girl grows up to be an RN, has blessing of seeing future husband come to the Lord (our twenty-fifth anniversary is next year), blessed with three kids (two of whom have special needs), and knowing that all three children know and love the Lord! Woven throughout is my praise and worship to Him! He is faithful! Thank you, Billy!

I SURRENDERED EVERYTHING TO HIM

Billy Graham—yes the name certainly rings a tone of *strength*, *courage*, *honor*, and *humility*. To be honest, I can't remember when I first heard Billy Graham preach a sermon. It seems he has always been a part of our lives, kind of like an uncle we see only once or twice a year, but we're always happy to hear his stories. For me personally, those strong and fervent messages always got to my heart. I can remember my husband and me sitting or standing in our living room praying the sinner's prayer with Billy Graham, and it would be a relief knowing we said that prayer. If we died that night, we were going to heaven! We both had asked Jesus into our hearts when we were young—twelve for me, and thirteen or fourteen for my husband—and rededicated our lives later after we were married.

I was always amazed at the crowds of people that filled stadiums to hear Billy Graham. I never knew what that was like until he came to Texas Stadium just a few years ago. For the first time in our lives, we were getting to experience the Billy Graham crusade live! What was so awesome was the fact that our son was with us. He was fifteen. Even though two years before he had invited Jesus into his heart, it was awesome to be saying the sinner's prayer with our son and the huge crowd that day

In 1997, for the first time in my life, after a visitation from the Lord, I surrendered everything to Him. I hunger and thirst after righteousness. Instead of trying not to sin, I have such a desire to live for my Savior instead, and that can only be because of His Holy Spirit.

To say that Billy Graham has been an influence in our lives would be a *yes!* Thank you, Billy and Ruth Graham and family, and of course the Billy Graham team, and their families, too! And thank you for the opportunity to share what is on my heart. We love and appreciate all of you and your dedication to our Lord!

MY FAVORITE MEMORIES

I've been affected by Billy Graham for as long as I can remember. (I'm fifty-seven now.) I've always had a wonderful admiration for him as a man of God—a humble, loving man of God who was never afraid to speak the truth clearly and plainly, but always in love. Wow! But I also have always felt this kinship to Billy Graham—like he was part of my family and I could sit and chat with him and it would be comfortable and great. (In heaven one day, I look forward to doing just that!)

My folks always loved Billy Graham, and we went every night to the crusade in Atlanta when I was a little girl. We got there early because my mom sang in the choir. I remember it being an amazing and exciting time. I think my favorite memories of Billy Graham are his message after 9/11—absolutely the truth, but so kind and loving—and the time he was asked what he would do if one of his kids came home and said he was a homosexual. Billy's response: "I'd love that one even more." I loved it—so much like Jesus.

Thank you, Billy Graham; you have humbled yourself before your God, you have sought justice and loved mercy. You have done your best to love the Lord your God with all your heart, soul, mind, and strength, and you have loved your neighbor as yourself. Thank you for being God's man in this time and place. God bless you.

I DISLIKED BILLY GRAHAM

When I was young and foolish, I disliked Billy Graham. I would even mock him and his preaching to my friends. But as I got older, I found myself listening to him every time there was a crusade on TV. It was not long before God began tugging on my heart and I became a Christian. I have now been a pastor for more than thirty years, by the grace of God and the faithful preaching of Dr. Graham. God bless you, Billy.

A MINISTRY YOU CAN TRUST

I was first introduced to Billy Graham when I was living in public housing under the worst conditions. We had a give-away room where people would place so-called junk for people to take if they wanted to. One of these pieces of junk was Billy Graham's *The Jesus Generation* book from the 1970s. This was way before my time, but I was interested in reading it because, at the time, I was struggling and so many friends were atheists, so I wanted to read about a time when young people were proud of their love for the Lord.

When I first started reading *The Jesus Generation*, I expected an easy read, stories of the Bible and journeys of faith and devotion. What I found was an intellectual, academic book about God. This was a new concept for me. I always expected to read such knowledgeable books only in seminary. I think Billy Graham may have understood what my old Baptist preacher understood, and that is that young people are drawn to intellect. They want to see how the Bible and Jesus can not only stimulate their lives but also their minds.

Later, I went on to read books like *The Journey* and *Angels*. I also started tuning in to old Billy Graham crusades on Daystar and TBN. I think the most catchy and potent of all mottos is one I saw while watching these crusades. It was after the program was over and there was an advertisement for giving donations. It simply read, "A ministry you can trust," and I think that's why I watched and read Billy Graham's TV broadcasts and books. It is because you could trust in his faith and obedience to God, as well as his teaching of the Good Book. I never felt as if Billy Graham would lead me astray, like some of the uneasy feelings I get when watching some televangelists or listening to some preachers on the radio.

I have also respected how Billy Graham took politics out of his ministry. He would pray and guide a Democrat as well as a Republican. Jimmy Carter respects Billy Graham as much as George H. W. Bush does. I don't know of any other preachers who can say that. He ministered to anyone, despite color, religion, political affiliation, etc., just like Jesus did. Billy Graham is an upright, righteous man who has probably ministered to more people than the apostle Paul himself. I know all the praise I give Billy Graham won't really matter to him, because he would rather give this praise to His and our Savior, Jesus Christ, and that's what makes him so special.

MY MOM'S STORY

This story is really my mom's story. My mom would often tune in to the crusades Billy held on TV, and the Holy Spirit began to work in her during those times. He plowed the fertile soil of her heart, so that in 1978, both she and I were ready to hear of His precious salvation when a coworker shared with my mom. Thank you, Billy and Ruth, for being faithful servants to the Lord, so my mom would be ready to hear in person of your free gift for all.

MOTHER'S DAY 1976

Billy Graham was preaching at the new Kingdome in Seattle. We had just survived the wild sixties and seventies. My dear friend had come to Jesus and kept pestering me to go to this crusade that Billy was going to be preaching at the Kingdome. Well, I didn't want to go! But Johnny Cash was going to perform, I could see the new Kingdome, I could get my friend Kathy, the new Jesus Freak, off my back, and since it was Mother's Day, I had some leverage with my husband to take me.

My life has never been the same since that day. . .praise God!

God is so faithful and gentle, but I think He also has a sense of humor with some of us who suffer from the sin of pride. I was always very faithful to Jesus as a child and through adolescence. My family expected me to become a nun, but somehow I just got further and further away from my faith. Oh, I still believed in Jesus, especially in emergencies and on Christmas and Easter sometimes.

So there I was at Billy's crusade. The Kingdome was three thousand people over capacity, so there was no altar call that night. It was so crowded that, after Billy's Spirit-filled sermon, he just asked us to stand up from our seats if we wanted Jesus in our lives. Well, I knew that I really wanted Jesus back in my life. I wanted His peace, love, and the forgiveness for my sins that can only come from Him. But I had a problem. You see, I am a devout Catholic, and my understanding of an altar call is when we stand up for Christ and go forward at Holy Communion to receive Him—Body, Blood, Soul, and Divinity in the Eucharist. Then to carry Jesus and His Gospel in our very beings, in all we say and do and think, out into the world. So, I had no idea what this sort of altar call was or what would happen to me if I stood up and acknowledged that I really wanted Christ in my life.

Well, Billy just kept asking, and I kept sitting there bargaining with God that "this wasn't my style," all this emotion and preaching. "I can't do this. God, I promise to start going back to church, read the scriptures more often—anything but this oversimplified act of just standing up for You." I was talking real fast to God by now, but He just kept saying, "Stand up, surrender your pride and all you think you know about Me. Stand up and live for Me."

I can honestly say I felt two heavy weights on my shoulders, keeping me in the chair. This mysterious, cosmic struggle between good and evil was going on. I summoned all my strength and stood up. I let God back in (of course He had never left me). He is always calling me to a deeper union with Himself. I just had too much pride and head knowledge about God to allow my heart to open up for Him to really enter.

Since that difficult, grace-filled moment at a Protestant crusade that I went to for all the wrong reasons, my life was changed, grace upon grace, mercy upon mercy, forever and ever, eternally. Thank you, Billy, for calling a young, stubborn Catholic woman back to the fullness of the Faith.

THE SPIRIT AWOKE IN HIM

Back in 1991 or 1992, your ministry came to Portland, Oregon. My mother-in-law had been praying a very long time for my father-in-law. The Spirit awoke in him, and he asked if she would like to go to the Billy Graham gathering. She could hardly say yes fast enough. After the invitation, my father-in-law said "yes" to our Savior, Jesus Christ. He passed away suddenly in January 1993, and we're sure that he's living in his heavenly home. I so appreciate all that you've done through the years; so much has touched my heart and spirit, too. As you have said, time and time again, you must be *reborn* before you can enter the Kingdom of God. So much of my understanding from the Bible has come about because of your ministry. All praise be to God for your guidance throughout your ministry years.

9/11

Thank you for pastoring a grieving nation after 9/11. It was the best sermon I have ever heard preached, and it touched my soul.

"HE WHO BEGAN A GOOD WORK. . ."

I cannot remember a day in my life any more clearly than when I was a teenager and I heard the Rev. Billy Graham preach at the Houston Astrodome in the mid-1960s. Even though I had accepted the Lord at a young age and had been baptized in church, it was that day that I knew what accepting God as one's Lord and Savior really meant. I truly felt the presence of the Holy Spirit. That day has given me encouragement and strength all of my life. I truly believe that "He who began a good work in you will bring it to completion at the day of Jesus Christ." God in my life is what life is all about. I am thankful for the day Rev. Graham helped me understand that. Thank you, Rev. Graham, for being such a part of God's plan for my life.

Donna

I ASKED GOD TO SHOW ME A REASON

I was a twenty-four-year-old woman living in Lake Tahoe, California. I worked with several people, but most notable were two men who would discuss the Bible. It was through these two men that I learned about a personal God, a personal Jesus, and what the Bible was really all about. As I listened, I struggled with what I believed and about giving my heart to the Lord. I asked God to show me a reason and then I'd commit my heart. I went to Reno to see Billy Graham. *Wow!* He spoke so eloquently, so passionately, so committed. But after hearing Billy speak, I knew right then and there that accepting Jesus was the best choice I could ever make. I knew that walking with the Lord was far more than what I thought it was, it was more than what I knew, and it would be a life-long journey. It was great! I will always keep the picture of you, Billy, walking around on the stage, effortlessly holding forth with that big Bible splayed open on the flat of your hand. Thank you, Billy, for cementing my love for the Lord in my heart.

YOUR CINCINNATI REVIVAL

Dearest Billy, I want you to know how much your stadium appearance touched my life and the life of my children. I have only been saved for five years, and right after I found my home church, I was able to attend your Cincinnati revival at the Coliseum. I will never forget the message and all the lost souls that walked forward at the end. "Just As I Am" played, and the tears flooded my soul, since that was the song that played when I gave my life to the Lord. Your passion for the Lord is so obvious, and you have been blessed with a long life and many lost souls found due to the calling on your heart.

Mrs. Albright

In 1960, I was living in Lexington, Kentucky, where my dad was stationed at the army depot. I attended Brian Station School, and my sixth grade teacher was Mrs. Albright. She looked to be of retirement age, but she commanded our attention and got our respect as the year went on. One of the expressions we heard frequently, when she rapped a hand with her ruler, was, "This was good enough for Billy Graham when he sat in my class, and it is good enough to teach you, too." I had no idea, then, who Billy Graham was, but I knew he must have grown up to be quite a great man, because Mrs. Albright thought so.

I became a Christian when I was forty years old. Since that time, as I look back to the events that led me to the Lord, I know that Mrs. Albright is one of those people used by God to help me find Jesus. I eventually learned who Billy Graham is (and he *is* a great man) and marveled that Mrs. Albright taught both of us. I enjoyed knowing that we were both blessed by a woman who loved to teach more than just reading, writing, and arithmetic.

A Prophetic Gesture

In June 1972, when my husband, Clay, was a youth pastor, we drove an RV full of kids from San Bernardino, California,

348

to an event in Dallas. We had just had our first child, Billy, six weeks earlier. It was a big step of faith to take our baby with a bunch of teenagers all the way to Texas, but I am so glad we did. The highlight was when Billy Graham preached one night. It was an awesome evening! The most memorable moment for us, however, was when Clay held our little son up high in the grandstands in a prophetic gesture and said to him, "Billy Ford, meet Billy Graham. He is a great man of God. May you serve God faithfully one day, too." Today, Billy Ford is a faithful Christian pastor. Thank you, Billy Graham.

THE RIPPLES GO ON AND ON

It is hard to believe the impact the Billy Graham family has had on our lives over the years. In addition to the innumer-able TV broadcasts and books we have enjoyed, and from which we have benefitted, my husband and I were privileged to have firsthand contact with two crusades. In Birmingham, Alabama, in 1973, while my husband was attending Southeastern Bible College, we sang in the choir and served as counselors. A few years later, singing in the choir, counseling, and working with follow-up assignments at the crusade in Norfolk, Virginia, were a blessing. In July 2007, the Franklin Graham Festival in Norfolk put "frosting on the cake."

The ripples from the Grahams' ministry go on and on. I have lost track of the number of people I've met who, years ago, were led to our precious Savior and Lord via the BGEA. Ruth's books, example, and encouragement over the years will be greatly missed.

Having a ministry that we can trust to be financially above reproach is an inestimable blessing. My daily prayers are with you all that you will continue to "walk worthy of the vocation wherewith ye are called."

Heaven alone will reveal what your faithful service to the Lord has accomplished. And what an indescribable joy to realize that we have eternity together praising Him for His faithfulness in and through the Graham family.

SPIRITUAL NOURISHMENT

I remember watching your crusades on television when I was a child growing up in the 1960s. We always heard our mother say how much she loved and admired you. Now that I am a parent, "training up my children in the way that they should go," I, too, watch your programming and have read so many of your books. In my Christian walk, these books have given me spiritual nourishment when the road has been narrow. I have registered both of my children to "Dare to be a Daniel." I can only hope and pray that my children will live to serve the Lord just as yours are doing. In this wicked and perverse generation, we need angels like you to keep us close to the truth and knowing His all-powerful Word. Thank you for your inspiration and ministry to an all-hurting world.

I WAS AMAZED

In the summer of 1957, when I was a teenager growing up on Staten Island, I was privileged, along with some of my friends, to sing in the choir at the Billy Graham crusade at Madison Square Garden. At the time, I didn't know if my father and mother had a relationship with the Lord. I prayed for them constantly. A couple of years later, my dad passed away.

It wasn't until several years later, while serving as a missionary in France, that I wrote my mother to ask if she knew the Lord. I was amazed at her answer. Without my knowing about it, my mother had attended the crusade that summer and had gone forward in a meeting, and had accepted the Lord.

You cannot imagine how thrilled I was to hear that news. My mother lived until she was eighty-four and went home to be with the Lord in 1983.

Thank you, Billy, for proclaiming the message of salvation in such a simple and straightforward manner. We wish the Lord could give you another lifetime to proclaim the message, but we know He has His own plans for your life.

A CONFERENCE AT THE COVE

In June 2002, I attended a prophecy conference at The Cove in Asheville, North Carolina. I went up the mountain a believer, but I came down the mountain as a believer with a renewed passion to get out of the spectator seat and onto the playing field for our Lord. Had you not been obedient to the vision for The Cove, maybe my life would still be just sitting in the stands, being comfortable and complacent, waiting for my time to be over on this earth. But God used that seminar to speak to me and show me that I could have a part in His Kingdom's plan on this earth. How can I say thanks for the life-changing days I spent at The Cove? I pray God's continued blessings on each member of the Ruth and Billy Graham family. I believe our time on this earth is short, and there is still a multitude of people who are waiting to hear the simple truth of the Gospel. Thank you for this opportunity to share how God has blessed me through your obedience.

I WONDERED WHY MY MOM TOOK ME WITH HER

I can remember when Billy Graham came to Memphis for a crusade. I was probably still in grammar school or junior high. I remember sitting in the Coliseum listening to the singing in the choir, because that's where my mom was. If I didn't sit in the choir, I was very close by. I listened to the testimonies and the Gospel preached. Billy Graham touched a lot of hearts when he preached. I was saved at six years of age. I wondered why my mom took me with her. I thought sometimes I was preventing someone else from hearing the Word preached by being there. So, I just sat and listened and prayed for anyone who might not have been saved that night.

God bless you, Billy Graham, for the ministry that you so faithfully did for God. I know that you will have a crown that will be so very special in heaven for your dedication and your faithfulness. Thank you for letting God lead and direct you for all these years.

I FOUND MYSELF TURNED AWAY FROM GOD

In 1968, I was drafted into the US Army. It wasn't long, maybe a year and a half, before I found myself turned away from God. I was away until the spring of 1997, when I found my way back to an altar of prayer, asking God to please forgive me and allow me to return to His precious care. The answer came instantly, and I have been serving Him since that time. During my time away from God, every time I saw Billy in the *TV Guide,* I had to watch the crusade service. In 1999, I had the opportunity to serve as a counselor in a Billy Graham crusade. Working in this crusade and volunteering solidified my commitment to Christ. I still watch all the Billy Graham films and crusade services, both the Classics and the new ones. Thank you, Billy. Your ministry was so very instrumental in my life.

MY OWN PERSONAL APOLLOS

I have been a Christian for more than twenty years. Although the message of the Gospel was not introduced to me by Mr. Graham, his simple presentation of it has had an impact on my life. Rev. Graham came along in my life when TV evangelists were gaining steam on the airwaves in the 1980s. Sadly, many pastors later fell to life's common temptations, causing their followers to faint or seek a better way. I thank God for His grace for helping me to seek the latter. The Lord used Billy Graham as my own personal Apollos. As I observed from my living room, he taught me that God's love was the message! The overuse in other ministries of themes of prosperity, and the badgering to have showy spiritual gifts, clouded my way. Returning to God's love was the answer! Finally, despite rejection, unemployment, or the death of a loved one, God's unwavering announcement of love through the ages still stands eternally to bring hope to man. Thank you, Dr. Graham.

GOD WAS DRAWING ME CLOSE

I want to thank Billy Graham for obeying the way God planned to use him to impact and touch my life along with millions of others. I was unsaved and in a failing marriage. I did not know at the time that God was drawing me close through Billy Graham. I sat on my couch and listened to him many days and nights, with tears and sorrow in my heart, as he ministered the Word of God to me. Today, I am saved and love the Lord because of the way God used Billy to touch my life. May the good Lord's blessings continue to be in your life. Thank you, Billy.

INSPIRED AND REASSURED

Since I was a little girl, I remember watching Billy Graham crusades on TV. I accepted Jesus Christ as my personal Savior on June 25, 1995. I thank God for anointing you, because my decision was due to one of your amazing sermons. At age seventeen, I accepted a call to full-time ministry in Christian counseling. Watching Billy Graham crusades and reading his books inspired me and reassured me that, as a Christian, if you only believe, God can use you to do great things for His Kingdom. I want to thank you with all my heart for living a life so dedicated to the Lord. Thank you also for being an encourager and inspiration to me in my walk with the Lord. May the Lord continue to bless you.

QUIET, HUMBLE, AND JUST AWESOME

I grew up listening to Mr. Graham on TV. As a little girl, I would be glued to the TV every time he came on. Having grown up in church and a Christian home, I really wanted to please God, and my relationship with God was enhanced so much every time I watched one of his crusades. I consider him to be my spiritual grandfather. He always had a word of encouragement, and I would have tears running down my cheeks every time, asking God to make me into the person He wanted me to be. I guess that's why I really did not fit in, growing up with my peers. I would rather watch Billy Graham on TV than go see a movie. He always presented Jesus as the most important person in your life, and I really wanted Jesus. Mr. Billy is the most humble person I know, and to watch him is like watching Jesus when He was here: quiet, humble, and just *awesome*. Billy has a majestic personality that shines all the time. I so admire him and the late Mrs. Ruth Graham. They were a perfect couple in the Lord. My role models. Thank you, Billy.

SOMETHING ABOUT YOUR WORDS CAPTURED MY HEART

Dear Billy Graham, I have a fond love for you through our Lord Jesus Christ. In 1972, just a newlywed, I was watching one of your televised crusades. I don't recall which state it was held in. There was something about your words that captured my heart, and when you gave the call, and the song "Just As I Am" played, I tearfully accepted Jesus Christ into my life.

I had been going to church with my husband and understood intellectually what was being said, but it didn't affect my heart until that wonderful night. God is so gracious and merciful. My life has been forever changed, and the Lord used you to do it. The works our Lord has worked through you and your family are far and wide. I praise God for your diligent service to Him. Someday we will meet in heaven. Until that day, may God continue to richly bless you.

YOU'RE LIKE MY PREACHER GRANDPA

Thank you for your spiritually uplifting messages and the reminder that God is always ready for us to ask Him into our hearts! I grew up watching your telecasts from all over the world. My mother enjoyed your messages over the years. It gave her strength and comfort as she battled a lifelong illness. I know she felt down at times, but she was always renewed in her faith to see her through. I have always had a respect and admiration for your honest, hard-driving truth. You're like my preacher grandpa, in that you both have the peace of God in your life, and that makes everyone feel comfortable to be around you listening to life-changing messages. Thank you for the gifts God has given you and your wife to make a difference in so many lives.

I AM ON MY WAY!

Raised in Christian households, my grandparents both contributed to your ministry. They went many times to The Cove—and yet, I still grew up never fully submitting my life to Christ.

My youth was rather difficult, and my young adult life held no value other than my pain and mistakes. One day, I was listening to the radio and found your ministry on. I can't say now what exactly it was that made me listen, but that was six years ago and I haven't changed the radio station yet. My life is changed because of your ministry. Your station seems to be everything I need, at exactly the right moment in my car or at home. I have learned so much and grown so deep in my faith. Thank you so much for your ministry! When you get to heaven, please say hello to my grandparents for me. Without their prayers and your ministry, I wouldn't be able to join you all in the future. Shake hands and pat each other on the back—tell them I am on my way!

CALLED TO THE MINISTRY

I grew up watching videos of your crusades, and it was then that I knew I was called to be in the ministry. I have read many of your books. I have learned so much just by watching your obedience to the Lord. Thank you so much for listening to

God and doing what He had for you. Your obedience touched millions and taught people like me to follow the Lord's plan first. Thank you for being the man of God you are.

BILLY REACHES ME FROM 1958

I had an amazing experience on the night of March 5, 2008. I was home alone, channel surfing, and I found a Billy Graham broadcast, originally from Memorial Day 1958 in San Francisco. Billy was preaching about God saving Noah, Job, and Daniel.

At one point while Billy was preaching, he looked right at the camera—I mean, right into it—and I swear he was looking right at me, it was so personal! Even though I had already given my life to Jesus Christ, I prayed along with Billy that night, asking for forgiveness and rededicating my life to Jesus.

Billy had no way of knowing, in 1958, that fifty years later he would come into my living room and get me to pray with him. Do you think God continues to work through Billy Graham? I *know* He does!

In 2004, I got to see and hear Billy at the Rose Bowl, and I cherish the experience. I have a large picture book of Billy that stays on my bookshelf, facing out so I can see Billy's face and be reminded of a dedicated man of God. Billy, thank you so much.

GRATEFUL TO "DADDY BILL" AND THE GRAHAM FAMILY

I was blessed to grow up in a Christian home, so I learned early what it means to walk with the Lord. As a young girl, I went with my parents to a Billy Graham revival in New

York City. I will never forget this experience; it's as if it happened yesterday. It helped me understand how important it is to always remain close to Jesus. It left a lifelong impression on me.

After graduating college and getting married, my husband and I moved to Florida. I was further blessed by meeting and becoming dear friends with Gigi Graham and her family. To this day, we remain close. Little did I know, as a young girl at the Billy Graham revival, that one day I would cross paths with one of "Daddy Bill's" daughters! As I think about this, as believers we really are all one family. Someday this family will join together with our heavenly Father. . . .

Amen!

MY TESTIMONY

I was a senior in high school in 1970. I was one of the few long-haired kids at my school. With the divorce of my parents, the Vietnam War, the drug scene, etc., I was looking for the answers to life. I met a fellow classmate at school one day. It was the first day of one of my classes, and this guy was sitting across from me with a Bible on the table in front of him. My first thought was, *Oh no!*

We talked a little and I told him that if religion was good for him it was okay with me. Throughout the semester, we got to know each other, and he invited me to church many times. Eventually, he won and I went to church with him a few times. He gave me a small Gideon Bible, and I took it home with me. I finally started to read the Gospel of John. I read that Bible a little bit just about every night. The more I read it, the more I thought this Jesus guy was right on! I still hadn't made a decision to believe in Christ.

One day, my friend and some of the folks at the church invited me to a Billy Graham crusade in Oakland. By that time it was 1971. We were at the Oakland Coliseum, and it was packed. Billy Graham preached that day on how King David's son Absalom was caught up in his long hair. He then went into the Gospel message. At the end of the sermon, thousands went forward to receive Christ. I was blown away. I did not go down with the others, but I made a decision in that stadium seat to accept Christ and follow Him.

After the crusade, I started attending church regularly with my friend from school. It wasn't long before we both graduated from high school. We had become close friends by then. He decided to go to San Jose Bible College that year, and I tagged along. I wasn't ready for college, but I learned a lot from all the activities, street ministry, and fellowship at SJBC. The school was about half "Jesus People" and half regular church kids wanting to be pastors. I only attended one year and then moved into a "Jesus House." There I learned more about the Word and more about outreach ministry. We had outreach meetings at the house, attended all the church services, and some of us would minister at the local juvenile hall. It was there at the Jesus House that I became more involved in music.

I eventually realized that I needed to learn a trade of some kind, and I enlisted in the US Air Force. The Vietnam War was still going strong, but I was sent to the US Army base at Fort Campbell, Kentucky. I continued to attend church and participate in outreach. I even spent a year or so as a live-in counselor in a Christian children's home. After four years, I got out of the Air Force, went back home, and eventually got married. My wife was not alone, but had three children.

I then decided to go back into the Air Force to provide for my new family. We traveled from base to base and even did a tour of duty in Italy. All those years, I became more involved in worship teams and being in Christian outreach bands.

Eventually, I left the service and finished my military career in the National Guard and Reserves. We then moved to our current location in Humboldt County, California. I continue to be involved in church and participating on worship teams. Through these latter years I have been a minister at the local jail, a member of the Christian Motorcyclists Association, and a chaplain in the United Bikers of Northern California (a secular group). I am also involved in men's ministries and am a member of the local camp of the Gideons. Throughout my life, I have been committed to tell others about Jesus. I have had many opportunities to spread the Gospel and see it as a direct result of Billy Graham and his ministry.

MY FIRST BILLY GRAHAM CRUSADE

When Texas Stadium opened in Irving, Texas, the first event was a Billy Graham crusade. I was lucky to be raised in a great Christian environment by my parents and grandparents. I accepted Christ as my Savior and Lord on September 18, 1968. To make a long story short, I thought I knew what salvation was all about—being raised in the church and all— but when I had the opportunity to go with my family to the crusade, it seemed as if Billy was speaking directly to me. A lot of things fell into place in my young mind, and I answered the altar call and rededicated my life to Christ.

I still feel blessed to this day. I am still learning and growing in the Word and have learned from many great teachers over the years. But Billy Graham is the one who stands out above the rest. He really was the one who started me down the right path, and for that I am truly grateful. May God bless and keep him and his family.

MY FATHER'S FAVORITE PREACHER AND SINGER

I come from a small, First Nation Cree community in northern Saskatchewan. My parents were trappers and fishers, raising a family of thirteen children. It was hard work, but my childhood memories of life in the bush are good.

As a child, I would wake up on Sunday mornings to the powerful singing of George Beverly Shea on the radio and the powerful preaching of Billy Graham. It did not matter whether we were out living on the trapline in our log cabin for the winter, or in our summer fishing camp in a tent, my father always listened to the weekly radio program. His favourite song (and mine) was "How Great Thou Art."

My father, who passed away two years ago, was one of the first Christians in the community, and it wasn't an easy journey. But today we are blessed because of his faithfulness to God and that of the ministry of Billy Graham. Through Billy's ministry, the whole community was reached. It was through programs like *The Hour of Decision* that my own faith was awakened and the Gospel message made simple and easy to understand. God bless Mr. Graham and his family.

A DEDICATED FOLLOWER OF YOURS

Mr. Graham, you are truly an apostle of our Lord Jesus Christ. I believed in God before I knew you, when I was a child, but from the moment I saw you on television, I could never miss a program. When you were on TV, I just had to be there—my hero was on!

My faith deepened as I watched and listened to you, read your books and the Bible, and went to church every Sunday, like you said. At one point in my life, I was not certain if I was saved. *If I had died, would I live with Jesus—would I go to heaven?* Therefore, I wrote to you, and you sent me a little package (which I still have). After I had read and followed everything it said to do, then, and only then, did I feel I was saved.

I am a dedicated follower of yours and a disciple of our Lord Jesus Christ—in great part because of you, Mr. Graham. This is why I want to thank you from the bottom of my heart. You will be forever in my heart. I also want to thank you for all the wonderful work you did for Jesus, and for all the souls you helped save throughout the world. I know you'll have a special place in heaven.

FROM BLANKET TO BLESSINGS

When I was two years old, my mother and father took me to a Billy Graham crusade in Augusta, Georgia. I don't remember much—I slept on a blanket on the floor just in front of the first row—but perhaps what Dr. Graham shared planted a seed that sprouted when I was nine years old. That's when I received Christ as my Savior. Through my growing-up years, we listened religiously to Dr. Graham on the radio. Seeds were planted, watered, and were growing. After calling me to vocational ministry, the Lord allowed me the privilege of working on committees to bring Billy Graham to Tallahassee. God used both father and son to introduce hundreds of people to Christ. To God be the glory.

ONE OF THE HAPPIEST DAYS OF MY LIFE

In 1963, when I was ten years old, I attended a Billy Graham crusade at our local high school in Lancaster, South Carolina. I was saved that night, but being a very shy little girl, I didn't go forward during the invitation. My heart was beating so fast that I thought I was going to die, but I knew it was the Lord talking to me.

I went home and told my parents, and the next night they had our pastor come to our house and talk and pray with me. The following Sunday morning, I went before the church, along with one of my friends who was also saved at the crusade. We were both baptized that night. That was April 10, 1963.

I still remember that day as being one of the happiest days of my life; and even though I have had a lot of ups and downs in my spiritual life, I have gotten back on the correct path and try to live every day for the Lord to the best of my ability. Thank you, Rev. Billy Graham, on behalf of everyone who has been led to the Lord through one of your sermons.

A GREAT LIFE EXPERIENCE

I had the pleasure of seeing Billy Graham twice when he was in the Dallas area. The last time was at Texas Stadium, and I remember the traffic moving so slowly and being so excited to see Rev. Graham in person again. I had watched him on television, but to see the people respond and move down at the invitation in person was a great life experience. There was a powerful moving of the Spirit that night. During the time when other evangelists were under scrutiny, Rev. Graham shined bright, without blemish or question of his integrity. Thank you for reaching so many with God's message and for being the inspiration you have always been.

BILLY GRAHAM, THE HOLY SPIRIT, AND ME

My parents started taking me to church every Sunday from the time I was about six. When I was nine, a well-meaning Sunday school teacher pressured me into accepting Christ. I said I accepted Him so she would leave me alone. In my young mind, I was afraid to tell my parents, because I knew it was not true, yet I felt trapped in a situation with my Sunday school teacher. So I lived a lie around her, hoping Mom and Dad would not find out and confront me. The thing is, I believed that Jesus existed, I believed He died for our sins, and I believed He rose from the grave. I believed everything in the Bible that I was taught. However, I did not believe *in* Him, I would not give myself to Him, confess Him as my Savior, or believe in Him with all my heart.

One night, at a church revival, I came under conviction; I was around thirteen. I started crying, and my dad took me outside to see what was wrong. I told him I was afraid that if I died I would go to hell. He read some passages in the Bible to me and asked me if I understood. He said he would take me to talk to a minister who was a close friend of our family's. It was over a week before we met with the minister.

We went to the minister's home, which was full of adults and children. When he talked to me and shared some passages with me, I still did not understand everything about true salvation, but I was afraid to ask in front of the adults in the room, who were all staring at me. I thought they would think I was stupid. So I said that I understood and I believed what he said, but at that time I wanted to be out of the room and away from the adults' eyes.

During the next several years, I ran from the Lord, coming under conviction at least three other times. While in college, I dropped out of church, living however I wanted to without thinking of the consequences. After college, I married a woman who was a Christian, and I started going to church every so often with her. I could act like a Christian and I could talk like a Christian, but I was not truly walking like a Christian, nor did I really want to. Besides, I saw what I thought were a lot of hypocrites in the church, and I fell into Satan's trap of selfish pride.

One evening at home, tired and alone after working all day roofing a house, I turned on the TV. As the screen lit up, Billy Graham was just starting to speak. I started to change the channel, but I had always respected Dr. Graham, so I lay on the floor and listened. Although he was speaking on TV to thousands of people, it was as if he had stepped into my living room and was talking just to me. At that point, it was Billy, the Holy Spirit, and me, together in the room. Every word of the Gospel out of Romans that Billy spoke cut through me like a knife, and that night, at the age of twenty-five, I confessed the Lord Jesus as my Savior.

Jesus has walked with me and picked me up after so many times I have failed Him. He has taken me places where I was afraid to walk. He has delivered me time and time again when I didn't want to go on, when I wanted to quit.

When I was sixty, the Lord called me to be a minister. I was so afraid when He started calling me to this church, but I remembered something I once heard Billy say, which is found in Philippians 4:13: "I can do all things through Christ who strengthens me." In one of my recent sermons, I used a story I found about Brother Graham. Apparently, for his first sermon, he prepared four sermons and preached them all in ten minutes. I certainly can relate to that. I am so thankful that he didn't decide to quit after that first sermon. Where would I be if Billy and the Holy Spirit had not been in that room with me that night? Where would hundreds of thousands of others be without the Lord putting Billy and the Holy Spirit in their living rooms?

I praise the Lord for Billy Graham and his wonderful family, who have allowed the Lord to use them as mighty vessels for Him. When we all get to heaven, I hope to see and thank Brother Billy for allowing his heavenly Father to use him to reach so many lost souls, and for the night that he was in my living room.

MY WISH CAME TRUE

When I was growing up in North Dakota in the early 1950s, I remember listening to Billy Graham on the radio, and later watching him on TV. I will never forget how big his crusades were and wishing I could attend one. My wish came true in 1987, when he appeared in Denver. I went forward to re-commit my life to Jesus, and I felt so honored to have been in the same stadium with Billy Graham. In his lifetime, he has made so much difference to people who needed to hear God's Word from a man who truly loves Him and His Son. Billy always stands by the Bible, and he taught the truth that it reveals. I thank God for putting Mr. Graham in our lives, and I pray that he will continue to be with us until Christ returns to take all His followers home. Thank you, Billy Graham, for your many years of evangelism to the world.

THE STIRRING VOICE OF GOD

I was raised Catholic, and I questioned whether there was more to knowing God than what I knew as a teenager. I watched Billy Graham's TV crusades back in the 1970s. At the time, my dad questioned my watching, but I would say, "If we are of the same faith, why the concern?" I watched because I could sense the stirring voice of God coming through the scriptures when Billy Graham spoke. And I always wanted more of that. In October 1974, I became born again.

Thank you, Billy Graham, for planting the seeds of faith in my life.

I Felt a Sense of Belonging

Thank you so much for your faithfulness and obedience to God. I have seen you preach on television and read books you have written, but what I will always remember is when I saw you preach in person. I was nine years old. My father was stationed with the US Army in Japan, and my mother and I rode a bus to Tokyo to attend a crusade. I had never seen so many people in one place! There were many more Japanese people than Americans, but I felt a sense of belonging. I don't recall the entire sermon, but even as a child I felt a peaceful spirit of unity. I was touched by the number of people responding to the altar call. I am so grateful my mother took me along with her. Thank you, Billy.

A Double Blessing

I was a children's counselor at the Billy Graham crusade in San Antonio. One of my close friends, who was not a believer, decided she wanted to attend the crusade with me one night. I decided I would sit in the stands with her rather than go down to help out after the crusade.

When my friend saw the sea of people on the floor, she

said, "Lisa, I think they need you, but I'd like to go with you." I was blessed to lead an entire family to Christ, and my friend told me afterward, "When you prayed with the family, I prayed as well and asked Christ into my life." I received a double blessing that night at the crusade! Thank you Billy.

THANKS FOR YOUR MINISTRY TO THE WORLD

In the Calgary crusade, in the early 1980s, I was a member of the choir. I recall how much I enjoyed the choir and Cliff Barrow's leadership of it. I also remember the news that Mr. Graham received during that crusade. Mrs. Graham was hospitalized with a broken hip, if my memory serves me correctly. He could have had another member of the team continue the crusade while he returned to Charlotte to be with her. However, he stayed and finished the crusade. I remember how struck I was with the dedication of this man of God. I have grown up with the Graham team, *The Hour of Decision*, and George Beverly Shea, and have enjoyed the movies made by World Wide Pictures. I thank God for this spiritual giant. His message has been consistent, and to my knowledge he has never strayed from the Gospel. Let us all remember the contribution of this man to the cause of Christ. He believes that God is keeping him here for a reason. I believe that to be true, and I trust that his godly legacy will continue until the Lord comes for His bride, the Church. Thank you, Billy Graham, for all you have done to help a lot of us grow in our faith, and for your example. I thank God for the crowns you will receive from the One whom you have served so faithfully.

YOU HAVE ALWAYS BEEN AN INSPIRATION FOR ME

I accepted Christ into my heart at the young age of ten. I

can still recall and feel the exhilaration of that moment. Over the years, I have watched and listened to your sermons, seen the multitudes respond to the invitations, and known the exhilaration that each of them feels at that moment. Thank you so much for all you have given us over the years, and for being such a faithful servant of God. May He bless you and all of your family.

MY FAITH JOURNEY

Mr. Graham has been one of God's greatest instruments in my faith journey. I remember listening to Billy Graham on TV when I was young, and it really pulled the strings of my heart. His words made me want to follow Jesus as the Lord of my life. I know if I hadn't heard him and believed, I might have taken a different way. Thank you, Mr. Graham, for your faith, and for the courage to speak publicly of our Savior so that people might come to believe. As they say, faith comes by hearing.

A MAN AFTER GOD'S OWN HEART

Dear Rev. Billy Graham, I just want to thank you for your ministry. Back when I was in high school in the early 1980s, my high school sweetheart and I went to a crusade you were having in Fort Lauderdale. During that crusade, we both went forward and received Jesus as our Savior. Today, I have been happily married for twenty-seven years to that man. We are doing well and continue to be thankful for you. Thank you for allowing Jesus to use you to help the lost sheep in this world. Your ministry changed my life. May God continue to bless you and keep you in good health. You are a man after God's own heart, and that makes my heart leap for joy!

"DON'T FORGET TO GO TO CHURCH"

After my mother died, I stopped going to church for ten years. During those years, I would always watch your broadcasts when they came on, and at the end you always said not to forget to go to church on Sunday. Those simple words were used by the Holy Spirit to convict me, and He worked in my life and I became a born-again believer, along with my husband and two daughters. Thank you for those words at the end: *"Don't forget to go to church this Sunday."* Because I listened, they changed my life.

LEGACY

I have loved listening to you preach ever since I was little. Thank you for your faithfulness to God. It's clearly evident in your family, of whom I have been doubly blessed by reading and learning from your wonderful children. Thank you, Dr. Graham, for simply loving Jesus and never being afraid to tell the world. I look forward to meeting you someday.

THE BEST CHRISTMAS GIFT

I thank God each day for someone like Billy Graham who stands for the truth, and for his family also. I admire the way Billy Graham has conducted his life in preaching the Gospel. My oldest son was only sixteen years old when we took the whole family to the crusade in Atlanta. At the end of the sermon, when Mr. Graham gave an altar call, my youngest son punched me and asked what was wrong with his brother. I turned and immediately knew that the Holy Spirit was talking to my oldest son. He was crying, and my husband and I talked with him about giving his life to Jesus and following Him. That next Sunday was Christmas, and he was baptized at our church. It was the best Christmas gift any mother could ask for. My other two children followed in their older brother's footsteps, and they, too, in the following months gave their lives over to Jesus. I am so thankful for that day in December when Billy Graham's crusade came to Atlanta. Thank you so much, Mr. Graham, and all of the people who worked with you. Your life and your family's lives have been a true blessing.

Billy Graham Stopped the Chaos

From the time I was a tiny girl, my father had a raging temper. He abused my mother physically and mentally. My two sisters and I would wake up to hear him cursing my mom, the church, the country, and anything else he could think of. When I was about eight or nine, I remember the only time my dad would quit was when he would listen to the many Billy Graham crusades on the TV. No one could talk when he was listening to the crusade message. I think my father liked the sincerity, honesty, and simple down-home way Billy Graham talked about God. He said, "I like that man."

My father seemed to mellow and soften when Billy spoke, especially of Jesus. No man was better than another in God's eyes, my daddy agreed. Thank you, Billy, for bringing peace and quiet into our little house and telling my daddy about the love of God. Mom took us to church every Sunday, but my daddy would never darken the doors. She prayed and prayed for my daddy's heart to be changed and clung to God's promises. She said God loved my daddy but that He was not pleased with the things he said and did. She wouldn't let us hate our father. Even though she took the brunt of violence in our home, he never touched us.

My daddy was saved when he was eighty years old, because of the seed you planted. Because of your obedience, I will see my daddy again.

—Carolyn

One Night, I Couldn't Sleep

Among the millions who have come to the Lord as a result of a Billy Graham crusade, I am only one, but the impact the Rev. Graham has had on my life is immeasurable. I was what I'd call a casual believer: I grew up in a parochial school and went through the usual customs of the denomination at the appointed times, but they didn't mean much to me. Looking back, I was kind of herded through the process of becoming an "official" church member.

I honestly can't remember really being touched by the message of the Gospel until I was twenty-two. I was newly married and had recently had a miscarriage. My father, a former alcoholic who developed stage 4 lung cancer at forty-six years old, had died about ten months earlier. I was sick, and I was scared.

One night, about three a.m., I couldn't sleep, so I started flipping through the channels on the TV. When I came across a rerun of a Billy Graham crusade, I wanted to change the channel, but I couldn't. I had always believed in God and loved Him, but I had never really known about salvation through the blood sacrifice of Jesus Christ. . .not until I heard it from the Rev. Graham. I was amazed. . .I had heard the stories about Jesus in church, but I didn't really "get it" until that night. I was a sinner. . .God hates sin. . .God loves me so much. He allowed His only Son to be tortured because of my sin, on my behalf, to be the perfect atoning sacrifice. Repentance and salvation from an eternity in hell are available to those who believe and receive. These were the truths I learned that night and have hung onto for the last five years. I have never looked back with regret about making my decision for Christ.

Other ways that Billy Graham has impacted my life? My husband's grandmother was a Christian Scientist until she went to a crusade as a young wife and mother. Because of those few hours she spent listening to Billy Graham, and as a result of God's grace in listening to her righteous prayers, her husband, her sons, their wives, and their children all have asked Jesus into their hearts. I know that Grandma's witness to my mother-in-law inspired her to pray for me before I was born and that those prayers have kept me safe in some incredibly unsafe situations.

Thank you, Rev. Graham, for your obedience to God's calling. Thank you for your fearlessness. Thank you for your honest biblical presentation of the Good News. We love you!

Answered Prayer

Bonnie's side of the story: I got saved on April 20, 1962, but by 1968 I had gone my own way. When I first saw my future husband, the Lord told me, "That's the man you are going to marry." We eventually married, and within a year of our marriage I gave birth to our first daughter. She had a problem with her heart, and the doctors told my husband to get ready for the worst. We prayed all night and I told God I would get back into church. The next morning, I arrived at the hospital and a nurse was singing and said, "Your little girl is all right. Something worked last night, and you can take her home in a couple of days." I knew God had answered my prayers, but even then I didn't get back to church.

In 1970, I was watching TV and a Billy Graham crusade was on. As I watched, Billy said, "Come back to Jesus," and then he looked right at me and said, "Go to church this Sunday."

While getting ready for bed, I prayed for Mike to stay home instead of playing basketball with his friends. When he came home limping, due to a sprained ankle, I thanked God again for answered prayer. I then began to pray that Mike would watch Billy Graham the next night. He likes to surf the channels, and every time he came to Billy Graham, I would pray, "Stay there, listen," and sure enough he did. He came to me afterward and said, "We are going to church tomorrow." Again I thanked God for answered prayer.

We went to the church where we were married, and that day God spoke to Mike, and the pastor watched him struggle in his seat. Afterward, the pastor asked if he could come by that afternoon. We agreed to a visit, and I once again began to pray for Mike's salvation. That afternoon, he prayed with the pastor and got saved. Thank you, God, for Billy Graham, for saving my husband, and for answered prayer. God has used you, Billy Graham, with your simple message and piercing eyes. (I felt God looking at me, and I rededicated my life to Him.) Thank you for your service to our Lord, and thank you to your family for sharing you with us.

Mike's side of the story: I had been familiar with Billy Graham since I was eleven years old. I remember the crusade at the Los Angeles Coliseum in 1959. I wanted my folks to take me so badly. But we were poor and did not own a car. I returned home from Vietnam, where I had served as a US Marine and been wounded three times in battle.

When I went to Vietnam, I took some Billy Graham crusade literature with me. I read it constantly. I did ask Jesus to save me in Vietnam, but I don't know that He did. My language was that of a typical US Marine. I attended services occasionally but got nothing out of the services. I remember writing in my diary how I left the Christmas services in 1967 feeling empty. The Gospel was not preached by the chaplain, and the service was more about how God was for us killing the godless Communists than about Jesus Christ.

I had a friend who was a Christian, and he talked to me about Jesus, and I later asked Jesus to come into my heart and save me. But because my job required me to kill so many human beings, both enemy and noncombatants, I felt as if God could never save someone like me.

I returned home in February 1968 and married my bride, Bonnie. We have been married forty years this past September.

One August day in 1969, I had gotten dressed to go play basketball with my friends. However, I noticed that the Billy Graham crusade was going to be on, and my wife begged me to stay home and watch it. My wife had been saved when she was twelve years old. Anyway, to make a long story short, I did not go to the game and I listened intently at the Word of God preached by Dr. Graham. Afterward, during the invitation, I gave my heart to Jesus Christ as my Lord and Savior. The next day, August 17, 1969, I went to church with my wife. When the preacher gave the invitation, I wrestled with the devil about going forward. I wanted to be saved but was fearful of all the people looking at me.

As we were leaving the church, the pastor must have seen the battle going on in my heart. As I left the church, he asked if he and his wife could come by our home and speak with us. I said, "I would like that, Pastor." He said he would be there at 1300 hours, and he was prompt. We spoke for a short time, and then he preached unto me Jesus Christ. Afterward, he asked me if I would like to ask Jesus to come into my heart and be my Lord and Savior. I said, "Yes, Preacher, oh yes." We kneeled at our coffee table, and I received Jesus as my Lord and Savior. All because of the Gospel I had heard preached to me by Billy Graham, the Prince of Preachers.

I went on to serve actively in our church in California for twenty-one years before the church was handed over to a Spanish ministry. My wife and I then went to a church in Long Beach. During the thirty-seven years I have been saved, I served in many capacities in the church. I was an assistant lay pastor, deacon, Sunday school bus driver, and Sunday school teacher, teaching from first grade through young adult, and also adult men. Who would have thought that the message of one man could have wrought such righteousness out of unrighteousness?

That August night, Dr. Graham preached on John 3:16. When he was done preaching and invited those who wanted to receive Jesus Christ as their Lord and Savior, I was on my knees at the same coffee table, crying and asking Jesus to save me. I was baptized August 24, 1969. Words cannot explain what Dr. Graham has meant to me. Like Christian in *The Pilgrim's Progress*, I felt the load of sin and guilt fall from me, and I became "a man made new by the grace of my Lord Jesus Christ." Billy, God bless you, thank you for being there for me. Though I was not personally at the crusade that August night, I felt the Holy Spirit calling me to salvation, and

I responded. You shall always hold a very special place in my heart and life.

SALVATION CALL

In 1993, when Mr. Graham came to Pittsburgh, I decided to volunteer and take the crash training course to help those who had dedicated their lives to Jesus. When I got back to my seat that day, I noticed that my twelve-year-old daughter had gone down and accepted Jesus as her Savior. It was the most satisfying moment of my life, for I had talked to her of the importance of having God in her life, but I didn't realize she was actually listening. Thank you, Mr. Graham, that the Lord placed you there for this salvation to take place. May our heavenly Father bless you abundantly.

Mabel

JACKSON, MISSISSIPPI, 1952

In Jackson, Mississippi, in 1952, when I was twelve years old, I watched my father join others and Billy in removing the ropes that separated blacks and whites. Then, in 2000, at Amsterdam, while working as a steward for the ten thousand itinerant evangelists, I saw how the power of God used Billy to influence His servants. Thank you, Billy Graham, for taking the stand that God wanted you to take.

A DEMONSTRATION OF GOD'S GRACE AND POWER

In 1954, on Easter Sunday in Winston-Salem, my dad asked Jesus into his heart while listening to Billy on the radio at *The Hour of Decision*. After his conversion, he wanted his three children to know the Lord, and shortly thereafter we all came to Christ. It is a demonstration of God's grace and power to see how God has worked in our entire family over the years. The Lord used you to change the course of our entire lives. Thank you, Billy, for your faithfulness in preaching the Gospel all over the world. The message stays the same, and our prayer is that the Association will be preaching the same Gospel when Jesus comes again.

UNCLE HERB'S AMAZING TRANSFORMATION

In 1965, on a cold winter Sunday night, my Uncle Herb was watching one of your crusades on TV. His wife had gone to church, and he was home alone. Though Herb wanted nothing to do with the things of God, as he listened to your message the Spirit of God convicted him of his sins. When his wife came home from church, she could see that something was bothering him. She asked him what was wrong, and he told her about your message and how God was dealing with him. She asked him if he wanted to give his heart to the Lord, and he eagerly said yes. From that moment on, Herb's life changed. Everyone who knew him was amazed at the change. Just looking at him, you knew that something had happened. Everywhere he went, he told people about Jesus. About eighteen months later, Herb and his wife and adopted baby boy were killed in a car accident. His life and his death changed the lives of many people. Billy, I thank you for your faithfulness to preach the simple yet powerful Word of God. Herb and many others are in heaven today because of you and your wonderful message.

Ron

I COULD WRITE VOLUMES ABOUT
HOW THE LORD HAS WORKED IN MY LIFE

Dear Billy Graham, I was born in 1946, but my life did not really begin until the spring of 1971 in Pittsburgh. At that time, I was a young mother of two, very unhappy, and feeling as if life had no meaning whatsoever. I could not understand why we had to die. I was fearful of many things, but most fearful of dying. At that time, I believed that when we die, that's it. No eternal life. I had never even heard of it. That is, until I heard Billy Graham's message on my TV. I was ill that evening, too ill with fever to get up and turn off the TV. (No remotes in those days.) So I was forced to hear his message. Something happened inside me when he spoke of eternal life and about Jesus. I knew of Jesus but had never heard that you could have a personal relationship with Him or with God for that matter. I jumped off the chair, ran into the kitchen to find some paper, and immediately wrote to Billy Graham that I had accepted Jesus into my heart. I mailed it the very next day.

I could write volumes about how the Lord has worked in my life and the lives of others because of that event. Today, I am a grandmother of six, of whom four are attending Christian schools, and they all love Jesus. My daughter has led many to Christ. I have been involved in ministry work for years, mentoring others, heading a Bible study, designing evangelistic bracelets that speak of God's love, helping with less fortunate children, all in the name of Jesus. I live my life for Him.

Life has not been perfect, but Jesus makes the difference in each and every storm that life takes us into. I am so grateful that Jesus makes the difference in my life. He has healed my body several times, healed my son's crooked foot when he was eight years old. (He is now thirty-seven.) I have seen the hand of God working over these past thirty-six years. I am truly grateful that Billy Graham made the sacrifice in his personal life so that others could have a better life in Christ.

When We Were Little

When we were little, my mom used to make my sister and me take a bath on Saturday nights so that we would be nice and clean for church the next morning. I remember that if Mr. Graham was on the television (this was back in the 1970s and it was a *huge* console television), my mom would wrap us up in towels and deposit us in front of the TV. We couldn't have been more than four and six years old. I can still remember seeing Mr. Graham on the TV and thinking what a wonderful person he must be. There wasn't a single time growing up that, if Mr. Graham was on TV, we weren't tuned in.

Learned as a Child

My grandmother raised me—and, to be honest, it wasn't the best of situations. I didn't have the usual grandma-in-the-kitchen-baking-cookies type of relationship. She was a hard person to live with. But as Billy Graham spoke to an audience that awed me even as a child, and as I watched him on the black-and-white television do what is now called an altar call, and all the people walked down from all areas of the football stadium with tears in their eyes and hands raised to accept Jesus as Lord of their lives, I knew there had to be something to this Jesus that made so many people want to be in a relationship with Him. I held on to those memories during my abusive childhood, and at the age of fifteen accepted Jesus as Lord of my life. I haven't regretted it since. Thank God for raising Billy Graham up for such a time as that. He still holds a very tender place in my heart today, when I see his programs aired on TBN. Thank you.

I Watched You on TV as a Little Girl

I used to sit with my parents while they watched you on TV when I was a little girl. When I grew up, I went my own way. Little by little, the turns of life became increasingly difficult. Then, one night in my living room, your program came on the TV. It was as if you were speaking to me personally. You encouraged me to accept the Lord as my Savior, so I did. That was more than thirty years ago. Thank you, Billy, for your faithfulness to God's call. Now I can call heaven my home and pray for my family like you prayed for me.

Kids Sure Are Smart!

My father, mother, brother, and I were watching the 1982 Billy Graham crusade on TV. At the end of the program, a mother and her young daughter were walking to the front. I asked my mother what the little girl was doing. She told me that the little girl was going to ask Jesus into her heart and that she was going to start living for Him. I thought for a moment and said to my mother, "I don't have Jesus in my heart, do I?" She told me I didn't and asked if I wanted to. I told her yes, and we prayed together. I was only three years old. I am very thankful that God has given me such a caring and loving mother. She has always been there for me. I have recently come to know the significance God's presence in my life and know that I wouldn't be able to get through these hard times without Him. Thank you, Billy!

BILLY GRAHAM SAVED MY LIFE. . .
WELL, JESUS DID, BUT THROUGH BILLY GRAHAM

When I was thirteen, I went to a Billy Graham crusade and accepted Christ. Now I am twenty-five and realize that accepting Christ was the most important and only eternal decision I will ever make. I'm so grateful to Billy Graham and his sharing the truth with so many people. I love Jesus! Bless you.

THAT NIGHT, I UNDERSTOOD

It was May 1980, in Indianapolis. I can remember the anticipation, waiting to attend my first Billy Graham crusade. Mom had always watched you on television when I was growing up, and I had learned to do the same. It was the first night of the crusade, and I could hardly wait for you to give the invitation. I don't think I really understood the concept of going forward, but I know that as soon as you gave the invitation, I was on my way down. As I walked down to the front, I remember thinking it was like I was walking into heaven. Everything changed that night. Raised a Lutheran, I knew that Jesus died on the cross for my sins, and I knew that was the way to heaven. But, that night, I understood that God wanted more than lip service from me. He wanted my heart, and He got it. I love Him. His Spirit fills me, and I cannot imagine what life would be without Him. Thank you, Billy, for your obedience to the call.

THE GIANT LAWN MOWER

One of the stories of my childhood is about the giant lawn mower. We had a huge lawn mower and a small lawn. The neighbors couldn't understand it. The reason was that, when tent revivals came to town, my dad loved to take his huge mower and go to help mow the fields and prepare them for the tents and chairs to be set up. We have a treasured snapshot, that my brother took with his little Brownie camera, of a young Billy Graham standing near our church. I can remember attending two-week cottage prayer meetings as a small child. I can remember the adults on their knees in the living room praying for the souls to come to the tent and accept Jesus. I just cannot seem to call Billy by any more formal of a name, because he was always referred to as Billy in our home. His simple message changed our lives. I saw him in a Chicago crusade in the 1960s. It healed my heart in many ways. Thank you, Billy.

THE FIRST REAL PREACHER I EVER KNEW

Dear Billy Graham, you were the first real preacher I ever saw on television. I say this because I listened to you and watched you on television when I was a little girl. You were real in every sense. I could not wait to see you on television. Your sermons were real, and you spoke of a real God who I came to know while watching your telecasts. You touched my life, and I came to know who God really is through your ministry. I must have been at least seven years old, but had it not been for the Spirit of God speaking through you to me wa-a-ay back then, I would never have had that foundation you laid within my heart. I am now fifty-four years old and still saved. I can't say thank you enough. I love you. You are so real.

THANK YOU, BILLY!

I attended your 1989 crusades at the old Wembley Stadium in London, and a little before that, the simulcast in my hometown.

Your preaching led a scared little eleven-year-old to Christ, and I will forever be grateful to you. Twenty years later, I feel such fondness for you and am thankful my dad took me to hear you preach. I am just sorry that, when I have children, I will not be able to take them to hear you as well.

MY LETTER TO BILLY GRAHAM

My mom told me this story one day. When I was a little girl, old enough to write, I did something very unusual—at least in my mom's eyes. It was around Christmastime. All the other kids in the country were writing letters to Santa Claus—giving him their wish lists. But not me. I wrote a letter to Billy Graham. I don't remember writing the letter, but I remember longing to know God from a very young age. Thank you, Billy Graham, for being a representative of Jesus. Somehow, as a child, I understood what you stood for. I understood that you could lead me to a relationship with God. Thank you for a life well lived. I'm sure you've put many smiles on the face of your heavenly Father.

NEVER TOO YOUNG. . .

In 1986 or 1987, the Billy Graham crusade came to Denver. My husband and our three-year-old son, Jon, came with me to the crusade. We enjoyed and deeply appreciated the music, testimonies, and message given that day. At the end of the day, Rev. Graham gave the opportunity to accept Jesus as Savior into our hearts. My husband and I were already believers, so we prepared to leave. Suddenly, Jon said that he wanted to go down front. He said that he wanted to receive Jesus, too. So my husband carried him down front, and Jon received Jesus that day, at the age of three. The Lord has done miracles in his life that have kept him on the right path. Thank you, Rev. Graham, for coming to Denver that day.

I Was the Enemy's Friend

I was an angry young man, worshipping Satan and trying to summon demons—anything that would satisfy me or make me happy. At the age of fourteen, I decided to watch Billy Graham. I heard about Jesus, and God instantly touched my heart, and I prayed the prayer of salvation and got saved! Now I'm saved by the blood of Jesus, and I'm a Christian. Thank you, Rev. Billy Graham, for being obedient to the call God had on your life. God has used you to spread the Gospel to hundreds of millions over the world. So again, thank you.

Matthew

A Great Inspiration

In Nigeria, in 1984, when I was just twelve, I heard about becoming born again. Then I received several books from Billy Graham, and after reading them, I decided to give my life to Christ. Billy and Ruth Bell Graham are a great inspiration to me, and I will always be thankful for those books that I was privileged to read during my formative years. God bless you both. Your crowns await you in heaven.

A White Velvet Dress
with a Red Satin Bow

I am one of seven children. We were raised Catholic, but my mother brought all of us to the local stadium in Arlington, Texas, back in the 1960s to hear Dr. Graham. I vividly remember wearing a white velvet dress with a red satin bow to the stadium gathering and coming down to the stage with my mother, brothers, and sisters as we accepted Christ into our lives.

Dr. Graham was instrumental then and remains so today. My husband and I follow the teachings of his children, and our faith has been strengthened by the foundation laid almost fifty years ago by my mother, who is now seventy-six years young. May God bless Dr. Graham, his family, and the ministry. I would not be the Christian I am today were it not for the foundation I got as a young girl, which helped to propel me toward my destiny, being a God-fearing, God-loving woman who promotes the love of the Father in everything I say and do, even when I don't do it as I should. Thank you for the opportunity to share. Being such a strong Christian has impacted so many other lives.

Dad Told Me to Sit Down
and Watch Billy Graham

I remember my father, an alcoholic atheist, telling me to sit down and watch Billy Graham on TV one night. He told me I needed to make some changes. I gave my heart to the Lord that evening sitting in my living room. Though my father never believed, thank you, Dad; but most of all, thank you, Billy Graham.

I Would Not Be Here Today

There is so much I could say about the Reverend Billy Graham. I grew up watching the Billy Graham crusades, using the first Bible my parents bought me for Easter 1965. I used to write down every scripture and every word that Reverend Billy said that inspired me as a young child. I still have that Bible, and I often look in the front and back to review the scriptures and words that I wrote there. Reverend Billy, I want to thank you so very much for all the years of ministry and service to our Lord and Savior Jesus Christ. If it had not been for your dedication to our Lord, I would not be the woman of God that I am today. I was raised in a very strict Christian home, and my mother made me go to church all the time. I enjoyed church until my mom went home to be with the Lord in 1978. It was then that I turned my back on God in anger for taking my best friend from me, my mom. But it was once again that the Lord, the Bible that my parents bought me with all the scriptures and inspirational words from Reverend Billy, and many words of prayer from family and friends, eventually turned me back to God. I repented and rededicated my life to the Lord and began my path to serve the Lord. If it had not been for the Billy Graham crusades to start me on the right path, I truly believe I would not be here today, serving the Lord Jesus with all my being. God bless you, Reverend Billy.

Giving It All to Him

It was the summer of 1963. I was thirteen and home alone one night. I turned on the TV, and a live crusade was on. We only had one channel in San Angelo then, so I stayed tuned to the crusade. When Billy Graham asked if I would surrender my life to Christ, I did. I gave all I knew of me to God. I accepted Jesus as my Savior. I ordered *Decision* magazine but didn't read much of it. I do remember reading one article about the Bible and either it all being true or you couldn't trust any of it. That made sense to me.

At that time, in my church, I didn't hear anything about getting saved, so I didn't tell anyone. In hindsight, I think being a loner made my relationship with God go up and down over the next eight years. I was sincere, and I remember reading the hymns we would sing each Sunday, almost studying them. I got most of my doctrine from them. Later, I described my salvation as being in two parts. The first was emotional and the second intellectual. I truly gave all I knew to give at age thirteen. At twenty-one, I realized that I hadn't fully given it all to Him. When I gave it all to Him, a new world opened. Scripture became alive and powerful. Now, at fifty-six, I continue to be grateful for my complete salvation, which started one night in 1963 while watching Billy Graham alone one night.

Tommy

A SPECIAL SPIRITUAL CONNECTION

I was raised up and blessed in a Christian home, the youngest of five children. My siblings and I had to attend church every Sunday. It was like knowing we had to go to school five days a week. So, every Sunday, it was Sunday school and church.

As far back as I can remember, I grew up watching Dr. Graham, with my mom and dad, sister and brothers. I was stretched out across our living room floor, "sponging" every word Dr. Graham had to say. Although I was a little girl, I knew there was something godly, special, great, and powerful about Dr. Graham. He preached in such a simplistic manner that even a little child like me could understand.

My mom and dad would always watch his programs; therefore, my sister and brothers and I would also. When his programs were on, we all would be quiet and listen to this great man of God and every word he had to say. I thank God for giving my mom and dad the tender spirits to listen to him. Dr. Graham is like my first spiritual father. There are a few others that I became close to later on in my life also, but he was the first. Therefore, there will always be a special spiritual connection with him. He has a great spirit and made a positive impact on my life.

I thank God for using Dr. Billy Graham to come into my life and home while I was a little girl—to share the love of Jesus Christ with me and my family. Also, my children grew up listening to him. To this day, as an adult, I still watch him on TV and listen to him every Sunday morning on the radio. His messages are as strong today as they were years ago. Whenever I am in a desperate situation, I think of a statement Dr. Graham made: "Jesus loves you, and come to Him just as you are." I tell my loved ones and others the same thing. Thank you, Dr. Graham, for obeying God's will to use you as His willing vessel, and for being my spiritual father to the full glory of God.

A TRUE PROPHET OF THE LORD

Growing up, one of the fondest memories I had was watching Billy Graham crusades on TV with my family. Throughout my entire life, the ministry of the Grahams has been a blessing to me and my family. I still remember seeing Billy Graham in person in Indianapolis, IN, about ten years ago.

Even though he was physically growing weaker, his message was as strong as ever. Now as I look back on his words—or should I say Christ's words through us, I remember the joy of the Gospel being in a place with a true prophet of the Lord.

Even years later, I still remember going forward for the altar call when I recommitted my life to Christ—something I have done frequently before and after that day. I honestly can't say that he brought me to the Lord, the Lord had done that many years before—but I can say that experience brought me closer to Him so that I could trust Him more and more. Even now after having received a degree in theology, I often think fondly of the memories I have of growing up with Billy Graham as a part of my life. To God be the glory, and my thanks to Billy for accepting the Lord's call.

The Lord Is Faithful

While I was growing up, my parents always tuned in to Billy Graham when his programs were shown. I was born in 1952, and I remember sitting down with the family and watching the Graham ministry on TV when I was a small child. When Billy Graham went to Denver, I was entering eighth grade. It was during that summer in Denver that I went forward and accepted Jesus as my personal Lord and Savior. It was through Billy Graham's ministry that I learned about needing to be saved from sin—my personal choices to separate myself from a holy God who loved me. I am now fifty-five years old and have witnessed the death of every person in my immediate family. I have survived breast cancer since my diagnosis in 1998. Only three days ago, I found out that I need to have a bone scan, because there seems to be a suspicious spot on my left thighbone. But through it all, I have learned that the

Lord is faithful, and He is with me. He has not promised life to be easy, but He has promised to be with me through life. He is my sanctuary. Where He is, I am safe. I thank Billy Graham for his ministry, his dedication to the Lord, his commitment to God's Word, and for the godly manner in which he has lived his life. His life is a witness to the abundant life promised to us by our Savior. He has been God's good and faithful servant, and I thank him for allowing God to work such blessings through him.

I Sang at the Crusades and Was Saved

My story starts in 1985. I was the youngest in our church choir (only fifteen years old at the time) and completely excited to have the chance to sing at Billy Graham's crusade at the Anaheim Angels' baseball stadium. To be honest, I think I was more excited to be at the ballpark than at the crusade. I was a huge Angels fan, and the thought of being at their ballpark made me so happy.

With as young as I was in my church choir, where the average age of a singer was fifty, the women really looked after me. But no one could have known what I was going to undergo the very first night I was singing with thousands of people at Billy's crusade. By this time in my life, I had been in the church for about three years. But looking back, I had never fully understood God's love for me. That night, I did! The rush of emotion, the feeling of pure safety and overwhelming love had come over me. As the words to those beautiful songs that we had been practicing for weeks started to sink in, I started to cry. What each word was doing to my heart, it was as if a one-ton weight had been lifted off of my chest. Relief and peace washed over me as God took over and

the Holy Spirit washed me clean. Billy Graham was the catalyst to my walk with Christ. He opened my eyes to the light
when I couldn't even see that I was in the dark.

I am now thirty-six years old, a wife and mother, and
with God's love and constant support I am still learning to
be the Proverbs 31 wife. Within my journey, my husband has
become saved; my son (of his own accord) has gone through
the classes and was water baptized; and as a family we went to
Africa in 2006 on a two-week missions trip to help the AIDS
orphans. We are constantly growing in the Lord with prayer
and Bible studies. But with every person I tell my story to, it
always starts with, "When I was fifteen years old, I sang at the
Billy Graham crusades and was saved." Thank you so much,
Mr. Graham. You saved me and my family!

Donna

REDEDICATED

When I was fourteen years old, I went to a Billy Graham
crusade for Christ at Anaheim Stadium. That was the beginning of my being born again; I stood up and went down the
aisle. I have fallen behind at times, but that inspired me to
pick up and keep going. I rededicated myself three years ago,
at age fifty, and am now happy to be a servant of the Lord's.
I am still learning, but my understanding has improved, and
I have been so blessed in that our Lord gave me the gift of
believing Jesus Christ is my Savior. Thank you, Billy.

BILLY GRAHAM VISITED MY ISLAND

I was born in Jamaica, West Indies. I came to know the Lord
in a personal way in January 1964, when Billy Graham visited my island. He preached so clearly that a ten-year-old
could understand. When the altar call was given, I still re-

member walking all by myself—with no fear and with tears streaming down my face. Billy led us all in the sinner's prayer, and right there I asked the Lord to be my Savior and friend. I never thought at the moment about being lost in that great crowd; I just wanted to give my heart to the Lord. Mr. Graham, because of your obedience to visit my island to preach God's Word, I know beyond any doubt that God is real in my life today. May heaven's blessings be yours continually. I am looking forward to meeting with you at the Marriage Supper of the Lamb.

A POEM FOR BILLY GRAHAM

I was nine years old when my family attended Explo '72 in Texas. When I came home, I wrote a poem for Billy Graham. I can still recite it today:

Preaching a sermon, Billy Graham
And singing a hymn were Jesus Christ's fans
Listening to the sermon, never bored,
And then one jumps up and shouts, "Praise the Lord!"

Attending that Graham crusade affected my life greatly. I owe much of my walk to your ministry. To this day, I say "Praise the Lord!" numerous times during the day. Thank you, Billy!

I REMEMBER BEING BLOWN AWAY

I remember as a child going to see Billy Graham with my two older sisters and my parents. He was talking at the Pontiac Silverdome in Pontiac, Michigan, back in the 1970s. I was probably nine or ten years old and had grown up in a Christian home. I had seen Mr. Graham on TV, so I knew what to expect when we got to the Silverdome. However, I remember being blown away by what I now know as the presence of the Holy Spirit, when thousands of souls were saved and people walked to the center of the field to ask Jesus into their hearts and lives. My family and I also walked down to the stage as we welcomed Jesus into our hearts. It was quite an experience. Since then, I have shared with my now Spirit-filled Christian husband how I was there when I was a child. I will never forget that life-changing experience. Thank You, Jesus, and Mr. and Mrs. Graham, for all the hard work and dedication to our God and heavenly Father.

THANKS FOR YOUR MINISTRY

My parents took my brother and me to the Billy Graham crusade as children. I remember, even as a child, how the Spirit of the Lord spoke to my heart through this powerful evangelist. My brother and I accepted Jesus Christ as Savior on the same day. We will always remember that great day! What an awesome preacher! Even as children, we were drawn to what he said. I will never forget how he laid out the simple plan of salvation so that even we could understand. And as so many other thousands of people came, as the song "Just As I Am" was being sung, we walked down that aisle to give our lives to the Lord.

We have been saved now for fifty-three years. It's not always easy, but the Lord has been there every step of the way. We are both now serving in ministry at our respective churches. But I will always be grateful for the wonderful evangelistic ministry of this great man of God, Billy Graham. God bless and keep you, until you hear the Lord say (and I *know* you will), "Servant, well done."

LONG WALK TO THE FRONT

It was—as I can best recall—1964, at a place called Jet Stadium in Columbus, Ohio. My mom, God rest her soul, took my siblings and me to the stadium to hear this man, Billy Graham. The place was packed, and the stadium seats were full, so we sat with the multitudes of others on the baseball field. There was music and singing, and of course the pressing of the crowd as the Lord was praised and worshipped. Rev. Billy took the stage and began to speak, and the words I heard as an eleven- or twelve-year-old boy were as if He were speaking directly to me. The story of Jesus and how He died for me to save my life. That was it in simplest terms, and though Rev. Graham spoke many words, the ones that pierced my heart and took to seeding were the ones of this man, the Son of God, Jesus.

As a child, I feared my earthly father, as he was many times drunk and abusive, both physically and verbally. I was confused that there could be a heavenly Father who was loving and forgiving and who would send His only Son to come save me. I heard these words as a child, and I try to think back as a child as I write. . .but now a child of God. That night, under the lights, this scared-to-death little boy walked seemingly forever through the crowds when the altar call was given by Rev. Graham. Mom held my hand, and my siblings went forward as well, pushing through the crowd that was gathering around the front of the stage area. Billy Graham led us all in prayer, the sinner's prayer; and not knowing fully why, I cried unashamed as I repeated those words as best I could.

I walked away from that night feeling a huge relief inside. I was clean, though I was sweaty from the summer heat. . . clean inside! Over the many years since that night, I have strayed somewhat from the path, but never once did God's Spirit let me stray too far away. Always, His Spirit spoke to me in what we Christians know as that "still, small voice," and I have always been brought back to the path called straight. I am getting along in age now, and I often reflect on that night at Jet Stadium. I think about the tumultuous times in family life as a child, and how I learned how a Father truly loves His children, even to the point of sacrificing His own for another's sake. Grace is truly amazing to walk in, and no matter what the world throws at me, at us, we are His children. I am because He is.

Thanks to Rev. Billy Graham for his simple approach to the Gospel and truth of Jesus as our Savior and Lord. So easy that even a child can understand it! I love the Gospel of Jesus Christ. God continues preparing your mansion, Rev. Billy, and one day I would like to visit you there!

A SHINING EXAMPLE

Billy Graham, you and your family are shining examples of who Jesus is. You give this country hope that if we give our lives to Jesus Christ, He will take care of things. Well, this is my story:

My mom was divorced when I was nine, and I had two younger sisters. Mom worked when she could, but we had no support from Dad, and food was a bit scarce—although Mom's family helped us when they could. Every time you were on TV, Sunday for special events, my mom would say, "Let's all get in front of the TV; Billy Graham is on." She told us that she watched you to give her hope in dark times. She told us that hearing you speak gave her goose bumps and made her feel good inside. (She didn't realize that was Jesus—

and I didn't either, until I got older.)

So I was watching you on TV one night, and on this particular night, I heard Billy say, as I had before, "Come on down, give your life to Jesus, we will wait." Then the song "Just As I Am" came on. I was thinking how badly I wished I were there so I could run down those stairs. Then I heard Billy say, "You at home, you can give your lives to Jesus right from your living room." I was thinking, *What?* If he had said that before, I certainly hadn't heard it. But I did this time, and I did just as he said: I bowed my head and gave my life to Jesus. I think I was ten years old.

Then I heard them say, "If you gave your life to Jesus today, write for this little book, it will help you get started." So I did. I still remember the address—it was simply, Billy Graham, Minneapolis, MN. (It was my sister's job to remember the zip code. I still don't remember it, but I bet she does.)

I remember getting that book, after checking the mailbox every day! When I got that book, it explained that I was clean and that I had no more sin in my life. I was kind of mean to my sisters, so I assumed I needed a lot of forgiving. It was the best time in my life. I went to church then, but I never heard it spoken like Billy did it.

Thank you so much, Billy and family. We truly love you all. Thank you for being that shining light when the world can get so dark. We so need prayer for our country now. Be blessed and know you are truly a man after God's own heart.

Rhonda

THE ROCK OF OUR LIFETIMES

As so many people have, I grew up with Billy Graham. I cannot remember a time when he wasn't on TV, preaching in those crusades. I remember listening with my family to some of them and being impressed by his total certainty in what he was saying. He had no doubt about Jesus Christ, and no doubt about expressing the message of God's Son to the rest of us. He was educated, forceful, and clear-cut in his sermons. And I have no doubt that whenever and wherever he preached, the Holy Spirit moved. Billy has always seemed as solid as a rock to me. Oh, I know he is human, and I'm sure he has made mistakes in life, but to my knowledge, they weren't public mistakes. He never did anything to disgrace his ministry or God's message. As Peter was the rock of the early church, Billy has been the rock of our lifetimes. I'm sure that the lives he has touched, and those who have come to accept and know God through Billy's preaching, is a staggering number.

When I was around ten years old, and not long after I was saved, I took a correspondence course from the Billy Graham Evangelistic Association. I still have the certificate of completion, with Billy's signature. It is one of my most prized possessions. That course not only added to my Christian education, but the memory of it kept me seeking after God all my life. I've been a Christian for forty-six years now, and I know the influence of Billy had a hand in that decision.

Billy has probably influenced this country and our world more than any other modern minister. Thank God for you, Billy! Thank God that you answered His calling, took courage, and stepped out in faith, so that so many could hear God's Word. I am sure that someday in heaven I will come to a long line of people who are waiting to give you a hug. I will get in line, and I will reserve a giant hug for you. May God bless you now and forever!

"CHARLOTTE, BILLY'S ON THE TV"

When I was a very young child, around five years old, my maternal grandmother would come and stay with us for several weeks at a time. During this period in my family's history, my father was a practicing alcoholic. My grandmother worried about the outcome of my life living in such an environment. I would often hear her "whispers" of prayer for me every night. She was hard of hearing, so they were whispers to her, but louder than she realized. Her other intervention in my life, frequently throughout my childhood, was to make me stop all that I might be doing and watch your crusade. She would yell to me, "Charlotte, Billy's on TV!" I knew exactly which "Billy" she was speaking about and that there was no choice but to stop and watch. Numerous times, I prayed with you, not only for my own salvation but for my family's. God was faithful and provided protection and deliverance from this situation. I truly believe that those prayers for salvation at such an early age opened the door for God's hand in my life. Thank you for sharing your crusades with those of us who never came to a coliseum but nonetheless felt God's Spirit move right in our own homes.

ONE NIGHT STANDS OUT IN MY MIND

I can remember as a young child watching the crusades on TV. I always attended church, and our family was very active in the church. My grandmother was also a great influence on me as far as becoming a Christian. But one night stands out in my mind as the night I believe I really began my walk with Christ. As I watched the crusade and Rev. Graham gave the invitation, he made it sound so simple and inviting. I just couldn't refuse. I got down on my knees and prayed with him, after walking toward the TV. It was like I was there, along with all those people going forward. Not long after that, I was baptized in a small creek and joined the church. It has taken years of growth, and I am still learning more about myself and how sinful I was and am without Jesus. But I am a born-again Christian raising four kids, and I am very thankful for God's grace that was revealed to me from Rev. Graham and his desire to serve God and lead others to Christ. Thank you, Billy Graham, for all your dedication.

I SPILLED A SNOW CONE ON A LADY'S DRESS

When I was only three years old, my mother and father took me to the local fairgrounds to hear a preacher they had seen on our small black-and-white TV, which my dad had just purchased from money he had saved and put aside for the family. I was so little at the time and yet I can still remember people from everywhere, coming from all directions, following one another inside the grandstand. They seemed so happy! Bibles were in their hands and smiles were on their faces.

They served snow cones that night, and I was so excited when my mom took me down to buy one. We were on our way back when, lo and behold, I accidentally dropped my snow cone down the back of a lady's dress! My mother was upset with me, but the lady was so sweet and never missed a beat singing and following along to "What a Friend We Have in Jesus."

I remember the night so well because everyone was so happy and full of love. Love that you don't really feel in a lot of the churches we have today. It was a peaceful type of love. When Billy Graham got up to speak that night, I remember it so well. His voice was full of love for our Lord Jesus Christ, full of love for the people he was talking to, and full of love for the Word of God.

He loved me! Jesus loved me! Even if I did spill that snow cone down that lady's back. Jesus still loved me, because Billy Graham told me so that night. Yes, I still remember the first night I heard Rev. Billy Graham. I thank him so much for telling me that night how much Jesus loves me. Since that time, I have always loved to hear him preach and tell everyone how much they are loved, because I feel as if someone, somewhere at that very moment, really needs to hear it just like I did that first night.

"I NEED TO DO THIS, TOO!"

It was a hot summer evening in 1956, at the Oklahoma City fairgrounds. My older sister and I, visiting our Oklahoma relatives with our mom, were sitting with aunts, uncles, and cousins, waiting to hear this "new preacher" who had come to town. My sis and I had attended church all our lives and been "good little girls" growing up, but this night, as I listened to this fiery preacher, I heard (with spiritual ears) some things I hadn't grasped before. I guess I understood for the first time that I was apart from God. And I understood why Jesus had to die for me. One of the verses stuck in my young head: "What shall it profit a man, if he shall gain the whole world, and lose his own soul?" (Mark 8:36 KJV). I had pretty much "gained the world" in my young teen eyes, but what Billy shared made complete sense in my mind and heart. I didn't want to lose my soul. . .I wanted God.

The choir started singing "Just As I Am," and I ached to go forward. But we were high in the bleachers, and there was a long line of relatives and strangers between me and the aisle. I chickened out.

Later that night, deeply troubled, I confided in my sis. "I really wanted to go forward tonight." My sis, who has always been there for me, told me she would take me back the following evening so I could follow through with my desire. And she did.

The following evening, I listened intently, knowing exactly what I wanted and needed to do when the right time came. But, to my surprise, when "Just As I Am" began, my sis hopped up and started down the aisle before me. I followed, unsure of her motives, until we met at the foot of the stage where Billy stood. My sis looked at me and said, "I need to do this, too!"

So it was that two sisters were ushered into the counseling tent and into the Kingdom. The counselor explained some things to us and gave us some "B-rations," which were verses on assurance to memorize. Billy actually came into the tent shortly afterward, and all of those who had received Christ went by, one by one, and shook his hand. When I shook his hand, I remember his piercing blue eyes looking into mine as he asked me, "Did you receive Christ as your Savior tonight? Do you want to live for Jesus?" I said yes, and I meant it.

I have now been saying yes to the Lord for more than fifty years, as He has led me through valleys and on mountaintops. I know Him as my Husband, my Friend, my Counselor, my Rock, my Light, my Joy, the "I Am" of my life. From memorizing those verses in that small pack given to us at the crusade, my sister and I went on to discover the joys of quiet time, scripture memory, Bible study, and sharing our faith with others. Though both married, we are very close and often pray for each other over long-distance wires.

What if I had not gone back to hear Billy the second time? I could not have made it through the years without Christ. I thank my God upon every remembrance of you, Billy. All glory to God for His message of grace brought to me through His dear and precious messenger, Billy Graham. May His peace and comfort and joy overwhelm you as you look forward to the day when you will place many, many crowns at the feet of our Lord Jesus!

Judy

GOD'S REMINDER AND BLESSING

I was a volunteer at a crusade. I don't remember my official title. I guess I was an escort. I had a wheelchair and helped (a few) people into the Cox Convention Center. I wanted to be a blessing, but I felt as if I wasn't doing enough. I "got lost" in the message, and I remember that I enjoyed it. (I was up in the nosebleed section.) As I worshipped the Lord, He reminded me that all my children would come to know and love Him, a promise He had given me a decade or so before. This time, He added that it would begin with my youngest daughter. What a blessing! I wanted to be there as a blessing, but God gave me a blessing instead!

ONE OF GOD'S TRUE GENERALS

I first learned of this great man of God as young boy. I once again encountered the teachings of Dr. Graham while serving as a US Marine on Okinawa in the late 1980s. The one thing that has remained the same is his unwavering love and commitment to our Lord and Savior Jesus Christ. One of God's true generals.

WE MET THE LORD IN 1959

Dear Billy, thank you for coming to Melbourne, Australia, in 1959. That was the start of both my husband Peter's and my walk with the Lord. We were both almost thirty years old, with two children and a mortgage. By the time the crusade was over, seven of our immediate family members had made a decision for Christ, and each one has continued in the walk, which began nearly fifty years ago. During those years, my husband and I have served the Lord in our church— my husband as an elder, and both of us in youth and Sunday school. We have also worked with Prison Fellowship for nearly fifteen years, and ten years with the Gideons.

We thank God for the opportunity we had to go forward for Christ. If you had not followed God's leading, Australia would be a sadder place. Both Peter and I recall vividly how God spoke to us and has led us every day. Thanks to you again, our daughters and their children have made a commitment for the Lord.

When God spoke to me through you, I learnt that "I had to come as a child, and God would teach me." One of the meetings was held at the Melbourne Showgrounds, and it was there that Peter asked the Lord into his heart. On that night, it was raining so heavily that it caused a delay in the program. The announcement was made as a road was blocked. Then the choir sang "There Shall Be Showers of Blessing." When they had finished, the rain stopped, the clouds parted a little, and the moon shone through the gap onto you. . .Billy.

This physical sign of God's presence softened Peter's heart. When you said from God's Word that "there is a wide way and a narrow way, and there will be many on the wide way and few on the narrow way," Peter knew that God was speaking to him. Praise God for the changes that have come into our lives, and the lives of others led to us for counseling or encouragement. We have, with His help, faithfully served God within our own family and with others we have met over our journey. We are both seventy-eight now and yearn for the unsaved in our family and friends.

We considered it a privilege to share in the counseling at your following crusade here in Melbourne, and also at your son's crusade. Thank you, Billy, from the bottom of our hearts.

Marion and Peter

Thank You, Billy Graham. . .
for Sharing Ruth with Us

RUTH AND RUTH

This morning in our prayer meeting at Desiring God, as we gave thanks for the life of Ruth Graham, I was moved. Probably because of her death in proximity to my father's (March 6). The connection is this: When I was growing up, there was a cluster of independent traveling evangelists in Greenville, South Carolina. My father, Bill, and his brother, Elmer, were in that group. Cliff Barrows, Billy Graham's partner in music for decades, was also part of the fellowship from time to time. That was our connection with Billy and Ruth Graham. So, in my mind, my mother, Ruth, and Ruth Graham were in the same business—supporting a traveling evangelist.

It was a hard calling. In those early days, when propeller airplanes with their single rear wheel would whisk away Big Billy (Graham) and Little Bill (Piper) to who-knows-where around the country, for two, three, four, five, or six weeks at a time, to preach the everlasting Gospel, Ruth (G) and Ruth (P) were left at home with house and lawn and rusting gutters and leaky faucets and weeds and utilities and checkbook and laundry and church and neighborhood and homework and discipline and sports and plays and teenage acne and fear and no one at their side at church or in bed. It was a hard calling. So when we gave thanks for Ruth (G), I was flooded with thanks for Ruth (P) and Little Bill (P), and that flood increased my thanks for Ruth (G). Only when the books are opened in eternity will we know the ten-thousand-fold fruit of their lives, as they bore the weight of sending their men into the greatest battle in the world.

John Piper

MEETING MRS. GRAHAM

For as long as I can remember, I have counted Dr. and Mrs. Graham among my heroes. While I never had the privilege of attending a Billy Graham crusade (though I've watched many on television over the years), the Grahams have nevertheless had a deep impact on my life and that of my family. My dad grew up just down the road from the Grahams' home in North Carolina, and when I was growing up I heard countless stories of their kindness to him over the years, kindness that continues to this day. Many years ago, I did have the honor of meeting Mrs. Graham at the reception following my grandfather's funeral. (I believe Dr. Graham was ill at the time.) And at the funeral home, I met George Beverly Shea. Although I was sixteen—an age at which many would be apathetic to such things—their simple presence meant the world to me and is something I believe I will never forget.

I HEAR HIS VOICE SPEAK EACH WORD

My grandparents, parents, and I sat around the TV watching the Billy Graham crusades. The impact the crusades had on our lives still rings in our ears today with Brother Billy's patented voice: "You can have eternal life today through salvation at the cross." Whenever I read one of Billy Graham's books, I hear his voice speak each word as if he were in the same room. . . . I do not know where I would be today if not for Billy and Ruth Graham. They are some the greatest Christians I have ever seen. I use Billy's books and magazine to aid me in teaching Sunday school. What an impact he has had on my life.

I LIKE RUTH'S FRANKNESS

I am an Ethiopian living in the United States. I have never been to any crusade physically, nor seen Billy Graham in person. But I've heard the testimony of a person I highly respect. He got saved in Ethiopia during one of the crusades conducted a long time back. He was desperate and almost at the end of his life, with years of sinful life without Christ. Today, he is a church elder and worships the Lord with his family.

I personally have been reading about Billy Graham and his family members in magazines, and watching crusades through TBN and other Christian TV stations. In a *Newsweek* magazine article, I read Ruth's response to the question, "Have you ever considered divorce?" Her reply was straightforward and dynamic: "Divorce, no. But murder, yes!" This great frankness and humility encourages those who struggle with the pain and stigma of divorce. I am not divorced, but the message helps to encourage others, not to be taken as excuse, but to understand the existence of struggles in every marriage, including great people of God. It also encourages enduring and looking upon God for solutions.

DEAR GRAHAM FAMILY

Words cannot describe the sorrow I feel for your loss. My family is devoted Baptist, and God-fearing people. I learned of religion on my grandmother's knee, and usually listening to you. Thank you for your wife's devotion to the Lord; it obviously rubbed off on you, Mr. Graham. Our thoughts and prayers are with you in this difficult time.

THE STANDARD THAT WIVES STRIVE TO BE

Dear Rev. Graham, first of all, I send sincere condolences on the loss of your wife. . . . What an amazing tribute to Mrs. Graham, to be the standard that wives everywhere strive to be. She truly was a special person, wasn't she? I grew up watching Billy Graham crusades on TV, and when you talked, it felt as if you were talking directly to me. Awesome! I would like to personally thank you for not ever letting your followers down. You never fell to the scandals and controversy that other evangelists did. You and Mrs. Graham are one of a kind, and there is a special place for both of you in heaven. Just know that a tear falls for you today, and may God hold the hand of Mrs. Graham on her trip home. God bless you and your family.

MINE IS A TYPICAL STORY, BUT MY OWN

My grandmother, who gave me my first Bible, recognized my interest in reading the Bible at an early age. Where it came from, I'm not sure. I was adopted at the age of two weeks, and my parents—the only ones I've ever known—don't remember where my interest in the Bible came from. They were typical holiday-only churchgoers.

Church for me as a child was a massive place where people came to hear someone speak way up front. Yes, we sat in the back primarily, or near the back. I don't know if it was because we were late or for an easy escape route. Sometime during my early years, I attended a Ladies-in-Waiting church function for a few weeks. We memorized scriptures and moved up the ladder to Ladies in Waiting. What we were waiting for, I don't know. But those events, reading the Bible, and memorizing scripture, affected me in ways I didn't know then, but I found out around the age of twelve.

My grandmother, who was an unbeliever herself, a hoper, was living with our family after the death of my grandfather. Her bedroom and mine were next to each other. As she focused on TV after dinner, she called out, "Billy Graham is on!" I asked, "What channel?" because I also had a TV in my room.

Had I watched him before? I believe so, but I'm not sure. I flipped to the channel and listened. And as so many have done before me, I laid my hands on the TV during the invitation to Christ. As a child, I didn't know where that decision would take me; but I'm still on that marvelous journey.

In my late teenage years, when I had tested everyone, including God, I found myself at my sorry-self end. As much as I was in control of my life, I wasn't. Subsequent to having my fiancé call off our wedding two weeks before the event, I was raped two weeks later. I tried numerous times to commit suicide, but for some reason, God physically saved me each and every time. As I look back, I realize the salvation events were miracles. Teenagers are unaware of their mortality, so I had tested anyway.

Following my last suicide attempt, I was dragged to a church retreat I had commited to. I was awful to everyone, and everyone was so gracious with me. I slept through most of the retreat and on the final night recognized again that I needed a savior. But it all started with the invitation from Rev. Billy Graham over the air forty-one years ago. That invitation holds a special memory in my heart! Thank you, Rev. Graham, for following God's leading and being obedient. Thank you for being our nation's pastor. Thank you for meeting with dignitaries and sharing the message of Christ with them and all of us. Thank you!

Years ago now, I purchased one of Mrs. Graham's books. I believe it was her first one, but I'm not sure. It was the same gentle and loving message that the women on the retreat shared with me. If I could have spoken to Mrs. Ruth Graham, I'd have embraced her and cried. I would have cried for her faithfulness, her commitment, her dedication to her Savior, her husband, and her children. I looked up to her as a godly woman! I still do. She left a lasting image and message, as does Rev. Graham. Now their children, and probably their grandchildren, are serving the Lord, along with thousands of others, because of Rev. Graham's messages. What a legacy!

I USED TO "GET SAVED" AT EVERY ONE

Thanks for the TV crusades of days gone by. I used to listen to them and get "saved" at every one. I loved them.

What a wonderful example Billy and Ruth have lived for the world, and especially for the Body of Christ. These things will never be forgotten by the many whose lives were touched by these courageous people. In Jesus' name, may all the family be blessed as Billy and Ruth live on in them.

HE STIRS UP MY SOUL

When I hear the names Billy and Ruth Graham, I always think of Jesus Christ. When I hear Billy's preaching, I am always attached to the television screen. He quickens and stirs up my soul. I thank God for his ministry, for he is an icon to evangelism. May you all be blessed beyond measure.

I CRIED LIKE A BABY

I love Ruth and Billy Graham! When I was a little girl, I loved watching Billy Graham on television. When they opened the new Billy Graham Library in Charlotte, I really wanted to go, but I have been so sick with my health, I just could not make it. Those words Billy said about Ruth made me cry like a baby. I want the entire Graham family to know that you're in my prayers. Could you please pray for me and my kids? I lost my husband last July, coming up on one year. My kids are constantly in my prayers. God be with you, Billy, and your family. Thank you, Billy and Ruth.

Emily

BRIGHTER THAN ANY CANDLE

Our thoughts and prayers go out to Rev. Graham and all the Graham family. When our news channel told us of Mrs. Graham's going home, my mind went to Proverbs 31:10–31. Mrs. Graham was the mother of all mothers. She may not have been in the spotlight as much as her husband, but she knew and taught other women their roles in being a Christian. She and Rev. Graham were a fantastic role model to the whole world. Their love for each other glowed brighter than any candle ever could. It was clear on both of their lives. Ruth lived her life strictly by God's Holy Word. Even though hearts are saddened and broken down, Sister Ruth is shouting on the Hills of Glory and is safe in the arms of Jesus. May each of you look to Jesus for comfort during these days of sorrow. We will have everyone in our thoughts and prayers.

SIMPLY, THANK YOU!

Dear Rev. Graham, I simply want to give God praise, and thank you for allowing God to use you in such a tremendous way throughout the years. I simply want to thank God for your wife, Ruth, and how God used her to be a blessing to us through your ministry. I simply want to thank you for being consistent throughout the years. I recently viewed one of your Classic crusades, and it was truly a blessing and just as powerful today as it was then. I simply want to say that I love and appreciate you and your ministry, and my prayers are with you and your family.

Finally, I simply want to thank you for not being ashamed of the Gospel of Jesus Christ and for lifting His name up all over the world. May God continue to bless and use you for His glory, for you have been a blessing to so many, and God is not finished with you yet!

AMERICA'S MESSENGERS FOR GOD

Dear Billy and Ruth Graham, thank you for being America's messengers for God! Thank you for the admirable relationship you have with one another in your marriage. What an example of the words *love* and *covenant*, especially in today's society.

I was born on a farm in rural Virginia in 1965. I was the baby of the family, with older siblings already married and out of the house. My mother always made sure I attended church. My father, who was a member of the local Masonic organization, didn't attend church, but we were always tuned in as a family watching you by television whenever there was a telecast on. My dad would sit and listen as George Beverly Shea sang and Cliff Barrows did the introductions. Daddy would comment on how long the two of them had been on the shows. I always had pen and paper ready to write for the free book you would offer, as my mother would suggest that I copy the information down for her. These memories will always be etched in my heart.

I have been married now for seventeen years, and for a long time, when all our friends were having children we couldn't. I prayed and prayed, and the Lord blessed us with a boy on December 2, 2004. I wanted him to have a special name, a different name, and I searched the things close to my heart and came up with *Graham*, so we named him Graham Alan. I would explain to people how I came up with the name: "Graham, like Billy Graham."

I'm so thankful to you for being in our home when I was growing up. Please pray for us now as the loss of my daddy has pulled our family apart. I pray also for you and Ruth. God bless you and your family and the ministry as it is continued.

ABOUT THE COMPILERS

Jerushah Armfield lives in South Carolina with her husband and two children. She helps her husband lead City Lights, a church planted in 2012 in Greenville. You can follow Jerushah's writings at http://jerushahruth.blogspot.com/

Aram Tchividjian grew up in South Florida and now lives in Boynton Beach. He is senior web developer for a Palm Beach Gardens, Florida, agency and father of three kids. In 2008, he coauthored the book *Invitation* about his grandfather's ministry.

Basyle "Boz" Tchividjian is a former child abuse prosecutor who currently teaches at Liberty University School of Law. Boz is the founder and executive director of GRACE (Godly Response to Abuse in the Christian Environment), designed to educate and equip the faith community to confront and address child abuse.